SS SL
LITG.CRM
EDW

I0683007

Fixed Fees in the Criminal Courts

The College of Law
of England and Wales

LIBRARY SERVICES

The College of Law, 14 Store Street, Bloomsbury, London WC1E 7DE
Telephone: 01483 216387 E-mail: bloomsbury-library@lawcol.co.uk

**This book MUST be returned on or before the last date stamped below.
Failure to do so will result in a fine.**

SHORT LOAN COPY

WITHDRAWN

Birmingham · Chester · Guildford · London · Manchester · York

The College of Law, Guildford
WITHDRAWN
S12590

Other titles available from Law Society Publishing:

CLSA Duty Solicitors' Handbook (3rd edn)
Andrew Keogh

Criminal Defence (3rd edn)
Roger Ede and Anthony Edwards

Drinking and Driving Offences, 2nd edn
Jonathan Black

Forensic Practice in Criminal Cases
Lynne Townley and Roger Ede

Immigration Advice at the Police Station (3rd edn)
Rosie Brennan

Police Station Skills Kit 3rd edn
Eric Shepherd

Prison Law
Margaret Obi

Related Family and Criminal Proceedings
Family-Criminal Interface Committee

Road Traffic Offences Handbook
Kenneth Carr, Frank Lockhart and Patrick Musters

Sentencing Handbook
Anthony Edwards and Joanne Savage

All books from Law Society Publishing can be ordered through good bookshops or direct from our distributors, Prolog, by telephone 0870 850 1422 or email lawsociety@prolog.uk.com. Please confirm the price before ordering.

For further information or a catalogue, please contact our editorial and marketing office by email **publishing@lawsociety.org.uk**.

FIXED FEES IN THE CRIMINAL COURTS

A Survival Guide

SECOND EDITION

Anthony Edwards

The Law Society

All rights reserved. No part of this publication may be reproduced in any material form, whether by photocopying, scanning, downloading onto computer or otherwise without the written permission of the Law Society and the author except in accordance with the provisions of the Copyright, Designs and Patents Act 1988. Applications should be addressed in the first instance, in writing, to Law Society Publishing. Any unauthorised or restricted act in relation to this publication may result in civil proceedings and/or criminal prosecution.

Whilst all reasonable care has been taken in the preparation of this publication, neither the publisher nor the author can accept any responsibility for any loss occasioned to any person acting or refraining from action as a result of relying upon its contents.

The views expressed in this publication should be taken as those of the author only unless it is specifically indicated that the Law Society has given its endorsement.

The author has asserted the right, under the Copyright, Designs and Patents Act 1988, to be identified as author of this work.

© The Law Society 2010

ISBN 978-1-85328-868-5

First edition published in 2008

This second edition published in 2010 by the Law Society
113 Chancery Lane, London WC2A 1PL

Typeset by Columns Design Ltd, Reading, Berks
Printed by Hobbs the Printers Ltd, Totton, Hants

The paper used for the text pages of this book is FSC certified. FSC (The Forest Stewardship Council) is an international network to promote responsible management of the world's forests.

Contents

CONTENTS

Abbreviations

ASBO	anti-social behaviour order
CCU	Complex Crime Unit
CJA	Criminal Justice Act
CRIMLA	decisions of the Costs Appeal Committee of the LSC
DSCC	Defence Solicitor Call Centre
HFL	higher fee limit
HSF	higher standard fee
LFL	lower fee limit
LSC	Legal Services Commission
LSF	lower standard fee
MHA 1983	Mental Health Act 1983
NAE	notice of additional evidence
PCMH	plea and case management hearing(s)
PPE	pages of prosecution evidence
SCCO	Senior Courts Costs Office
SCTO	[former] Supreme Court Taxing Office
TMC	Taxing Masters' Compendium
TIC(s)	[offence(s)] taken into consideration
UFN	unique file number
VHCC	very high cost case
X###	cases quoted in the Litigator's Graduated Fee Scheme Guidance, published by the National Taxing Team

Introduction

SCOPE

This guide covers only the following situations:

- police station cases where the first call is referred or reported on or after 14 January 2008;
- magistrates' court cases where the representation order is dated on or after 16 April 2007;
- unless otherwise specifically stated, Crown Court cases where the representation order is dated on or after 3 August 2009. This does not include orders issued before that date but transferred after it. Only if an old order is revoked and a new order issued after 2 August 2009 will the new regime apply. For orders dated on or after 14 January 2008 but before 3 August 2009, reference should be made to the first edition of this guide.

NOTE ON RATES

London rates apply to fee earners whose offices are situated within the LSC's London region. If an office outside London instructs as agents an office inside London, London rates apply. National rates apply when a London firm instructs a firm whose office is outside London.

All rates quoted in this edition are exclusive of VAT.

MISCELLANEOUS PAYMENTS

Reviews and supervisions of criminal files continue to be required by the LSC Unified Contract (Crime). Payments are claimed once annually. They are paid at the following rates, exclusive of VAT:

Face to face review	£31.18
Paper file review	£18.71

APPEALS

Crime lower

If dissatisfied with an assessment, appeal is to the Adjudicator within 28 days. If you wish to challenge further, seek a certificate that a point of principle of general importance is involved within 21 days. Appeal is then to the Costs Appeals Committee.

Litigators' graduated fees

Appeal to the ligitators' fee team (using Form LF2) within 21 days. Written reasons for further decision may be sought for 21 days. Then appeal to costs judge within 21 days. There is a further right of appeal to the High Court on matters of principle and of general importance.

Advocates' graduated fees

Seek redetermination within 21 days; thereafter obtain the officer's written reasons within 21 days and within 21 days from their receipt, appeal to a costs judge. There is a further right of appeal to the High Court on matters of principle and of general importance.

Guidance

Guidance is available on the websites of the LSC and the National Taxing Team but does not bind the appellate bodies (*R* v. *Sturmer and Lewis* (2008) SCCO 277/08). The Graduated Fee Scheme Guidance published by the National Taxing Team (November 2008) is at **www.hmcourts-service.gov. uk/cms/files/NTT-AGFSGuidanceNov2008.doc**.

References

References to 'CRIMLA' decisions are to decisions of the Costs Appeal Committee of the LSC; references to cases in the style 'X123' are to cases quoted in the Graduated Fee Scheme Guidance, published by the National Taxing Team; 'TMC' refers to cases in the Taxing Masters' Compendium; 'SCTO' and 'SCCO' decisions are those made in the former Supreme Court Taxing Office and now the Senior Courts Costs Office respectively.

RELATED PROCEEDINGS

These are the proceedings defined by the Criminal Defence Service (General) (No.2) Regulations 2001, SI 2001/1437, reg.3(2), conducted under representation orders, such as applications for anti-social behaviour orders, football banning orders, sexual offences prevention orders, violent offender orders, drinking banning orders, etc.

CHAPTER 1

Crime – lower work (provided for by the Unified Contract (Crime))

Appendix 1 contains a summary of all the claims that may be made under the Unified Contract (Crime) with the limitations upon them.

1.1 GENERAL

1.1.1 Work types

Record the final charge that your client faces. Where your client is facing multiple charges, you should identify the most serious charge.

Criminal matter type code table

Code	Description
1	Offences against the person
2	Homicide and related grave offences
3	Sexual offences and associated offences against children
4	Robbery
5	Burglary
6	Criminal damage
7	Theft (including taking vehicle without consent)
8	Fraud and forgery and other offences of dishonesty
9	Public order offences
10	Drug offences
11	Driving and motor vehicle offences (other than those covered by codes 1, 6 and 7)
12	Other offences
13	Terrorism
14	Anti-social behaviour orders
15	Sexual offender orders
16	Other prescribed proceedings

Notes

1. A full list of offences covered by each code appears in **Appendix 2**.
2. Code 12 is used when no other appropriate code exists or when the client is not subject to an investigation or proceedings or where the nature of the matter is not known.

1.1.2 Definitions

A 'business day' means a day other than a Saturday, Sunday, Christmas Day, Good Friday or any bank holiday.

The rates for unsocial hours apply to any work carried out by a duty solicitor or accredited representative after 17.30 and before 09.30 on each weekday or on weekends or bank holidays (non-business days).

1.2 CRIMINAL INVESTIGATIONS

1.2.1 Investigations conducted other than by a constable (e.g. Department for Work and Pensions, Department for Business, Innovation and Skills, local authority)

Claims and claim codes

- Means test applies. Care is needed to ensure that relevant evidence of means and necessary extensions on Form CDS5 are obtained. See **Appendix 1**. There must be an eligible client and valid Forms CDS1 and CDS2.
- Claim on Form CDS6 under code INVA. Guidance on completion of the form is at **Appendix 3**.

Outcome codes

Code	Description
CNO1	No further instructions
CNO2	Change of solicitor
CNO3	Client not a suspect
CNO4	No further action
CNO5	Simple caution, reprimand, warning
CNO6	Charge, summons or reported for summons
CNO7	Conditional caution
CNO8	Fixed penalty notice

An explanation for these codes appears in **Appendix 3**.

Payment

Payable at hourly rates including travel and waiting for work actually and reasonably undertaken.

Work	National rate	London rate
Preparation	£46.90	£49.70
Travel and waiting	£26.30	£26.30
Routine letters written and routine telephone calls	£ 3.70 per item	£ 3.85 per item

These claims will also be available in criminal related matters that do not involve interrogations, e.g. advice on restraint proceedings, when criminal proceedings have not yet been instituted.

1.2.2 Investigations conducted by a constable (e.g. police, HM Revenue and Customs)

Claims and claim codes

- No means test applied.
- Claim on Form CDS6.
- Guidance on completion of the form is at **Appendix 3**.
- A list of all police station and scheme references appears at **Appendix 6**.

Use the codes in the following table.

Code	Description
INVB	Police station: telephone advice only
INVC	Police station: attendance
INVD	Police station: (armed forces)
INVE	Warrant of further detention (including Terrorism Act 2000, advice and assistance and other police station advice where given). This would appear to be the appropriate code for applications at court to vary pre-charge bail conditions
INVF	Warrant of further detention (armed forces) (including Terrorism Act 2000, advice and assistance and other police station advice where given)
INVG	Duty solicitor standby (substantially redundant)
INVH	Police station: post-charge attendance – breach of bail/arrest on warrant
INVI	Police station: post-charge attendance – post-charge identification procedure/ recharge/referral back for caution, reprimand, warning
INVJ	Immigration matter

Outcome codes

Code	Description
CN01	No further instructions
CN02	Change of solicitor
CN03	Client not a suspect
CN04	No further action
CN05	Simple caution, reprimand, warning
CN06	Charge, summons or reported for summons
CN07	Conditional caution
CN08	Fixed penalty notice

An explanation for these codes appears in **Appendix 3**.

Payment

DEFINITION OF A MATTER

A claim may be made for each matter.

The contractual provisions as to the number of matters are complex and difficult to apply. Legal Services Commission (LSC) guidance (LSC, Police Station Advice and Assistance Fixed Fee Scheme Questions and Answers For Service Providers working under the Unified Contract (Crime) from 14 July 2008) does not cover every situation in strict accordance with the contractual terms and the contractual terms are contradictory.

The following propositions can be stated based on the contract and guidance:

- each suspect represents a separate matter;
- the number of custody records opened is not an essential consideration, though separate records may support separate claims (separate Defence Solicitor Call Centre (DSCC) references are not required to support separate claims, but each should have its own unique file number (UFN));
- if matters conclude on different occasions, or are bailed to return or charged to different court dates, there are as many claims as there are different outcomes or dates.

In its guidance (see **Appendix 5**) the LSC accepts:

> Two Matters advised on and advice continued on one of the Matters after first occasion. Two fees will be paid. [...] One fee for each Matter charged to different dates/courts.

Even if the first arrest is subject to no further action or diverted from prosecution, a bail to return on a further arrest will generate a further matter.

If that is not the case two further issues arise.

4

First, it is necessary to decide if there are 'genuinely separate' enquiries. These are enquiries that arise in new and different circumstances and are not merely the widening of the original enquiry, such as where a suspect is further arrested in an ongoing enquiry which continues as a single enquiry. If matters would become one case in the magistrates' court they will be a single matter, but the Unified Contract (Crime), Specification B provides:

B1.1.21(12) Examples of when more than one Police Station Telephone Advice Fixed Fee and/or one Police Station Attendance Fixed Fee:

(a) Client is arrested for theft from a shop and is bailed to return to the Police Station. The next day he is arrested for another theft from a shop.
(b) Client is arrested for burglary, he fails to appear at court and is arrested on the street for failing to appear.

If there are not genuinely separate enquiries only one claim may be made.

Second, if there are genuinely separate enquiries it must then be considered whether all the advice was given on a single 'occasion'.

The word 'occasion' is not defined, and will require careful application to the facts of a particular case. It does not, of necessity, require that the attendances be made on different days. 'Advice' is also undefined, but to rely on advice other than on the bail to return there will need to be a valid CDS1/2. However, if the client is at the police station, telephone advice would suffice:

- if all the advice is given on one occasion and all matters conclude, in whatever way, together there will be only one claim;
- if there is advice on more than one occasion in relation to the separate matters, there will be separate claims whatever the outcome of each one.

A matter ends when the client is charged or summoned or the case is concluded in any other way, e.g. no further action. A case remanded to the police station under Magistrates' Courts Act 1980, s.128(7) will generate a new matter.

For there to be more than one claim, there must be more than one offence. An arrest for breach of a conditional caution merely increases the value of the original claim but it is likely to remain within the same fixed fee.

If there is more than one matter, this will require apportionment of the relevant attendance between the possible claims to show an attendance was made, thus justifying the fixed fee.

Further guidance published by the LSC appears in **Appendix 5**. The position is summarised in Figure 1.1.

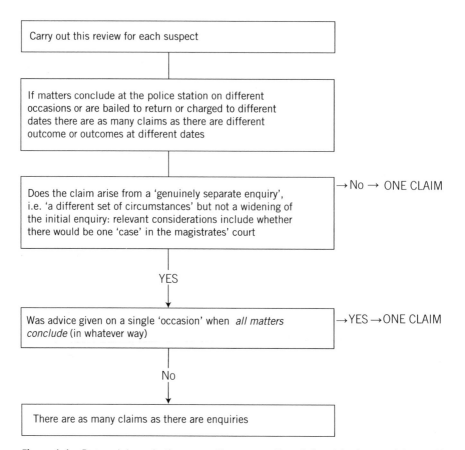

Figure 1.1 Determining whether more than one police station telephone advice and/ or attendance fixed fee can be claimed

A claim may also be made for a volunteer who attends at any place where a constable is present. By definition, he or she is not arrested.

Difficult issues will apply in the application of these rules where suspects are interviewed about matters to be taken into consideration (TIC). Separate claims would appear to be proper where there is no connection or similarity between the matters subject to the original investigation and those taken into consideration, and they conclude on separate occasions (as where such TICs are not accepted).

Telephone only advice

This covers all telephone attendances on a single matter dealt with only over the telephone. A single call in relation to a person in custody is required in order to generate a claim. It is wise to obtain a DSCC reference using the form at the end of **Appendix 3**.

It may not be claimed separately where an attendance is made and a fixed fee is claimed for that. It is relevant in identifying whether the escape provisions apply and as a stand-alone payment.

CLAIM RATES

Cases where CDS Direct has initially been involved:

Location	Fee exclusive of VAT
All areas	£8.00 per matter

Note: The DSCC and CDS Direct are separate organisations. Calls will normally come through the DSCC but only if CDS Direct is involved would this lower fee be payable or credited.

Cases where CDS Direct is not involved:

Location	Fee exclusive of VAT
London	£31.45 per matter
National	£30.25 per matter

Attendance cases

Note that no claim may be made unless the case has been registered at the DSCC. Use the form at the end of **Appendix 3**. Telephone 08457 500640 or fax 020 8763 3191, if the police have not already done so. The report must be made before attending the client if the solicitor is asked by a third party to attend a client already under arrest. If the client attends as a volunteer with the solicitor, or the client meets the solicitor who is at the police station, the case must be registered within 48 hours.

CLAIM RATES

It is still necessary to know the appropriate claim rates because:

1. The LSC requires the claim value to be inserted on Form CDS6 even if a fixed fee results.
2. They are required to identify whether an additional claim can be made because the value of the matter exceeds the escape figure.
3. They are payable for all work in the criminal investigations class represented by the following claim codes: INVE (warrants of further detention, including terrorism); INVF (warrants of further detention

(armed forces including terrorism)); INVH (post-charge attendance, breach of bail, warrants in cases where an attendance may be made); and INV1 (post-charge identification, caution, reprimand warning).

Important note: all these figures are exclusive of VAT.

Police station advice and advice and assistance other than by telephone

HOURLY RATES

At the police station	National rate	London rate
Duty solicitor (unsocial hours)	£69.05	£69.05
Duty solicitor (other hours)	£52.00	£56.20
Own solicitor	£52.00	£56.20
Duty solicitor – serious offences (unsocial hours)	£80.00	£80.00
Duty solicitor – serious offences (other hours)	£60.00	£65.00

Travelling and waiting	National rate	London rate
Duty solicitor (unsocial hours)	£69.05	£69.05
Duty solicitor (other hours)	£52.00	£56.20
Own solicitor	£28.80	£28.80

FIXED FEES

Work type	National fee	London fee
Police station telephone advice fixed fee (including all telephone calls whether routine or fixed 'advice', (except CDS Direct cases for which no such fee may be claimed))	£30.25 per claim	£31.45 per claim
Fixed acceptance fee (former CDS Direct cases referred to a duty or own solicitor for police station attendance only)	£8.00 per case	£8.00 per case

Definition of duty solicitor cases

A case is a duty case when allocated as such, or when a solicitor who is rota duty solicitor sees one of the firm's own clients in a relevant police station. Duty solicitor status lasts for the duration of the suspect's first continuous period in custody.

Enhanced duty rates apply in those circumstances to the following offences:

- treason (common law);
- murder (common law);

- manslaughter (Homicide Act 1957 and common law);
- causing death by dangerous driving (Road Traffic Act 1988, s.1);
- rape (Sexual Offences Act 2003, s.1);
- assault by penetration (Sexual Offences Act 2003, s.2);
- rape of a child under 13 (Sexual Offences Act 2003, s.5);
- assault of a child under 13 by penetration (Sexual Offences Act, s.6);
- robbery (Theft Act 1968, s.8);
- assault with intent to rob (common law);
- arson (Criminal Damage Act 1971, s.1(1), (2) or (13));
- perverting the course of public justice (common law);
- conspiracy to defraud (common law);
- kidnapping (common law);
- wounding or grievous bodily harm (Offences Against the Person Act 1861, ss.18 and 20);
- conspiracy to commit any of the above offences (Criminal Law Act 1977, s.1);
- soliciting or inciting to commit any of the above offences (common law);
- attempting to commit any of the above offences (Criminal Attempts Act 1981, ss.1 or 1A);
- any offence if the client is accused of possessing a firearm, shotgun or imitation firearm; and
- any offence if the client is detained under Terrorism Act 2000, s.41;

provided that duty solicitor rates would normally be payable and the attendance is personally undertaken by a solicitor.

Telephone only cases

Fees for attendance at a place where a constable is present are payable if the attendance is reasonable and not excluded by the contract.

An attendance cannot be claimed for in the following matters unless an exemption applies:

- detention for non-imprisonable offences;
- arrest on warrant (except where the solicitor has clear documentary evidence available that would result in the client being released from custody);
- arrest for driving with excess alcohol (driving unfit/drunk in charge/failure to provide a specimen); and
- arrest for breach of bail;

except where:

- there is to be an interview or identification procedure;
- the suspect is eligible for an appropriate adult;

- the suspect is unable to communicate over the telephone (this will include a requirement for privacy);
- the suspect alleges serious maltreatment by the police;
- the investigation includes another offence for which an attendance may be paid; and
- the solicitor is already at the police station (when the claim is limited to a telephone advice fee).

Fixed fees

These fees are payable, when there is a sufficient benefit in attending, for each claim made *only* under the following codes:

- INVC (police station attendance);
- INVD (police station attendance; armed forces); and
- INVJ (immigration matters).

The circumstances when there is a sufficient benefit include:

(a) providing advice prior to and during interview;
(b) advising at an identification procedure (including a video identification procedure when the client is not present);
(c) when appropriate, advising on the implications of the caution when the client is charged with an offence;
(d) advising when the advice may materially affect the outcome of the investigation and goes significantly beyond initial advice;
(e) advising a client who complains of serious maltreatment by the police.

If none of the above is satisfied further justification for attending should be provided on the file.

In relation to each matter the fee payable is a fixed fee *for the police station first actually attended* (from whichever scheme the work originated) *unless* the full value of the claim exceeds the escape figure.

The rates (together with the escape figure) are set out in the table at **Appendix 4**.

If a fixed fee is payable, no separate claim may be made for:

- advice and assistance related to the investigation;
- travel;
- waiting; and
- telephone advice.

An attendance fee is payable once a solicitor reasonably sets out to attend the police station, even if the call is later cancelled.

RESTRICTIONS ON NUMBER OF CLAIMS

In normal circumstances only one fixed fee may be claimed for each matter. It is therefore wise to register the claim at DSCC as soon as instructed directly (see **Appendix 3**).

Solicitors will also need to make particular checks, if asked to become involved after the start of a matter, to ensure that another firm has not already become entitled to the fixed fee.

However, the Unified Contract (Crime), B1.1.14(1) allows for a number of circumstances where more than one claim may be made:

(a) there is a gap in time and circumstances have changed materially between the first and second or subsequent occasions when the Police Station Advice and Assistance was sought;

(b) the Client has reasonable cause to transfer from the first supplier e.g. conflict of interest; or

(c) the first supplier has confirmed to you that he or she will be making no claim for payment for the Police Station Advice and Assistance.

These exceptions are significant. If a conflict is found to exist on attendance at the police station, the solicitor identifying the conflict and the new solicitor will both be able to claim a fixed fee. If a client cannot identify the earlier solicitor (and the custody record does not assist), an attendance will reasonably generate a fixed fee. The same would appear to apply when a client has entirely lost confidence in the original firm or wants a representative from a particular minority ethnic group, or the DSCC does not originally call the correct firm and the client will only work with the firm he actually named. Two solicitors instructed simultaneously may also claim if they attend.

All these explanations will need to be documented on the file. When a duty solicitor is called in as such because an earlier duty solicitor cannot continue both will be able to claim the fixed fee. The duty solicitor may return a matter (B.1.1.14(11)) when:

(a) You are unable to continue to act personally and there is no other suitable person in your firm able to act and you are unable to instruct a suitable agent. Examples of circumstances where it would be reasonable not to continue to act personally include:

   i.   Personal illness;
   ii. Pre-arranged annual leave/holiday
   iii. Unavailability due to other professional commitments to publicly funded Clients; or

(b) The Client removes/rescinds instructions from your firm;

(c) Your firm is unable to act because you have legitimate concerns about a breach of your professional code of conduct; or

(d) You confirm that you will not claim a Police Station Advice and Assistance Fixed Fee or any other remuneration for the Case.

The LSC expects reasonable enquiries to be made about whether there has been previous advice in the same matter in the last six months, and that these enquiries are recorded. The Contract (B1.1.14(4)) states that a second fixed fee should not be claimed where:

(a) The Client merely finds the first advice unpalatable and wants a second opinion;

(b) There is only a short time between the first and second occasions when the Police Station Advice and Assistance is sought and no material change of circumstances has occurred;

(c) The change requested is from a second to a third Supplier (unless exceptionally there is good reason for a further change); or

(d) There is no reasonable explanation for the Client seeking further Police Station Advice and Assistance from a new Supplier.

Particular problems arise when a suspect is transferred from one police station to another at a considerable distance. The LSC considers that the first solicitor should seek, within the fixed fee, to appoint a local agent, or attend himself. If neither is possible and there are substantial practical problems with both, the matter should be returned to the DSCC for allocation to the duty solicitor in the distant area. Each solicitor is then entitled to claim a fee.

BAILS TO RETURN

Because the fixed fee covers all attendances, solicitors will wish to examine carefully the need to return. It is unlikely that an attendance can be justified until it is known that the client is present and the police have confirmed that there is to be an interview or identification procedure or a need to make a prepared statement at charge.

This will make it essential that solicitors at the first attendance have signed Form CDS14 and Form CDS15 in case there is a charge at a later stage, having obtained authority to complete the details of the charge once known, and the client's agreement to provide details of any financial change of circumstances.

Escape provisions

VALUE OF CLAIM

If the value at prescribed rates of the work actually and reasonably done exceeds three times the fixed fee (the fee limit) for the relevant scheme then you claim **the fixed fee + the amount by which the value exceeds the fee limit**.

Thus, if in an area the fixed fee is £310, the escape limit is £930. If on assessment a claim is accepted at £1,400 the amount paid will be:

The fixed fee		£310
The excess of the claim over the fee limit (£1400 − £930) =		£470
	Claim	£780

This removes any incentive to push towards the fee limit as in most cases it will lead to significant loss. This work will be subject to individual assessment by the LSC and should be claimed on Form CDS18. To ensure that CDS18 is processed without difficulty it should be accompanied by:

- full file of papers (photocopies are acceptable);
- Form CDS11;
- completed Forms CDS1 and CDS2 if your claim includes any freestanding advice or assistance.

The file should also contain:

- times of when the solicitor arrived and left the station;
- interview times;
- times the solicitor had to wait and the reasons for doing so;
- a copy of the full custody record.

CALCULATING THE VALUE

Add value at the appropriate rate (including duty and enhanced duty rates) of:

- travel;
- waiting;
- advice and assistance (including letters and telephone calls) if there are valid Forms CDS1 and CDS2;
- attendances;
- relevant telephone advice fee.

Compare the total with the fee limit.

Cases outside fixed fees

These are claims made under the following codes:

- INVE (warrant of further detention);
- INVF (warrant of further defence (armed forces)).

The LSC has indicated that the same applies to:

- INVH (post-charge: breach of bail/warrant) – it must be emphasised that breach of police bail prior to charge is dealt with by fixed telephone or fixed attendance fee and not by hourly rates;
- INVI (post-charge: identification/recharge/referral back).

They are payable at the hourly rates specified above, including for travel and waiting.

Because the standard and particularly the litigators' graduated fee schemes provide for fixed fees, solicitors will normally wish to elect to claim this post-charge work as an additional police station claim (as is allowed by the decision of the LSC Costs Appeals Committee, CRIMLA 77).

Advocacy assistance on a warrant of further detention or at an Armed Forces Custody Hearing

Work type	National hourly rate	London hourly rate
Preparation		
– Standard rate	£46.90	£49.70
– Enhanced rate	£62.50	£66.30
Advocacy		
– Standard rate	£59.00	£59.00
– Enhanced rate	£78.65	£78.65
Travelling and waiting		
– Standard rate	£26.30	£26.30
– Enhanced rate	£35.05	£35.05
Routine letters written and telephone calls	per item	per item
– Standard rate	£3.70	£3.85
– Enhanced rate	£4.90	£5.10

Note: The enhanced rate applies to advocacy assistance provided by duty solicitors in **unsocial hours only**. The standard rate applies to advocacy assistance provided by duty solicitors **outside unsocial hours** and by **own solicitors at any time**.

Advocacy assistance (warrants of further detention before the High Court or senior judge)

Work type	National rate	London rate
Routine letter out	£7.50 per item	£7.50 per item
Routine telephone calls	£4.15 per item	£4.15 per item
All other preparation work including any work which was reasonably done arising out of or incidental to the proceedings, interviews with client, witnesses and other parties, obtaining evidence; preparation and consideration of, and dealing with, documents, negotiations and notices; dealing with letters written and received and telephone calls which are not routine	£75.00 per hour	£79.50 per hour
Attending counsel in conference or at the trial or hearing of any summons or application at court, or other appointment	£37.00 per hour	£37.00 per hour

Attending without counsel at the trial or hearing of any summons or application at court, or other appointment	£75.00 per hour	£75.00 per hour
Travelling and waiting	£33.25 per hour	£33.25 per hour

Note: No enhanced rates are payable for this unit of work.

Advocacy assistance in the magistrates' court in connection with an application to vary pre-charge police bail conditions

Work type	National hourly rate	London hourly rate
Preparation	£49.70	£52.50
Advocacy	£62.30	£62.30
Travelling and waiting	£26.30	£26.30
Routine letters written and telephone calls	£3.90	£4.05

Claims should include the time involved in giving any notice of appeal and any reasonable preparation and follow up work including reasonable preparation in the office, correspondence and telephone calls and advising the client of the consequences of the outcome.

DISBURSEMENTS

All disbursements actually and reasonably incurred continue to be payable. These will include items such as photographs, if required, but also hotel bills when the work cannot otherwise reasonably be done. The use of hotels during rota periods requires specific authority from the LSC.

Travel costs are also met. The mileage rate is £0.45 per mile. Solicitors will wish to use the fastest method of transport, as the value of the travel time will seldom be recovered.

METHOD OF CLAIMING

The fixed fee and remaining hourly rate claims and claims for advocacy assistance are made separately in the normal way on Form CDS6. In cases reaching the escape figures, the additional claim (for the amount in excess of the fee limit) is made on Form CDS18 and sent to the appropriate assessment centre with all the relevant papers (or photocopies) so that an assessment can take place.

1.3 PROVISIONAL REPRESENTATION ORDERS

1.3.1 Criminal Defence Service (Provisional Representation Orders) Regulations 2009

A provisional representation order may be granted, in cases continuing between 3 August 2009 and 31 December 2011, where:

- the case has been identified by the Crown as involving an individual in an allegation of serious or complex fraud; and
- the Crown has invited plea discussions in accordance with the Attorney General's Guidelines on Plea Discussions in Cases of Serious or Complex Fraud (18 March 2009); and
- the LSC considers that any trial would be likely to last for more than 25 days.

This will enable litigators and advocates to be remunerated for entering into pre-charge discussions.

The work to be undertaken will need to be agreed with a contract case manager from the complex criminal cases unit, but membership of the VHCC panel is not required. Payment is at special rates (see **Appendix 12**).

The order lasts for three months and may be extended once for up to three months from the date of extension.

1.4 MAGISTRATES' COURT CASES

A list of all magistrates' courts appears at **Appendix 7**.

1.4.1 Court duty solicitor

Attendance

Attendance is paid by hourly rates for all time actually and reasonably spent at court, when not undertaking own client work.

It is reasonable to arrive in sufficient time to have cases ready for the court's normal start time, and to remain at court to complete all relevant paperwork, including applications for a representation order. A claim cannot be made for a luncheon adjournment, although it is appropriate if the time is actually used. Solicitors will wish to ensure that any waiting time is undertaken as duty solicitor. The rates below are *exclusive* of VAT.

Type of rate	National hourly rate	London hourly rate
Standard rate (attendance and waiting at a magistrates' court)	£53.85	£55.15
Enhanced rate (only payable in respect of work done on a day which is not a business day)	£67.30	£68.90
Travelling (only payable where the duty solicitor is called out (including being called to return) to the court from the office or attends on a day that is not a business day). Reasonable travel expenses may then also be claimed	£26.30	£26.30

Travel

Travel is payable:

- when there is no rota and a solicitor is called in; or
- when a rostered duty solicitor has left court and has to return; or
- on a Saturday and bank holiday (the travel may be claimed from a home address if that is further than the office).

In these circumstances travel costs may also be recovered. The mileage rate is £0.45 per mile.

Claim code

PROD is used. No outcome code is required; nor are individual client details or case information.

1.4.2 Virtual courts

A claim for advocacy assistance may be made if:

- a case concludes at a virtual court;
- the case is adjourned and a representation order is not granted;
- the solicitor declines to represent the client at the next hearing and there is no application for a representation order; or
- the solicitor advises the client not to take part in the virtual court and does not represent the client at any adjourned hearing.

No such claim may be made if:

- a representation order is granted to the solicitor at the virtual court, when the time involved becomes part of the core cost of the magistrates' court claim; or

- a representation order already exists, and this includes when there is an arrest for breach of bail.

The fees are as follows, exclusive of VAT:

Work type	London	Outside London
Attendance in office hours	£200	£150
Attendance in unsocial hours	£240	£180

Claims for these fees are made not on Form CDS6 but on a virtual court solicitors' claim form available at **www.legalservices.gov.uk**.

1.4.3   Costs without a representation order

There are three other possible claims (under Unified Contract (Crime) B.2.3) which may be used when a representation order is not granted.

Pre-order costs

CONDITIONS

1. An application for a representation order is made but refused on merits (whatever the means position).
2. The designated fee earner documented why they considered the merits test met.
3. No claim is made for early cover.

CLAIMS

- Rates are the hourly or individual rates appropriate for magistrates' court preparation, advocacy, travel, waiting, and routine letters and telephone calls.
- The total claim is *limited* to (inclusive of any disbursements):

  - London: £52.55 + VAT
  - National: £49.70 + VAT

- A separate claim may be made for each client. The claim code is PROP.

Early cover

CONDITIONS

1. An application for a representation order is refused on means but granted on merits.

2. An application, properly completed, was received by the court by 09.00 on the sixth working day following the day of first instruction or earlier court hearing.
3. All reasonable steps were taken to complete and submit the form with supporting evidence.
4. No decision by the court was made before the first hearing.
5. You represent the client at the first hearing.
6. Progress is made at the first hearing or an adjournment is justified.

CLAIMS

- Disbursements cannot be claimed.
- A separate claim may be made for each client.
- The claim code is PROT.
- Fees: £75 + VAT).

Initial advice

CONDITIONS

1. No early cover.
2. Would satisfy merits test and solicitor should document the file accordingly.
3. Failed means test.
4. Advice within 10 working days of charge or process.
5. Not privately instructed.

CLAIMS

- Fees: £25 + VAT.
- Claim code: PROU.

1.4.4 Costs with a representation order

Claims

Payment for claims made for each case for which a representation order exists depends on the area in which the solicitor's office named in the representation order is situated and the court issuing the order.

'Carter' fees apply if the office or the court is situated in the 'designated' areas, which include the criminal justice areas of:

- Greater Manchester
- London
- Merseyside
- West Midlands

as well as the local or unitary authority areas of:

- Brighton and Hove
- Bristol
- Cardiff
- Derby and Erewash
- Kingston-upon-Hull
- Leeds and Bradford
- Leicester
- Nottingham
- Portsmouth and Gosport
- Newcastle and Sunderland (including Gateshead, North Tyneside, Blythe Valley and South Tyneside)
- Sheffield
- Southampton

For a claim on Form CDS6, Guidance for Reporting Work on Form CDS6 is at **Appendix 3**.

CLAIM CODES

Code	Criminal proceedings
PROE	Representation order – lower standard fee
PROF	Representation order – higher standard fee
PROG	Representation order – non-standard fee
PROJ	Second claim for deferred sentence
PROK	Carter fee – representation order – lower standard fee
PROL	Carter fee – representation order – higher standard fee
PROM	Carter fee – representation order – non-standard fee

OUTCOME CODES

Code	Criminal proceedings
CP01	Arrest warrant issued/adjourned indefinitely
CP02	Change of solicitor
CP03	Representation order withdrawn
CP04	Trial: acquitted
CP05	Trial: mixed verdicts
CP06	Trial: convicted
CP07	Discontinued (before any pleas entered)
CP08	Discontinued (after pleas entered)
CO09	Guilty plea to all charges put – not listed for trial
CP10	Guilty plea to all charges put after case listed for trial
CP11	Guilty plea to substitute charges put – after case listed for trial
CP12	Mix of guilty plea(s) and discontinuance – not listed for trial
CP13	Mix of guilty plea(s) and discontinuance – listed for trial

CP14	Committal: election
CP15	Committal/transfer: direction
CP16	Committal: discharged
CP17	Extradition
CP18	Case remitted from Crown to magistrates' court for sentencing
CP19	Deferred sentence
CP20	Granted anti-social behaviour order/sexual offences order/other order
CP21	Part-granted anti-social behaviour order/sexual offences order/other order
CP22	Refused anti-social behaviour order/sexual offences order/other order
CP23	Varied anti-social behaviour order/sexual offences order/other order
CP24	Discharged anti-social behaviour order/sexual offences order/other order

Note: An explanation for these codes appears in **Appendix 3**.

Payment

The number of cases must first be identified and any excluded case dealt with at hourly rates on Form CDS7.

EXCLUDED CASES

In all these cases, use Form CDS7 and claim the value of the full hourly rates. Cases fall outside standard fees:

- if any part of a claim is enhanced;
- if an advocate is assigned;
- if the proceedings are extradition proceedings.

The codes to describe the work undertaken appears at **Appendix 8**.

NON-EXCLUDED CASES

All other cases must be categorised. For each case, the core costs of the case must be calculated and the figure compared with the fee limit in the relevant category. If the value does not exceed the lower fee limit (LFL) a lower standard fee (LSF) is payable. If the value exceeds the LFL but not the higher fee limit (HFL) the higher standard fee (HSF) is payable. If the value exceeds the HFL a full claim may be submitted on Form CDS7. No claim can ever be made for a LFL or a HFL.

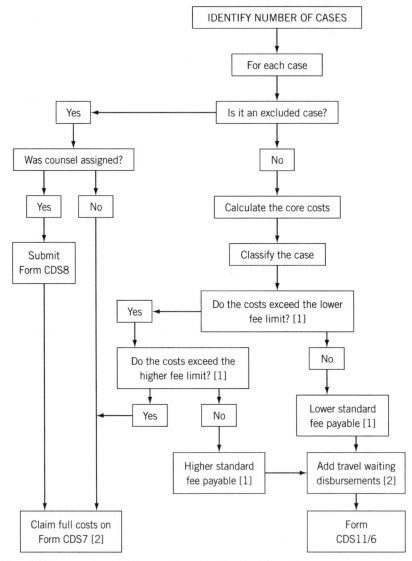

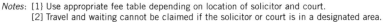

Notes: [1] Use appropriate fee table depending on location of solicitor and court.
       [2] Travel and waiting cannot be claimed if the solicitor or court is in a designated area.

Figure 1.2   Costs with a representation order – summary

If a second claim falls to be made for a case then (except for the conclusion of deferred sentence proceedings) credit must be given for the value of the claim already made.

In order to calculate payment the following must first be determined:

1. How many cases?
2. What is the correct category of the case?
3. What are the core costs of each case?

1. HOW MANY CASES?

(a) The number of defendants is irrelevant.
(b) The number of representation orders is irrelevant.
(c) There is one case if:

    (i)   the charges were preferred at the same time;
    (ii)   the charges are founded on the same facts (warrants/rearrest/alternative charges); or
    (iii) the charges are, or form part of, a series, i.e. is there a sufficient nexus of fact or law.

(d) Cases do not form part of a series merely because they all involve dishonesty and/or all conclude on the same day.
(e) Bail Act offences and breach proceedings cannot be a separate case if they are at any point heard at the same time as substantive proceedings. The existence of such matters may affect the *category*, which must also be identified.
(f) Stand-alone Bail Act or breach proceedings will represent a separate case.

2. WHAT IS THE CORRECT CATEGORY OF THE CASE?

Category 1	Category 2	Category 3
1.1 Guilty pleas	2.1 Contested trials	3.1 Committal proceedings
1.2 Uncontested proceedings arising out of a breach of an order of a magistrates' court (including proceedings in a magistrates' court relating to a breach of a Crown Court community rehabilitation order, community punishment order or suspended sentence)	2.2 Proceedings which were listed and fully prepared for trial in a magistrates' court but are disposed of by a guilty plea on the day of trial before the opening of the prosecution case	3.2 Proceedings transferred under Criminal Justice Act 1987, s.4 or Criminal Justice Act 1991, s.53

1.3 Proceedings (other than committal proceedings) which are discontinued or withdrawn or where the prosecution offers no evidence	2.3 Proceedings which were listed and fully prepared for trial in a magistrates' court but are discontinued or withdrawn or where the prosecution offers no evidence or which result in a bind over on the day of trial before the opening of the prosecution case
1.4 Proceedings (other than committal proceedings) relating to summary or either way offences which result in a bind over	2.4 Contested proceedings relating to a breach of an order of a magistrates' court (including proceedings relating to a breach of a Crown Court community rehabilitation order, community punishment order or suspended sentence)
1.5 Proceedings arising out of a deferment of sentence (including any subsequent sentence hearing) under Powers of Criminal Courts (Sentencing) Act 2000, s.2	2.5 Proceedings where mixed pleas are entered
1.6 Proceedings prescribed under Criminal Defence Service (General) (No.2) Regulations 2001, SI 2001/1437 (as amended), reg.3(2), except where the case was listed and fully prepared for a contested hearing to decide whether an order should be made	2.6 Proceedings prescribed under Criminal Defence Service (General) (No.2) Regulations 2001, SI 2001/1437 (as amended), reg.3(2) where the case was listed and fully prepared for a contested hearing to decide whether an order should be made

Notes on categories:

1. A case which is committed for sentence is in category 1.
2. Committal proceedings exist once the court has declined jurisdiction or the defendant elects trial on indictment.
3. A case is listed for trial when a not guilty plea is entered and the case is adjourned.
4. Whether a case is fully prepared for trial will depend on the individual circumstances of the case. Regard will be had to the existence of a proof and evidence of consideration of issues relating to disclosure and relevant witnesses.

5. Discontinuance should only be claimed in category 1 if a better claim cannot properly be made in the other categories.
6. Two claims are made when a sentence is deferred, the second is always in category 1.
7. A mixed plea can be claimed whether or not there is any preparation.

Special rules on categories:

1. If a case would have been in category 2 but a warrant is issued for the defendant, that defendant's categorisation is changed to category 1.
2. If a case would have been in category 2 but there is a change of firm assigned, the former firm must claim in category 1. If a solicitor merely moves from one firm to another, or the change is caused by matters such as a merger or because the old firm has lost its contract, only one claim, in the appropriate category, may be made.
3. Once a case is in category 3, it is always in category 3 whatever then happens (discontinuance, new firm assigned, warrant issued) unless the totality of the case reverts to summary trial under Magistrates' Court Act 1980, s.25(3). If any part of a case is in category 3, the whole claim is in category 3.
4. If part of a claim is in category 1 and part in category 2 (e.g. two defendants tried but one absconds), the solicitor may choose whichever category produces a larger fee.

Indictable only proceedings: If a case is sent to the Crown Court under the Crime and Disorder Act 1998, s.51 no claim may be made in the magistrates' court. This will not apply to any part of the proceedings that are not sent, for which a claim may be made in the appropriate category.

3. WHAT ARE THE CORE COSTS OF EACH CASE?

The core costs include the value of the work actually and reasonably done by way of:

- routine letters and telephone calls;
- advocacy;
- attending assigned advocate at court;
- preparation and attendances including all post-charge work up to 10 days before first hearing, if CDS forms are submitted within five days, and representation order granted to the firm making the claim.

Preparation includes:

- taking instructions;
- interviewing witnesses;

- ascertaining the prosecution case;
- advising on plea and mode of trial;
- preparing and perusing documents;
- dealing with letters and telephone calls (which are not routine);
- preparing for advocacy;
- instructing an advocate and expert witnesses;
- conferences, consultations and work done in connection with advice on appeal; and
- listening to or viewing any tape or video recording of interview or evidence.

To be chargeable the item claimed must be such as might reasonably be undertaken by a fee earner and not be purely administrative work. In determining the reasonableness of work done and whether the time is reasonable, account should be taken of all relevant circumstances of the case including the nature, importance, complexity or difficulty of the work and the time involved.

Routine letters written are those that are not items of preparation and are more than a compliment slip (*R* v. *Hudson* (TMC SJ2)). LSC guidance in the Integrated Criminal Bills Assessment Manual suggests a letter is routine unless outside the range of an average letter, substantial in length or complex in content. The additional guidance that letters should be more than one page in length and take more than 10 minutes to prepare does not appear to be based on authority. Individual letters are chargeable even if standard (*R* v. *Brown* [2002] 3 Costs LR 539) and each letter in similar terms to a number of different people may be charged. Fax messages and emails may be charged as letters (but only one claim for each item).

Routine letters received may only be charged if the reading time becomes an item of preparation. Routine telephone calls made or received are all calls that are neither an item of preparation nor abortive (*R* v. *Hudson* (TMC SJ2)). Guidance in the LSC Integrated Criminal Bills Assessment Manual suggests that for a telephone attendance to amount to preparation, it must be of such substance as to constitute an attendance and should materially progress the case.

Advocacy includes advocacy at bail applications made in the magistrates' court or an appeal during magistrates' court proceedings to the Crown Court.

More than one advocate may reasonably attend different defendants represented by the same firm in a single case (even though there is no conflict), if issues of presentation require it (CRIMLA 11). Advocacy time should be charged while a Bench is considering its verdict (*R* v. *Wanklyn* (TMC 528)).

Dictating time is properly charged as preparation (*Brush* v. *Bower Cotton & Bower* [1993] All ER 741) and this will include the dictation of file notes that add value to the file.

Preparation includes long telephone calls and letters written that are more than routine (*Bwanaoga* [1979] 2 All ER 105). Decisions must be made

26

without the benefit of hindsight (CRIMLA 38). Drafting time and time spent reading and updating case papers is properly charged.

Supervision which enables a less experienced fee earner to conduct a file may be charged, as may time spent in arranging appropriate delegation. The test is whether there is an overall saving to the fund. In larger cases requiring the work of more than one fee earner, the time spent in their meeting may be chargeable (CRIMLA 39).

Completion of LSC forms including CDS4, CDS14, CDS15, CDS16 and CDS17, but not billing forms (which are administrative), may be chargeable (CRIMLA 67).

Longer periods of time may reasonably be spent in attendance with those under 18 than an older client.

Checking transcripts is fee earner work. Routine research and updating of the law is not normally work for which a fee earner can charge to an individual file, but claims may properly be made for time spent in the application of the law to the facts of a particular case. In addition, research may be chargeable if it is a new, developing or unusual law (*Perry* v. *Lord Chancellor* (TMC SJ4); *R* v. *Great Western Trains* [2004] 2 Costs LR 331).

The total preparation time must be justified (*R* v. *SCTO ex p John Singh & Co* (TMC SJ3)) and is often best done by a case plan identifying the use of the time involved. If disallowed, the LSC must give reasons for doing so (*Miller Gardner* v. *Lord Chancellor* [1997] 2 Costs LR 29).

At each stage the claim should include the work undertaken by agents (at the rate appropriate for the agent) and unassigned counsel.

The value of the time involved in a bail appeal to the Crown Court during magistrates' court proceedings forms part of the core costs.

The work is valued at the following rates.

Work	National hourly rate	London hourly rate
Preparation (including taking instructions, interviewing witnesses, ascertaining the prosecution case, advising on plea and mode of trial, preparing and perusing documents, dealing with letters and telephone calls which are not routine, preparing for advocacy, instructing counsel and expert witnesses, conference consultations, views and work done in connection with advice on appeal or case stated)	£49.70	£52.55
Advocacy (including applications for bail and other applications to the court)	£62.35	£62.35
Attendance at court where assigned (including conferences with advocate at court)	£34.00	£34.00
Routine letters written and telephone calls	£3.90 per item	£4.05 per item

These rates are *exclusive* of VAT. They also apply to related proceedings undertaken under a representation order in the Crown Court.

With fees fixed for litigators in the Crown Court there may be financial advantage in doing reasonable work while the case is still in the magistrates' court. This will increase core costs and may lead to a higher fee at that level while earning the same fee at the Crown Court. It is usually good practice to take witness statements and observations on evidence at the earliest time while memories are fresh. It will help to listen to tapes at this stage to advise on the strength of the evidence.

CRIMLA 30 states as follows:

POINT OF PRINCIPLE

Where a legal aid order is made to defend criminal proceedings in the magistrates' court and the case proceeds by way of committal to the Crown Court, the costs payable under the order will be limited to items of work relating to proceedings in the magistrates' court. It is for the solicitor to justify work undertaken while the proceedings are in the magistrates' court, taking into account the nature of the case and the issues involved, the time when the work was undertaken, the then stage of proceedings, the nature of any evidence obtained and the effect of delaying the work to a date subsequent to committal.

HEAD OFFICE GUIDANCE ON DECISION CRIMLA 30

The Costs Appeals Committee did not wish to make a decision which could lead to delay in the Crown Court. However, whilst early preparation should be encouraged in certain circumstances, there is a limit on the amount of preparation for trial that should be carried out in the magistrates' court. That is where it would be more appropriate for the preparation to be carried out post committal.

In some cases it may be essential to obtain witness statements at an early stage, i.e. whilst the proceedings are still in the magistrates' court. For example, where there are witnesses whose evidence relates to issues of fact, such as witnesses to a fight, an accurate record of their recollection is important and it is therefore good practice to see such a witness as soon as possible. Similarly alibi witnesses whose recollection of where somebody was at a specific time may need to be spoken to whilst the events are fresh in their mind. On the other hand, character witnesses are the sort of witnesses whose evidence can be obtained at any time. Such witnesses do not need to be spoken to immediately and the taking of witness statements from them may properly be regarded as work to be done post committal. The same may be said of other witnesses whose evidence is not time critical, but who are just a part of the whole picture.

The same applies to disbursements, for example, experts' reports. If a medical report is being obtained on a defendant's medical state of health, it may be that the report will go to their state at the time of committing the offence in which case an early report may be necessary, or it may go to their general state of health such as, e.g. whether they could survive a sentence of imprisonment. Such evidence can reasonably be obtained post committal.

If solicitors see witnesses of fact as to the event very soon after receiving instructions, it will be easier for them to justify that it was necessary to do that work immediately, and prior to committal, than if there is delay of some weeks or months, and then long after the event, they take witness statements very shortly before the committal.

Standard fee tables

The standard fee tables are set out below.

1. OFFICES AND COURTS INSIDE LONDON

LSF	LFL	HSF	HFL
£284.35	£382.90	£611.15	£646.85
£484.60	£651.00	£1,005.49	£1,041.60
£406.46	£548.25	£888.85	£888.86

2. OFFICES AND COURTS INSIDE OTHER LISTED AREAS

LSF	LFL	HSF	HFL
£221.59	£298.45	£477.41	£517.10
£378.46	£512.70	£792.71	£854.40
£357.87	£452.20	£734.56	£789.50

3. OFFICES AND COURTS OUTSIDE LISTED AREAS

LSF	LFL	HSF	HFL
£173.45	£298.45	£417.20	£517.10
£306.25	£512.70	£702.40	£854.40
£276.50	£452.20	£626.50	£789.50

All figures are *exclusive* of VAT.

A claim is made for a LSF or a HSF or on Form CDS7.

No claim may be made for a fee limit (LFL or HFL). These limits merely identify which fee is payable.

Form CDS7 is used if the core costs exceed the value of the higher fee limit in the relevant category. The codes to describe the work undertaken appear at **Appendix 8**.

Additional payments

TRAVEL AND WAITING

When both court and firm are located outside the 'designated' areas, travel and waiting actually and reasonably undertaken are valued at £26.30 per hour exclusive of VAT. If a firm or the court is in a 'designated' area no travel and waiting may be claimed, even on a Form CDS7 claim.

ENHANCEMENT

An item in a bill only enhances if, taking into account all the relevant circumstances of that case, the work was done with any one or more of six exceptionalities, including:

(a) exceptional competence;
(b) exceptional skill;
(c) exceptional expertise;
(d) exceptional dispatch;

or the case involves:

(e) exceptional circumstances; or
(f) exceptional complexity.

Exceptional means unusual or out of the ordinary when compared with the generality of criminal cases.

If enhancement applies, a percentage uplift is applied to relevant items. The percentage takes account of:

(a) the degree of responsibility accepted by the solicitor;
(b) the speed and economy with which the case was prepared; and
(c) the novelty, weight and complexity of the case.

However, because of the rule in *Backhouse* (*R* v. *Backhouse* (TMC S30)) the percentage uplift is never less than 100 per cent which is normally also the maximum. However, an uplift of up to 200 per cent may be paid where the proceedings relate to serious or complex fraud (the allegation itself need not be of fraud).

If any single item in a bill enhances, the whole bill is excluded from standard fees, and this may be advantageous if a heavy loss would otherwise be made. Reasons must always be given for enhancement. Enhancement should be considered when the case has substantially increased the burden on the solicitor. Relevant factors include the character of the defendant, the weight and complexity of the case and the nature of the allegation, the degree of public interest in the case, the use of expert evidence – particularly if contested (CRIMLA 22), the length of any trial and issues arising over defence witnesses. The preparation of a case for imminent hearing may show exceptional dispatch (CRIMLA 18). The use of foreign languages by the solicitor's staff avoiding the need for interpreters may significantly improve efficiency (CRIMLA 4) and exceptional skill may be required to represent a number of defendants with different needs, though that factor alone will not be enough (CRIMLA 17). In the magistrates' court, a hearing lasting more than two days may be exceptional (CRIMLA 24). Preparation which avoids a trial may enhance (*R* v. *Smith* (SCTO 117/93)) and cases involving child witnesses, particularly where there is sexual abuse, will often enhance, particularly in the Youth Court (*R* v. *P* (SCTO 158/93)).

DISBURSEMENTS

Disbursements actually and reasonably incurred are always recoverable including travel costs. The mileage rate is £0.45 per mile. This is so in *all* claims (including those in 'designated' areas).

CHAPTER 2

Crown Court work (provided for by the Criminal Defence Service (Funding) Order 2007 as amended)

Litigators' fees are always added to advocacy fees and because the fees are fixed there are substantial advantages in having the work done by the same person.

2.1 GENERAL

Certain concepts are at the heart of both advocates' and litigators' graduated fee schemes. They are:

1. Classification of the case.
2. Numbers of pages of prosecution evidence (PPE).
3. Whether the case is a trial, 'cracked trial' or 'guilty plea'.
4. Number of days of trial.

It is also necessary to identify the number of cases for which a fee may be claimed.

2.1.1 Classification of the case

For both advocates' and litigators' fees there are 11 classes of work. They are summarised as follows and the full schedule appears in **Appendix 9**.

A. Homicide and related grave crime (and Mental Health Act 1983, s.41).
B. Serious violence or damage and serious drugs offences.
C. Lesser offences in same groups as B.
D. Sexual offences and offences against children (and unfit to plead (on election) but also see J below).
E. Burglary.
F. Other offences of dishonesty (but see G and K).
G. Other offences of dishonesty if exceeding £30,000 (and see also K below).
H. Miscellaneous (and residuary).
I. Offences against public justice.

J.   Serious sexual offences.

K.   High value offences of dishonesty (exceed £100,000).

The fee is based on the charges faced by the particular defendant represented (*R* v. *Mira* (X4)).

If a case involves offences which do not appear in the schedules, the claim is in Class H. Inchoate offences fall in the same class as the completed offence. If a case involves allegations in more than one category, the lawyer may choose whichever is more profitable. Class A may be used if the case concludes with a restriction order under the Mental Health Act 1983, s.41. If a defendant is unfit to plead or stand trial, the lawyer may, if they choose, select Class D. A robbery (Class C) is an armed robbery (Class B) if either the defendant was armed with a firearm or an imitation, or the victim so believed, or the defendant was in possession of an offensive weapon (*R* v. *Stables* (X12)).

Allegations of dishonesty may fall into one of three classes depending on the amount alleged to be involved. In undertaking this calculation, the value of alternative charges cannot be used more than once. The value of offences taken into consideration (TICs) may not be used (*R* v. *Knight* (X35)). However, the values are otherwise aggregated. The burden of proof as to the value is on the lawyer. If the full value does not appear on the face of the indictment, it is necessary to produce other evidence to satisfy this requirement, such as the prosecution case opening or summary or a letter from the prosecution or court. Sexual offences fall into categories D and J, depending on the specific offence charged. A claim should include a copy of the indictment and be sent to the Litigator Fee Team. The content of a representation order is not acceptable to them.

2.1.2   Number of pages of prosecution evidence

A page is counted however much or little appears on it. However, title pages and separator pages should not be counted (*R* v. *El Treki* (X26)). The number of pages of prosecution evidence (PPE) – served on the court – includes:

- all witness statements;
- documentary and pictorial exhibits;
- records of interview with the legally assisted person and with other defendants;

forming part of the committal or served prosecution documents, or included in any notice of additional evidence. If a transcript has been expanded, the fullest transcript is used for page count as well as the transcript in the committal bundle. Transcripts of video evidence asked for by the judge should be included in the page count (*R* v. *Brazier* (X5)); PPE does not normally include any documents provided on CD-Rom or by other means of electronic communication for which specific provision is made. This should be distinguished from video and audio recordings. The LSC accepts that where evidence is served electronically but has been served on the court in a paper bundle, it may be paid as PPE in the usual way as the litigator fee may otherwise be unfairly reduced. (See Litigator Graduated Fee Scheme Guidance, 3.43.)

In the case of proceedings on indictment in the Crown Court initiated otherwise than by committal for trial, the appropriate authority shall determine the number of PPE as nearly in accordance with the preceding scheme as the nature of the case permits.

Unused material only counts as PPE for graduated fees if served by formal 'notice of additional evidence' (NAE) (*R* v. *Sturdy* [1999] 1 Costs LR 1 (X9)) – otherwise unused material cannot be taken into account.

Pages only count if they were produced by the prosecution (rather than merely referred to in general terms). Defence papers do not count.

NAEs are included in page count for graduated fees whatever their nature – e.g. transcript of first aborted trial (*R* v. *Taylor* [2005] 4 Costs LR 712).

Forms and procedures have been introduced to reduce the number of disputes over page count and appear at **Appendix 13**. The costs judges have accepted an advocate's page count paid by the court as sufficient evidence (*R* v. *Goodridge* (SCCO 312/08)) though the LSC refuses to do so. The LSC is under a duty to examine the papers (*R* v. *Rovis* (SCCO 175/09)). It will accept the content of a letter from the prosecution or court or fully paginated list of exhibits and statements from the prosecution, together with any NAE. See generally the Litigator Graduated Fee Scheme Guidance, 3.32–3.33 and 3.35–3.36.

2.1.3   Categorisation of the case

There are three possible categories for each case in order of desirability for maximising fees. If defendants represented by the litigator are dealt with differently, the litigator chooses the best categorisation and applies the mark-ups below.

Trial

A trial begins once a jury is sworn or at the start of a formal preparatory hearing, but it also includes a Newton hearing (see *R* v. *Newton* (1982) 4 Cr App R (S) 388). If the planned Newton hearing does not take place, even by the reading of a s.9 statement or the making of s.10 admissions, the case reverts to its original classification (*R* v. *Riddell* (X3); *R* v. *Hunter-Brown* (X2); *R* v. *Ayres* (X32)). If a Newton trial is listed but does not proceed due to the absence of a prosecution witness, the defence version then being accepted, it is the supplementary fee for an ineffective trial that is for that day payable (*R* v. *Ayres* [2002] 2 Costs LR 330). See **2.3.4** below.

A case is a trial notwithstanding that a trial jury could not agree (*R* v. *Finn* [2006] 3 Costs LR 525). A trial which 'settled' at the close of the prosecution case by a guilty plea to an additional lesser charge was a trial (*R* v. *Aloys* [2007] Costs LR 321). Once a trial has begun, there cannot be a cracked trial (*R* v. *Maynard* (X19); *R* v. *Kara* (X19)).

Cracked trial

A cracked trial exists if there is no trial but a case in relation to any count proceeds beyond the plea and case management hearing (PCMH). If there was no PCMH listed there is a cracked trial if the case was listed for a trial which for any reason does not take place (*LC* v. *Taylor* [2000] Costs LR 1).

It is disadvantageous if the PCMH is itself adjourned as a change of plea between plea and case management hearings is a guilty plea (*R* v. *Beecham* (X11)). Where a PCMH is completed and the case adjourned for a mention, a cracked trial exists (*R* v. *Dawson* [1999] 1 Costs LR 4). If at or after PCMH counts are severed and following acquittal on the first indictment no evidence is offered on the second, that second is a cracked trial (*R* v. *Chubb* [2002] 2 Costs LR 333).

A retrial is a cracked trial if it cracks notwithstanding that a jury could not agree at the first trial (*R* v. *Frampton* [2005] 3 Costs LR 527). It is not an extension of the earlier trial. If a jury is selected but not sworn before the defendant pleads guilty, there is a cracked trial (*R* v. *Sanghera* [2008] Costs LR 823).

Guilty plea

All other cases, including the Crown discontinuing or offering no evidence at or before the PCMH, are classified as guilty pleas. A case where a trial date had been fixed at the preliminary hearing and an indication of guilty plea given before the PCMH was still a guilty plea when that plea was entered at PCMH (*LC* v. *Frieze* [2007] EWHC 1490).

2.1.4 Number of days at trial

This is the number of days or part of a day that a trial (including a Newton hearing) lasts. In the case of a Newton hearing, the first day of trial is the day on which the plea is entered (*R* v. *Gemeskel* (X2) (W7)) It includes all days or part of a day spent considering ancillary matters during the course of the trial. Non-sitting days do not count (*R* v. *Nassir* (X1)). If a trial is aborted and another jury sworn that day or the following day there is one longer trial. If there is a longer gap there is a retrial (*R* v. *Gussman* (X14)).

2.1.5   Number of cases

A case means Crown Court proceedings against a single defendant arising from a single indictment or notice of appeal or committal for sentence or breach of a Crown Court order. This is significant for advocates as a fee is payable for each advocate properly attending. Cases tried concurrently earn the fee for the main hearing with a mark-up for the second case.

The summary hearing of a Bail Act allegation ahead of the main trial is treated as a standard appearance (see **2.3.2** below). When a defendant is tried and acquitted on the third day on the first indictment and a second indictment is then cracked on that day the cases are not concurrent and two fees are payable (*R* v. *Tooth* [2007] Costs LR 302). For two cases to be heard concurrently, the main hearing in each case must have been heard at the same time (*R* v. *Fletcher* (X6); *R* v. *Fairhurst* (X6A)). If an indictment is severed these are separate cases.

2.2   LITIGATORS' GRADUATED FEES

Claims are made on Form LF1. Great efficiency is required as the fixed fee allows no room for unnecessary or repeated work. See Figure 2.1.

2.2.1   Non-indictable jurisdiction

This jurisdiction is normally dealt with by fixed fees to which there are no additions, though the exceptional provisions on confiscation below may apply and hourly rates apply to 'related' proceedings. The fee includes any attendance upon an advocate at the Crown Court and such attendances, unless required by professional duties, are unlikely to be made. The fees are given in the table (see page 38) and are exclusive of VAT.

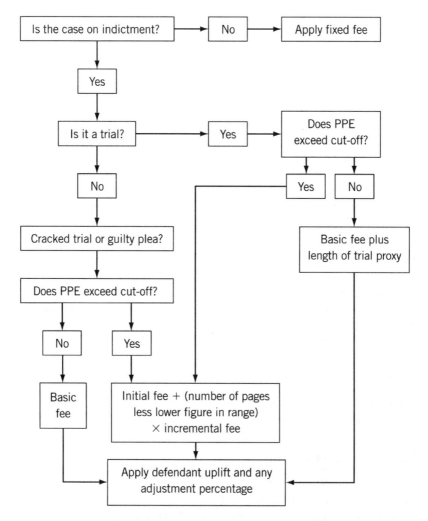

ALWAYS USE CORRECT TABLE FOR RELEVANT OFFENCE AND TRIAL OR CRACKED TRIAL/GUILTY PLEA. ADD VALUE OF CONFISCATION PROCEEDINGS AND ELECTRONIC EVIDENCE

Figure 2.1 Summary of calculation of litigator's fee

Attendance type	Fee
Appeal against sentence	£170.21
Appeal against conviction	£382.98
Committal for sentence	£255.32
Contempt proceedings – involving a non-defendant [for defendants the work is covered by the normal fee]	£170.21*
Breach of Crown Court order	£85.11
Section 1CA of the Crime and Disorder Act 1998 (variation and discharge of orders under section 1C)	£170.21
Section 155 of the Powers of Criminal Courts (Sentencing) Act 2000 (alteration of Crown Court sentence)	£170.21
Section 74 of the Serious Organised Crime and Police Act 2005 (Assistance by defendant; review of sentence)	£170.21

*Note: The Litigator Graduated Fee Scheme Guidance puts this figure at £127.66 but this is not in accordance with the Criminal Defence Service (Funding) (Amendment) Order 2009, SI 2009/1843.

There are no mark-ups for acting for additional defendants (*R* v. *Sturmer and Lewis* (SCCO 277/08)) but a separate fixed fee is paid for each appeal or committal (usually designated by different Crown Court reference numbers).

Solicitors will, prior to appeal or committal, need to consider with a client whether they can provide a professional service at such fees and advise clients appropriately where there are alternative ways to proceed.

Appeals in related proceedings

The Unified Contract (Crime) provides that hourly rates apply as if the work was carried out in the magistrates' court.

2.2.2   Indictable jurisdiction

To calculate the appropriate fee you require six pieces of information, below. Subject to very limited exceptions (see **2.2.7** below) there are no additional payments and no payment is made for attendance upon an advocate. If the case was sent to the Crown Court under the Crime and Disorder Act 1998, s.51 the fees from the magistrates' court are lost in the litigator's fee.

1. *The offence classification* (see **2.1.1** above).
2. *The number of PPE*. If a case which is not a very high cost case (VHCC) has more than 10,000 pages, it is treated as having 10,000 pages.
    Special preparation can be claimed where a case is heard on indictment and any of the relevant prosecution material is served in electronic form only and it is reasonable to make an additional payment based on the number of hours considered reasonable to view the material at the hourly rates appearing below. Electronic evidence is any document provided on CD-Rom or by other means of electronic communication. It does not include

audio or video cassettes. If the electronic evidence includes prosecution evidence it may still be financially advantageous to claim the PPE mark-up described at **2.1.2** above. To claim the time reasonably spent considering a CD-Rom, it must contain evidence (and not unused material) which falls within the definition of the Criminal Defence Service (Funding) Order 2007, Sched.1 para.1(2), as amended. This includes pictorial exhibits and would appear to include both still and moving images such as surveillance film or material obtained from CCTV.

Special preparation may also be claimed when the number of PPE exceeds 10,000. The fee is calculated on the number of hours it reasonably takes to read the excess.

3. *Whether the case is a trial, cracked or guilty plea.* A case is a trial if a jury is empanelled or there is a Newton hearing. A case is a cracked trial if it is not resolved by a guilty plea or an acquittal at the PCMH or an adjourned PCMH. A case is a guilty plea if it is resolved by an acquittal or conviction at or before the PCMH or adjourned PCMH.

Special rules apply if there has been a s.51 sending and an application is made to dismiss (see **2.2.4** below).

4. *The length of a trial* (see **2.1.4** above). If a case which is not a VHCC lasts more than 200 days, it is treated as if it lasted 200 days.

Special rules apply to determine the number of days of a trial if a hearing is held to determine whether the defendant is unfit to plead or stand trial. The litigator may elect for the most profitable of the following:

(a) if the trial continues, adding the length of the fitness hearing to the trial length;

(b) if the trial does not continue, the length of trial is the combined length of hearings to determine fitness and under Criminal Procedure (Insanity) Act 1964, s.4A;

(c) a cracked trial fee; or

(d) if there is a guilty plea, a guilty plea fee.

5. *The number of defendants for whom you acted.* The multipliers applicable appear at **Appendix 10(3)** and are set out below:

Total number represented	Percentage uplift
2–4	20%
5 +	30%

6. *The proportion of the case on which the litigator represented the defendant.* If a firm does not represent a defendant throughout a case, only a percentage of the calculated fee will apply. The details appear at **Appendix 10(4)** and are set out below.

Scenario	Percentage of the total fee	Case type used to determine total fee	Timing of claim
Cracked trial before retrial where there is no change of litigator	25%	Cracked trial	–
Retrial, where there is no change of litigator	25%	Trial	–
Up to and including plea and case management hearing transfer (original litigator)	25%	Cracked trial	–
Up to and including plea and case management hearing transfer – guilty plea (new litigator)	100%	Guilty plea	–
Up to and including plea and case management hearing transfer – cracked trial (new litigator)	100%	Cracked trial	–
Up to and including plea and case management hearing transfer – trial (new litigator)	100%	Trial	–
Before trial transfer (original litigator)	75%	Cracked trial	–
Before trial transfer – cracked trial (new litigator)	100%	Cracked trial	–
Before trial transfer – trial (new litigator)	100%	Trial	–
During trial transfer (original litigator)	100%	Trial	Claim up to and including the day before the transfer
During trial transfer (new litigator)	50%	Trial	Claim for the full trial length
During trial transfer – retrial (new litigator)	25%	Trial	Claim for the full retrial length
Transfer after trial and before sentencing hearing (original litigator)	100%	Trial	–
Transfer after trial and before sentencing hearing (new litigator)	10%	Trial	–
Transfer after retrial and before sentencing hearing (original litigator)	25%	Trial	–
Transfer after retrial and before sentencing hearing (new litigator)	10%	Trial	–
Transfer before retrial (original litigator)	25%	Cracked trial	–

Transfer before cracked retrial (new litigator)	50%	Cracked trial	–
Transfer before retrial (new litigator)	50%	Trial	Claim for the full retrial length
Transfer during retrial (original litigator)	25%	Trial	Claim up to and including the day before the transfer
Transfer during retrial (new litigator	50%	Trial	Claim for the full retrial length

A litigator may not be treated as both the original and a new litigator in the same case. A transfer occurs if the defendant had previously represented himself. A case is not treated as transferred where:

(a) a firm of solicitors is named as litigator in the representation order and the solicitor or other appropriately qualified person with responsibility for the case moves to another firm;

(b) a firm of solicitors is named as litigator in the representation order and the firm changes (whether by merger or acquisition or in some other way), but so that the new firm remains closely related to the firm named in the order; or

(c) a solicitor or other appropriately qualified person is named as litigator in the representation order, and responsibility for the case is transferred to another solicitor or appropriately qualified person in the same firm or a closely related firm.

Where a case is transferred to a new litigator and then transferred again, that litigator is treated as follows:

Transfer before trial or retrial	Original litigator
Transfer during trial or retrial	New litigator
Transfer after trial or retrial but before the sentencing hearing	No payment to be made

These proportions are of the total fee so that a page count is included. The Litigator Graduated Fee Scheme Guidance, 3.34 suggests that it is the page count at the first involvement in the case used but this is not supported by the Criminal Defence Service (Funding) Order 2007.

When a case is transferred to a new litigator because it is a VHCC, the outgoing solicitor is paid by the Complex Crime Unit (CCU) at VHCC rates for the work actually and reasonably done by them.

2.2.3 Calculation

The calculation is best done on the LSC litigator fee calculator available at **www.legalservices.gov.uk**. However, as with all computer systems, care is needed in their operation. For instance, if a case committed to the Crown Court is discontinued prior to PCMH, this should be entered as a guilty plea. If it is entered as a discontinuance, the computer generates the lower fee payable following a s.51 sending.

In managing a case solicitors will wish to calculate in advance the likely fee. The manual calculation is carried out using the tables at **Appendix 10**. The following stages apply:

Stage 1

Identify whether the number of PPE exceeds the relevant cut-off identified at **Appendix 10(1)(a)** or **10(2)(c)** for cracked trials, guilty pleas and trial.

Stage 2

If the number does *not* exceed the cut-off, the payments below are due.

NUMBER OF PAGES NOT EXCEEDING CUT-OFF FOR CRACKED TRIALS AND GUILTY PLEAS

(a) A basic fee set out in **Appendix 10(1)(b)**.
(b) A defendant uplift on the basic fee for the number represented by the firm (see **Appendix 10(3)**).
(c) An adjustment of the basic fee if the firm did not act throughout the case (see **Appendix 10(4)**).

NUMBER OF PAGES NOT EXCEEDING CUT-OFF FOR TRIALS

(a) A basic fee as set out in **Appendix 10(2)(b)**.
(b) A length of trial uplift/depending on the number of days of trial (see **Appendix 10(2)(d)**).
(c) A defendant uplift on (a) and (b) for the number represented by the firm (see **Appendix 10(3)**).
(d) An adjustment of the total of (a) and (b) if the firm did not act throughout the case (see **Appendix 10(4)**).

Stage 3

If the number of PPE *exceeds* the 'cut off', the payments below are due.

NUMBER OF PAGES EXCEEDING CUT-OFF FOR CRACKED TRIALS AND GUILTY PLEAS

A 'final' fee as defined below and set out in **Appendix 10(1)(c)**. A final fee (F) is represented by:

$$I + (D \times i)$$

where:

I	is the initial fee specified in **Appendix 10(1)(d)** and **(e)** and as appropriate for the class of case;
D	is the number of pages minus the lower figure and of the relevant PPE range specified in **Appendix 10(1)(d)** and **(e)**; and
i	is the incremental fee per page set out in the tables in that appendix;

and a defendant uplift on the final fee for the number represented by the firm (see **Appendix 10(3)** and an adjustment on the final fee if the firm did not act throughout the case (see **Appendix 10(4)**).

NUMBER OF PAGES EXCEEDING CUT-OFF FOR TRIALS

A 'final' fee as defined below and set out in **Appendix 10(2)(a)**. A final fee (F) is represented by:

$$I + (D \times i)$$

where:

I	is the initial fee specified in **Appendix 10(2)(e)** and as appropriate for the class of case;
D	is the number of pages of relevant prosecution material *minus* the lower figure of the relevant PPE range specified in **Appendix 10(2)(e)**; and
i	is the incremental fee per page set out in that appendix;

and a defendant uplift on the final fee for the number represented by the firm (see **Appendix 10(3)** and an adjustment to the final fee if the firm did not act throughout the case (see **Appendix 10(4)**).

The uplifts for the number of defendants represented by a firm are as follows:

Total number represented	Percentage uplift
2–4	20%
5+	30%

The adjustment for firms who do not act throughout apply when this is a transfer of legal aid or a representation order is withdrawn or a VHCC is agreed, or there is a retrial. These appear above and at **Appendix 10(4)**.

2.2.4   Proceedings without a committal

Special rules apply where proceedings have been sent (Crime and Disorder Act 1998, s.51) or transferred (Criminal Justice Act (CJA) 1987, s.4 (serious fraud) or CJA 1991, s.53 (children)). If such proceedings are discontinued or dismissed fees are payable as follows:

Scenario	Fee
If indictable only proceedings discontinued prior to service of the evidence	50% of the appropriate basic guilty plea fee (**Appendix 10(1)(b)**)
If any other of these proceedings discontinued or dismissed on a defence application (with any surviving allegations remitted to the magistrates' court)	The full fee appropriate for a guilty plea (**Appendix 10(1)(e)**)

Defendant uplifts apply to these figures. An application to dismiss which does not succeed adds no value to the litigator's fee.

2.2.5   Escape provisions

These are very limited. The fees include any attendance upon an advocate at court and the number of such attendances, unless required by professional duties, is likely substantially to reduce.

No additional fee is normally payable for any work done in connection with a sentencing or deferred sentencing hearing.

Unused material in long cases

Significant risks of injustice arise in cases with significant amounts of unused material as no additional provision is made for the situation. A firm's only remedy, in a case that may exceed 25 days at trial, is to seek a VHCC contract if the firm is on the VHCC panel or can reach a suitable agency agreement with such a firm.

Confiscation proceedings and electronic evidence and PPE in excess of 10,000

Work in connection with confiscation proceedings will continue to be paid at hourly rates and should be separately recorded. Where all or any of the prosecution material is served in electronic form only, and it is considered reasonable, an extra payment will also be paid in this way. So will the consideration of PPE in excess of 10,000. The work is remunerated depending on the grade of fee earner engaged in the following areas:

(a) for preparation, including taking instructions, interviewing witnesses, ascertaining the prosecution case, preparing and perusing documents, dealing with letters and telephone calls, instructing an advocate and expert witnesses, conferences, consultations and work done in connection with advice on appeal;

(b) for attending at court where an advocate is instructed including conferences with the advocate at court;

(c) for travelling and waiting; and

(d) for writing routine letters and dealing with routine telephone calls.

For this work, enhancement remains available on the following terms:

1. Enhancement is available for preparation, attendance at court where more than one representative is instructed, routine letters written and routine telephone calls in respect of offences in Classes A, B, C, D, G, I, J or K in the table of offences.

2. Enhanced fees are payable if taking into account all the relevant circumstances of the case:

   (a) the work was done with exceptional competence, skill or expertise;

   (b) the work was done with exceptional despatch; or

   (c) the case involved exceptional complexity or other exceptional circumstances.

   Exceptional means unusual or out of the ordinary compared with the generality of criminal proceedings.

3. Enhancement is paid by a percentage uplift dependent on:

   (a) the degree of responsibility accepted by the fee earner;

   (b) the care, speed and economy with which the case was prepared; and

   (c) the novelty, weight and complexity of the case;

   but because of the decision in *Backhouse* will not be less than 100 per cent which is also the maximum (see page 30 above on enhancement generally).

2.2.6 Hourly rates

These rates are exclusive of VAT.

Class of work	Grade of fee earner	Rate	Variations
Preparation	Senior solicitor	£53.00 per hour	£55.75 per hour for a fee earner whose office is situated within the London region of the LSC
	Solicitor, legal executive or fee earner of equivalent experience	£45.00 per hour	£47.25 per hour for a fee earner whose office is situated within the London region of the LSC
	Trainee or fee earner of equivalent experience	£29.75 per hour	£34.00 per hour for a fee earner whose office is situated within the London region of the LSC
Attendance at court where more than one representative instructed	Senior solicitor	£42.25 per hour	–
	Solicitor, legal executive or fee earner of equivalent experience	£34.00	–
	Trainee or fee earner of equivalent experience	£20.50	–
Travelling and waiting	Senior solicitor	£24.75 per hour	–
	Solicitor, legal executive or fee earner of equivalent experience	£24.75 per hour	–
	Trainee or fee earner of equivalent experience	£12.50 per hour	–
Writing routine letters and dealing with routine telephone calls		£3.45 per item	£3.60 per item for a fee earner whose office is situated within the London region of the LSC

2.2.7 Special circumstances

Warrant cases

Where a defendant fails to appear and a warrant is issued and not executed for three months, special rules apply.

INDICTABLE CASES

1. If the warrant is issued at or before the PCMH a guilty plea fee is payable.
2. If the warrant is issued after the PCMH but before trial a cracked trial fee is payable.
3. If the warrant is issued during trial and the trial aborts, a trial fee is payable as if the trial ended on that day.

FIXED FEE CASES

The appropriate fee is paid.

If the warrant is then executed within 15 months and the matter proceeds, credit has to be given for the amount already paid. After 15 months it appears that a further full fee would be paid.

Retrials

Two bills are delivered; one for the original and one for the retrial. The second bill abates in accordance with the table in **Appendix 10(4)**.

Disbursements

Disbursements including travel expenses connected to preparation or court attendance are payable in addition to the litigator's graduated fee. Vouchers for disbursements over £20 should be sent to the Litigator Fee Team; vouchers for those over £10 should be kept on file.

2.3   ADVOCACY IN THE CROWN COURT

These fees are always additional to a litigator's fee. References are to the Criminal Defence Service (Funding) Order 2007, SI 2007/1174, Sched.1 as amended. Use Form 5144F sent to the appropriate Crown Court.

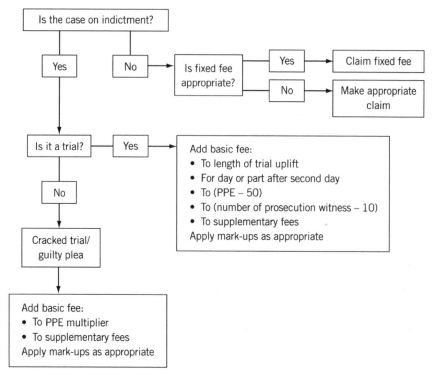

Figure 2.2   Summary of calculation of advocate's fee

2.3.1   Non-indictable crime

This includes committals for sentence, appeals against conviction and sentence and committals for breach of Crown Court orders.

Normal fees

The following fees are prescribed for the main hearing, i.e. the hearing at which sentence is imposed or the appeal against conviction is heard in routine cases. The order also allows fees for a QC and leading juniors but in any event, such cases would always fall into the exceptional group described below.

The fee is payable for each day of the main hearing (*R* v. *Hines* (X4)).

All figures in these tables are exclusive of VAT.

Hearing type	Paragraph no. (SI 2007/1174, Sched.1)	Rate
Appeals to the Crown Court against conviction	17(1)	£150 per day
Appeals to the Crown Court against sentence	17(1)	£125 per day
Proceedings relating to breach of an order of the Crown Court	17(1)	£125 per day
Committal for sentence	17(1)	£150 per day

The order also allows for subsidiary fees (see table below).

Hearing type	Paragraph no. (SI 2007/1174, Sched.1)	Rate
Adjourned appeals, committals for sentence and breach hearings, e.g. failure of the assisted person or a witness to attend, the unavailability of a pre-sentence report or other good reason	17(2)	£100 per day
Bail application mentions and other applications in appeals, committals for sentence breach hearings	17(3)	£100 per day

Mark-ups

Where two or more cases involving the same advocate are heard concurrently, the advocate is paid an additional 20 per cent of the fixed fee for each additional case, whether that involves separate allegations or separate defendants.

Escape provisions

The Criminal Defence (Funding) Order 2007, SI 2007/1174, Sched. 1, para. 17(2) allows for fees greater than these fixed fees:

> If the fixed fee for the main hearing is inappropriate taking into account all the relevant circumstances of the case the determining officer at the National Taxing Team may instead allow fees in such amounts as appear to him to be reasonable remuneration for the relevant work. This discretion will apply to all the work undertaken by the advocate.

Such fees are claimed on Form 5145, at present, from the appropriate National Taxing Team.

There is now no requirement for exceptional circumstances. At a time when that was a requirement, National Taxing Team guidance indicated that a reasonable fee beyond the fixed fee could be paid if work was carried out substantially in excess of that required in an average case of the same type when:

- a magistrates' court would have declined jurisdiction;
- an appeal committal or breach lasted more than a day;
- a Newton hearing took place.

The current Regulations set a lower standard than this guidance required.

The method of calculation is provided for by the Criminal Defence Service (Funding) Order 2007, Sched.1, para.17(5). It allows:

(a) a fee for preparation including, where appropriate, the first day of the hearing including, where they took place on that day –

    (i)   short conferences;
    (ii) consultations;
    (iii) applications and appearances (including bail applications);
    (iv) views at the scene of the alleged offence; and
    (v) any other preparation.

(b) a refresher fee for any day or part of a day for which a hearing continued, including, where they took place on that day –

    (i)   short conferences;
    (ii) consultations;
    (iii) applications and appearances (including bail applications);
    (iv) views at the scene of the alleged offence; and
    (v) any other preparation; and

(c) subsidiary fees for –

    (i)   attendance at conferences, consultations and views at the scene of the alleged offence not covered by paragraph (a) or (b);
    (ii) written advice on evidence, plea, appeal, case stated or other written work; and
    (iii) attendance at applications and appearances (including bail applications and adjournments for sentence) not covered by paragraph (a) or (b).

The fee to charge is a judgement dependent on the facts of the case, but a good indication is given by calculating the appropriate graduated fee for the offence(s) in question upon a guilty plea.

Related proceedings

Appeals in relation to anti-social behaviour orders (ASBOs) and similar orders referred to in the Criminal Defence Service (General) (No.2) Regulations 2001, SI 2001/1437, reg.3(2) are payable at hourly rates in accordance with the Unified Contract (Crime), at the rates for work conducted in the magistrates' court.

2.3.2 Indictable crime

Preliminary hearings

The law is still uncertain as to the fee payable to an advocate for an appearance at a preliminary hearing. The Bar Council suggests that it is comprised in the brief fee which forms part of the graduated fee for the offence, but there are substantial reasons to doubt this. The case is not yet on indictment and as was accepted in *R* v. *Smith* [2004] 2 Costs LR 348, there is no reference in the relevant provisions to such a hearing. This could easily have been included had it been intended, as the decision in *Smith* has been widely publicised. The appropriate fee for the advocate depends on the facts of the individual case. It is not only the time in court that is relevant if preparation has been undertaken by the advocate as such. The fee is unlikely to be below £100 (see *R* v. *Davies* [2007] 1 Costs LR 116 where there was preparation of 72 minutes, an attendance of 30 minutes and a hearing of six minutes).

If a preliminary hearing becomes a PCMH, the fee will become part of the basic fee. If a guilty plea is entered, the hearing becomes the main hearing and generates the basic guilty plea fee with such additional payment as may be due (see **2.3.3** below).

Bail hearings

If a defendant is arrested for breach of Crown Court bail conditions and produced before a magistrates' court the hearing is in Crown Court proceedings and will receive a standard appearance fee (*R* v. *Richardson* [2008] Costs LR 320; *R* v. *Bailey* (X16)), which under the arrangements set out below will merely form part of the brief fee. It may be better for these arrests to be handled by the duty solicitor (which is permitted as there is a new arrest) although if the instructed advocate (see **2.3.7** below) is not employed by the firm an invoice for £100 may be delivered to that person.

Graduated fees

To calculate the correct graduated fee it is necessary to collect a quantity of basic data about the relevant case.

The offence classification

See **2.1.1** above and **Appendix 9**.

The number of PPE

See **2.1.2** above.

Whether the case is a trial, cracked trial or guilty plea

See **2.1.3** above.

The length of a trial

See **2.1.4** above. The length of trial uplifts depends on the total length of the trial undergone by the particular defendant represented, whatever the length of the overall trial (see *Secretary of Stage for Constitutional Affairs* v. *Stork* [2006] 1 Costs LR 69).

The basic fee includes the first two days. Days beyond 40 are paid at the rate specified in **Appendix 11(e)**.

The number of prosecution witnesses

This includes witnesses served under CJA 1967, s.9 and whose evidence is read as admissible hearsay as well as those who, by whatever method, give live evidence. It includes witnesses in notices of additional evidence.

The category of advocate

The categories are:
1. QC
2. Leading junior
3. Led junior
4. Other advocate

The main hearing: the basic fee

It is then necessary to identify, for each case, the main hearing, as it is for the hearing that the primary fee is payable.

For example:

- **trial:** it is the trial;
- **guilty plea:** the hearing at which the plea is taken, or if there is more than one, the last of them;
- **cracked trial:** the hearing at which the case became a cracked trial or at which a formal verdict of not guilty was entered if the Crown offered no evidence, whether or not the parties attended the hearing. Where an indictment has two counts and one guilty plea is entered and the case adjourned for sentence when the other not guilty plea is accepted, the case 'cracked' at the first hearing (*R* v. *Johnson* [2007] Costs LR 316).

A basic fee, varying in amount, is always payable. The fee is payable for a single trial advocate representing one assisted person on one indictment in a trial. If the trial exceeds 40 days, the table at **Appendix 11(e)** applies.

Mark-ups are payable where there is more than one assisted person and/or more than one indictment.

If two advocates can be justified, this will result in higher total payments, but the Criminal Defence Service (General) (No.2) Regulations 2001 (as amended), SI 2001/1437, reg.16A provides that when a right to representation is granted for one of two or more co-defendants whose cases are to be heard together, the individual must select the same representation as a co-defendant unless there is or is likely to be a conflict of interest. Since 1 November 2007 a representative has included an advocate.

Included within the basic fees are preparation by the advocate, including:

(a) reading the papers in the case;
(b) contact with prosecutors;
(c) written or oral advice on plea;
(d) researching the law, preparation for examination of witnesses, and preparation of oral submissions;
(e) viewing exhibits or undisclosed material at police stations;
(f) written advice on evidence;
(g) preparation of written submissions, notices or other documents for use at the trial; and
(h) attendance at views at the scene of the alleged offence.

This is limited to preparation done before the trial, except in proceedings in which a preparatory hearing has been ordered under CJA 1987, s.8 (commencement of trial and arraignment), in which case it is limited to preparation done before the date on which the jury is sworn (or on which it became certain, by reason of pleas of guilty or otherwise, that the matter would not proceed to trial).

The basic fee includes:

- the first two days of any trial;
- any work carried out in the magistrates' court on a case which is sent to the Crown Court under the Crime and Disorder Act 1998, s.51;
- any work on audio or video recording and the first three conferences; and
- the fee payable in respect of an appearance at the first PCMH hearing and up to four standard appearances (this is the case for all proceedings not withstanding a drafting error in the Criminal Defence Service (Funding) Order 2007, SI 2007/1174).

'Standard appearance' is defined in the Criminal Defence Service (Funding) Order 2007, Sched.1 as:

an appearance ... in any of the following hearings which do not form part of the main hearing –

(a) a plea and case management hearing, except the first plea and case management hearing;

(b)   a pre-trial review;

(c)   the hearing of a case listed for plea which is adjourned for trial;

(d)   any hearing (except a trial, a plea and case management hearing, a pre-trial review or a hearing referred to in paragraph 2(1)(b)) which is listed but cannot proceed because of the failure of the assisted person or a witness to attend, the unavailability of a pre-sentence report or other good reason;

(e)   custody time limit applications;

(f)   bail and other applications (except where any such applications take place in the course of a hearing referred to in paragraph 2(1)(b)); or

(g)   the hearing of the case listed for mention only, including applications relating to the date of the trial (except where an application takes place in the course of a hearing referred to in paragraph 2(1)(b)), ...

2.3.3   Calculations

For trials

Where the main hearing is a trial, select the appropriate basic fee for the offence(s) in question, depending on the advocate making the claim, from the tables in **Appendix 11(a)**. It is important to select the correct table for the advocate in question.

To this **basic fee** ADD each of the following:

- length of trial uplift for each day or part thereof after the first two;
- payment for each page of prosecution material **after the first 50**; if the number of pages exceeds 10,000 or there is electronic evidence, a special preparation fee is payable as a supplementary payment;
- payment for each prosecution witness whether oral or written **after the first 10**; and
- supplementary payments as set out below.

For guilty pleas

Where the main hearing is a guilty plea, select appropriate basic fee for the offence(s) in question depending on the advocate making the claim. See **Appendix 11(b)**.

To the **basic fee** ADD:

- Payment for each page of prosecution material:

  - if the number of pages exceeds 1,000, the additional sum is payable per page in addition to the payment for the first 1,000 pages;
  - if the number of pages exceeds 10,000 or there is electronic evidence, a special preparation fee is payable as a supplementary payment.

For cracked trials

It is necessary to know at which point the case cracked: whether in the first third, second or last third.

This is determined by calculating the number of days from the date on which the case is first put in a warned list, or given a fixed date of hearing to the start of that warned list or the date of that fixture.

The number of days is divided in three equal parts and any days remaining are added to the last third.

A case that does not begin on the fixed date or in the period of the first warned list is treated as cracking in the last third. Retrials fall in the last third if they crack. Depending on when the case cracks, the fees are in **Appendix 11(b)** or **11(c)**.

To the **basic fee** ADD:

- appropriate cumulative payments for each page of prosecution material. If the number of pages exceeds 10,000 pages or there is electronic evidence, a special preparation fee is payable as a supplementary payment.

Mark-ups

A trial under the Bail Act 1976, s.6 no longer attracts a separate fee but is paid as if it were a bail hearing. Otherwise, where two or more cases are heard concurrently the advocate must select the principal case, and at the main hearing in each of the cases there is paid an additional 20 per cent of the appropriate basic or fixed fee.

Mark-ups of 20 per cent of the fee are payable for additional defendants and are also payable for certain supplementary fees for hearings dealing with abuse of process, disclosure, admissibility, or withdrawal of plea hearings.

Defendants unfit to plead or stand trial

Where a hearing is held to decide whether a defendant is fit to plead or stand trial (the fitness hearing), the following apply:

1. If the trial continues, the length of the fitness hearings is added to the length of the trial.
2. In other circumstances the fee is whichever of the following the advocate elects:

   (a) a trial fee adding the length of the trial, the length of the fitness hearing and any hearing under the Criminal Procedure (Insanity) Act 1964, s.4A; or
   (b) a cracked trial fee.

3. If there is a guilty plea, whichever of the following the advocate elects:

(a)   a trial fee adding the length of the fitness hearing; or

(b)   a guilty plea fee.

2.3.4   Supplementary fees

See **Appendix 11(d)**. It is then necessary to add to these figures any relevant supplementary fees. These are considered as follows:

1.   Interim hearings.
2.   Sentencing hearings.
3   Hearings paid by daily and half daily fees.
4.   Work paid by hourly rates.
5.   Special circumstances including –

(a)   sent and transferred proceedings;

(b)   retrial;

(c)   cross-examination of a witness.

A number of subsidiary hearings are, however, included within the basic fee, as is the value of any time spent on audio or video recordings and up to three conferences.

Interim hearings

Hearing type	Paragraph no. (SI 2007/1174, Sched.1)	QC rate	Leading junior rate	Other advocate rate
Standard appearance not included within basic fee	9(2)	£200 per day	£150 per day	£100 per day
Paper PCMH	9(3)	£30 per case	£30 per case	£30 per case

Standard appearances mean (Criminal Defence Service (Funding) Order 2007, Sched.1):

> an appearance ... in any of the following hearings which do not form part of the main hearing –

(a)   a plea and case management hearing, except the first plea and case management hearing;

(b)   a pre-trial review;

(c)   the hearing of a case listed for plea which is adjourned for trial;

(d)   any hearing (except a trial, a plea and case management hearing, a pre-trial review or a hearing referred to in paragraph 2(1)(b)) which is listed but cannot proceed because of the failure of the assisted person or a witness to attend, the unavailability of a pre-sentence report or other good reason;

(e)   custody time limit applications;

(f)   bail and other applications (except where any such applications take place in

the course of a hearing referred to in paragraph 2(1)(b));
(g) the hearing of the case listed for mention only, including applications relating to the date of the trial (except where an application takes place in the course of a hearing referred to in paragraph 2(1)(b)), . . .[which relates to fixed fees]

Advocates will often seek to classify such hearings as one of those for which daily or half daily rates are payable as these will generate additional fees. As any issue as to admissibility of evidence or disclosure falls into such payments, this will not uncommonly be possible.

Sentencing hearings

Hearing type	Paragraph no. (SI 2007/1174, Sched.1)	QC rate	Leading junior rate	Other advocate rate
Sentencing hearing (not part of main hearing)	12(1)(b)	£300 per day	£200 per day	£125 per day
Deferred sentencing hearing	12(1)(a)	£375 per case	£275 per case	£200 per case

Where an ASBO is sought at the sentencing stage in criminal proceedings, it is the fee under SI 2007/1174, Sched.1, para.12(1)(b) that is payable if it is not dealt with as part of the main hearing (*R* v. *Brinkworth* [2006] 3 Costs LR 512).

Hearings paid by daily and half daily fees (when not part of main hearings)

Note that a half day ends before lunch or begins after lunch. Mark-ups are payable for the first four groups.

Scenario	Paragraph no. (SI 2007/1174, Sched.1)	QC rate	Leading junior rate	Other advocate rate
Abuse of process. In these cases an additional 20% is paid for each additional defendant	10(1)(a)	£300 per half day £575 per full day	£225 per half day £400 per full day	£150 per half day £275 per full day

Hearings as to disclosure or witness summonses. In these cases an additional 20% is paid for each additional defendant. A hearing relating to a failure to disclose is likely to be classified as a standard appearance (*R* v. *Russell* (X31))	10(1)(b) and (c)	The same	The same	The same
Hearing as to admissibility of evidence. In these cases an additional 20% is paid for each additional defendant	10(1)(d)	The same	The same	The same
Hearings on withdrawal of guilty pleas made by a different advocate from that present when plea entered. Hearing of an unsuccessful application to withdraw a guilty plea made by a different advocate from that present when the plea was entered. In these cases an additional 20% is paid for each additional defendant	10(1)(e)	The same	The same	The same
Confiscation hearings Where the number of pages relevant to confiscation is 50 pages or less (or other cases see **2.3.5** below)	11	The same	The same	The same
Hearing of an application to dismiss which does not succeed	18(6)	The same	The same	The same
Ineffective trial	13	£325 per day	£225 per day	£150 per day
Noting brief	19	–	–	£125 per day
Contempt in the face of the court other than by a defendant (advocate alone)	17A	£300 per day	£225 per day	£150 per day
Contempt, etc. When there is advocate and litigator appointed	17A	£175 per day	£125 per day	£100 per day

If a Newton trial is listed but does not proceed due to the absence of a prosecution witness, the defence version then being accepted, it is the fee under para.13 that is payable (see *R* v. *Ayrs* [2002] 2 Costs LR 330 (X32)).

Work paid by hourly rates

Scenario	Paragraph no. (SI 2007/1174, Sched.1)	QC rate	Leading junior rate	Other advocate rate
Conferences and views	16	£85 per hour	£65 per day	£45 per hour

The basic fee includes the first three reasonable pre-trial conferences or views. Beyond that number, and subject to conditions, hourly rates are paid for:

- attendances at pre-trial conferences with prospective or actual expert witnesses other than at court;
- attendance at the scene of the alleged offence;
- attendances at pre-trial conferences with the assisted person not held at court.

In addition, the hourly rates will be paid for reasonable travelling time to attend the view of the scene or for a pre-trial conference where it is reasonably held away from chambers or office.

The conditions for reasonable hourly rates to be paid are:

- for trials (or the anticipated length of a trial that cracks) lasting not less than 21 days and up to 25 days: 1 further pre-trial conference of up to 2 hours;
- for trials (or cracked trials) lasting not less than 26 days and up to 35: 2 further pre-trial conferences of up to 2 hours;
- for trials (or cracked trials) lasting not less than 36 days and up to 40 days: 3 further pre-trial conferences of up to 2 hours.

Scenario	Paragraph no. (SI 2007/1174, Sched.1)	QC rate	Leading junior rate	Other advocate rate
Special preparation	15	£85 per hour	£65 per hour	£45 per hour

This fee is payable where:

(a) it has been necessary for an advocate to do work by way of preparation substantially in excess of the amount normally done for cases of the same type because the case involves a very unusual or novel point of law or factual issue; or

(b) the number of PPE, as defined in **2.1.2** above, exceeds 10,000 and the appropriate officer considers it reasonable to make a payment in excess of the graduated fee payable under the Schedule; or

(c) any or all of the prosecution evidence, as defined in **2.1.2** above, is served in electronic form only, and the appropriate officer considers it reasonable to make a payment in excess of the graduated fee payable under the Schedule.

Under (a) above there is a three-part test:

1. The work must be necessary.
2. That work must be substantially in excess of the amount normally done for cases of the same type. This is not to be given too narrow a meaning, i.e. manslaughter, not manslaughter by drugs.
3. A point of law or factual issue which is very unusual or novel means in relation to factual issue: 'a factual issue which is outwith the usual professional experience' (see *R* v. *Ward-Allen* [2005] 4 Costs LR 745).

There must be a very unusual or novel part of law or factual issue whatever the quality of the preparation may have been (see *Meeke and Taylor* v. *Secretary of State for Constitutional Affairs* [2006] 1 Costs LR 1).

For a further description of relevant case law, see also *R* v. *Marandola* [2006] 1 Costs LR 184 and the overview in *R* v. *Janjit* [2006] Costs LR 541, but the cases are inevitably fact specific.

The hourly rate is payable for the number of hours appropriate for the excess work or which are reasonable to view the prosecution evidence. The same hourly rate is also paid, as special preparation, to an advocate whose only role is to give written or oral advice. It is also paid for the length of reasonable preparation time spent by an advocate solely appointed to mitigate a sentence.

Scenario	Paragraph no. (SI 2007/1174, Sched.1)	QC rate	Leading junior rate	Other advocate rate
Wasted preparation	15	£85 per hour	£65 per hour	£45 per hour

These fees are payable provided:

- there are at least eight hours' preparation and there is a trial of at least five days; or a cracked trial with more than 150 PPE;
- in the following circumstances, where a trial advocate is prevented from representing the assisted person in the main hearing because:

  (a) the trial advocate is instructed to appear in other proceedings at the same time as the main hearing in the case and has been unable to secure a change of date for either the main hearing or the other proceedings;

(b)   the date fixed for the main hearing is changed by the court despite the trial advocate's objection;

(c)   the trial advocate has withdrawn from the case with the leave of the court because of his professional code of conduct or to avoid embarrassment in the exercise of his profession;

(d)   the trial advocate has been dismissed by the assisted person or the litigator; or

(e)   the trial advocate is obliged to attend at any place by reason of a judicial office held by him or other public duty.

2.3.5   Special circumstances

Cases sent or transferred

Under the Crime and Disorder Act 1998, s.51, CJA 1987, s.4 and CJA 1991, s.53 if the Crown discontinues or such proceedings are dismissed:

(a)   **before the evidence is served** the advocate's fee is one half of the basic fee payable to such an advocate for such an offence on a guilty plea;

(b)   **after the service of evidence** the appropriate guilty plea fee applies (including page mark-up) – even if other charges are remitted to the magistrates' court.

Where there is a failed application to dismiss, daily and half daily fees are payable (see **2.3.4** above).

A 20 per cent uplift of the guilty plea *basic* fee is paid for each additional defendant beyond the first.

Confiscation proceedings

For confiscation hearings on or after 21 August 2009, a special scheme applies where the number of pages involved in the confiscation proceedings exceeds 50.

Pages for this purpose include:

- the s.16 statement served and relied upon by the prosecution for the purpose of the confiscation hearing together with any annexes or exhibits attached thereto;
- documents served as part of the main trial bundle, where such documents are specifically relied upon and referred to in the s.16 statement but are not served again; and
- any defence expert report and the documents and exhibits attached, provided that the report had been obtained with the prior approval of the

LSC or is allowed on taxation, excluding any documents annexed to the report which have already been counted under either of the two sections above or which consist of financial records or similar data.

Where the relevant page count is between 51 and 1,000, there will be a payment as set out in the PPE table below for preparation and the first day of the confiscation hearing. Thereafter, the normal daily and half daily supplemental fee for confiscation hearings is payable (see **2.3.4** above).

PAGES OF PROSECUTION EVIDENCE

	Fees for QC	Fee for leading junior	Fee for junior alone	Fee for led junior
51–250	£750	£625	£500	£375
251–500	£1,125	£938	£750	£562
501–750	£1,500	£1,250	£1,000	£750
751–1000	£2,250	£1,875	£1,500	£1,125

Where the relevant page count exceeds 1,000, then in addition to the rates set out above for a page count between 751–1,000 there will be paid a reasonable fee for the time spent considering the pages in excess of 1,000 at the hourly rate below.

PREPARATION

	Fees for QC	Fee for leading junior	Fee for junior alone	Fee for leading junior
Hourly rates	£85	£65	£45	£45

Retrials

If the same advocate (but not otherwise) appears at original and retrials and:

(a) the defendant is assisted at both trials; or
(b) the defendant is involved only in the retrial; or
(c) the new trial is a guilty plea or cracked trial (in which situation the case is always in the final third);

the advocate must at their election, reduce the graduated fee for one of the two trials by the percentage applicable below.

Scenario	Percentage
If retrial start within one month of conclusion of first	30%
If retrial starts later than that	20%
If retrial becomes guilty plea or cracked trial within one month of the conclusion of the first	40%
If retrial becomes guilty plea or cracked trial later than that	25%

Cross-examination of a witness

An advocate appointed solely to cross-examine a witness under the Youth Justice and Criminal Evidence Act 1999, s.38 is paid a trial graduated fee with a daily fee calculated by reference to the number of days actually attended by the advocate after the first two days.

Mitigation only

An advocate appointed solely to mitigate is paid the supplementary fee for a sentencing hearing but in addition a special preparation fee.

Warrants

A hearing at which a warrant is issued is a 'standard appearance' and if there is no main hearing, extraordinarily, no fee is payable.

2.3.6 Disbursements

Travel expenses are payable to advocates for all reasonable attendance at the conference and views permitted for the relevant proceedings (see **2.3.4** above).

Travel and other expenses incidental to court appearance may also be paid if the advocate appears at a court not within 40 kilometres of their office or chambers, provided that they cannot exceed those payable to any local Bar or nearest advocate's office unless previously authorised or justified in all the circumstances.

2.3.7 Payment and distribution of the advocacy fee

Only one fee will be paid for advocacy in each case. Payment is made to the 'instructed advocate'. There are substantial advantages in solicitors being appointed as the instructed advocate as it gives to them control of the distribution of the payment to the advocates who have been instructed throughout the case. This distribution is entirely a matter for negotiation. However, the Bar have established a protocol which provides a workable basis for distribution in the absence of any other arrangement. Between solicitors, an advocacy fee is often 'protocol minus 10 to 20 per cent' or makes an allowance for work undertaken in the magistrates' court when a case is sent to the Crown Court.

Where there is more than a single advocate, the leading 'instructed advocate' pays for work of that level and the junior pays for work at the level undertaken by other advocates.

Where there is more than one defendant, the court must be notified in writing of the name of the additional instructed advocate as soon as he or she is appointed to ensure each is paid a full fee. This is particularly significant if a single advocate appeared at the PCMH.

Identifying the instructed advocate

In summary the position is as follows:

(a) if appointed before PCMH, the advocate may be nominated by a letter to court;
(b) if none is notified, it will be advocate at PCMH;
(c) if no PCMH, it will be advocate at next hearing;
(d) if more than a single advocate authorised, same procedures apply to each level of advocate.

Exceptionally in fixed fee cases, the instructed advocate will be deemed to be the advocate who attends the main hearing.

An instructed advocate once appointed must remain such except where they:

(a) are unable to attend trial fixed at or before PCMH;
(b) are dismissed; or
(c) withdraw for professional reasons.

Careful consideration should be given to this issue if there is a transfer of the representation order.

The instructed advocate has to account for VAT but, where the advocate is a solicitor, accounts should be rendered by the firm. Moneys held for the Bar should be paid into client account or if none exists into office account as long as it can be paid out within 14 days.

All appeal actions must be taken by the instructed advocate, as must the provision of information for supplementary fees.

Protocol fees

Because the basic fee covers a number of preliminary hearings, a method of distribution is required and is provided by the protocol. The essential concept is that if the basic fee is reduced below 70 per cent then all fees are reduced by the same percentage (whether the work is done by that advocate or others and including the main hearing). Fees added to the basic fee (e.g. page count) are always paid to the advocate attending the main hearing.

For the purpose of the protocol, a PCMH is paid at 15 per cent of the basic fee and other preliminary hearings (by a standard appearance fee at £100 for junior advocates).

EXAMPLE 1

Thus the basic fee is £755 and there is a PCMH and one other interim hearing:

Basic fee		£755.00
30% =		£226.50 less
PCMH (15%)	£113.25	
Standard appearance fee	£100.00	£213.25
		£13.25

As this is a positive figure result, PCMH and standard appearance fees are paid in full and balance is paid to the advocate at main hearing.

Thus basic fee now	£755.00
Minus PCMH and standard appearance fee	£213.25
Paid for main hearing	£541.75

EXAMPLE 2

If in the same case there are a PCMH and two other standard appearance fees:

Basic fee		£755.00	(70% = 528.50 (A))
30% =		£226.50 less	
PCMH (15%)	£113.25		
Standard appearance fee	£100.00		
Standard appearance fee	£100.00	£313.25 (B)	
		£86.75 DR (C)	

As this is a negative result *all* fees abate.
    The abatement is:

$$\frac{C}{A + B\%} \ \%$$

i.e. £86.75 (C) divided by £528.50 (A) + £313.25 (B). As percentage this is 10.31 per cent. Thus all fees are reduced by 89.69 per cent.

Payments:

Basic fee	£528.50 x £89.69%	£474.01
PCMH	£113.25 x £89.69%	£101.58
Standard appearance fee	£100.00 x £89.69%	£89.69
Standard appearance fee	£100.00 x £89.69%	£89.69
		£755.00

CHAPTER 3

Very high cost cases

3.1 Definition

The Criminal Defence Service (General) (No.2) (Amendment No.3) Regulations 2007, SI 2007/3550, reg.23 requires the notification in writing as soon as possible of any case likely to fall within the definition of a very high cost case (VHCC) – essentially a case that may last for no less than 25 days. The notification form appears at **Appendix 12**. The full definition (Criminal Defence Service (Very High Cost Cases) Regulations 2008, SI 2008/40) is:

> a case in which a representation order has been granted and which the Commission classifies as a Very High Cost Case on the grounds that –
>
> (a) if the case were to proceed to trial, the trial would in the opinion of the Commission be likely to last for more than 40 days, and the Commission considers that there are no exceptional circumstances which make it unsuitable to be dealt with under its contractual arrangements for Very High Cost Cases; or
>
> (b) if the case were to proceed to trial, the trial would in the opinion of the Commission be likely to last no fewer than 25 and no more than 40 days, and the Commission considers that there are circumstances which make it suitable to be dealt with under its contractual arrangements for Very High Cost Cases,
>
> ...

If the LSC decides to treat the case as a VHCC, the representation order must be in favour of a firm on the VHCC panel. Each such firm has entered into an individual contract as to the basis on which it will undertake the work. The rates appear in **Appendix 12**.

3.2 Provisional representation orders

Where the Crown invites the defence to enter plea discussions, in accordance with the Attorney General's Guidelines on Plea Discussions in Cases of Serious or Complex Fraud (18 March 2009) and the Commission considers that any trial would last at least 25 days, a provisional representation order may be granted to remunerate lawyers ahead of charge. Details appear at **Appendix 12**.

3.3   Cases ceasing to be very high costs cases; advocacy fees

Where a case ceases to be a very high cost case, the fee reverts to the normal methods of payment to an advocate, who must repay any money paid under the VHCC contract. However, if the advocate was a case manager there will, in addition, be payable an administration fee for the administrative work associated with the VHCC contract. The fee is calculated as a fee for three hours' work for each stage or part stage except stage O until the case ceased to be a VHCC.

Claims summary under the Unified Contract (Crime)

The availability of advice and assistance, advocacy assistance and representation is summarised in the following table.

See Contract Specification B1 for criminal investigations, B2 for criminal proceedings, B3 for appeals and reviews, B4 for prison law, and B5 for associated CLS work.

Advice and assistance claims	Merits	Means	Authority	Limits
Criminal law (excluding criminal proceedings)	Sufficient benefit test	Regs (evidence needed)	Devolved power [1]	£300 but 2 hours if no evidence of means Zero until seek such evidence
Police station telephone advice*	Sufficient benefit test	None	Devolved power	Fixed fee
Police station attendance*	Sufficient benefit test (see above)	None	Devolved power	None
Prison	Sufficient benefit test	Regs [2]	Devolved power	£300
Appeal: CCRC	Sufficient benefit test	Regs	Devolved power	£500
Appeal: others	Sufficient benefit test	None	Devolved power	£300
Associated CLS	Funding Code	Regs	Devolved power	£500

Advocacy assistance claims	Merits	Means	Authority	Limits
Warrant for further detention*	None	None	Devolved power	None
Armed forces custody hearing*	None	None	Devolved power	None
Duty solicitor session* [3]	None (unless non imp and not in custody	None	Devolved power	None
Prison law	Merits [4]	Regs	Devolved power	£1,500
Pre-order costs	Interests of justice, submission and refusal of Forms CDS14/15 B2.3	None	Devolved power	1 hour + VAT (limit)
Early cover	B2.3	None	Devolved power	£75 + VAT
Initial advice	B2.3	None	Devolved power	£25 + VAT

Representation claims	Merits	Means	Authority	Limits
Magistrates' court/ Crown Court	Interests of justice [5]	Magistrates' court: Regs Crown Court: none	Court	None No separate bill
High Court applications for a voluntary bill of indictment/to quash a tainted acquittal	Interests of justice	None	Court	None: bill to High Court
High Court representation on appeal by way of case stated	Interests of justice	None	High Court	None: bill to High Court
Associated CLS investigative help and legal representation [6]	Funding Code (proceeds of crime: interests of justice)	CLS regs	LSC	Limitation on certificate

* No application form needed

[1] Power to grant or refuse is solicitor's.
[2] See relevant financial regulations.
[3] If a case concluded by duty solicitor, no application for a representation order may be made.
[4] Merits test in Contract Specification B4.3.
[5] See *R (David Sonn)* v. *West London Magistrates' Court* [2000] CLW 40/13; *R (Punatar & Co)* v. *Horseferry Road Magistrates' Court* [2002] CLW 24/02.
[6] Solicitor may grant and refuse emergency civil legal representation.

APPENDIX 2

Criminal matter type code descriptions

[*LSC Manual*, Vol.4, Part E, release 06]

Offences against the person

- Assault (common) (Criminal Justice Act 1988 s.39)
- Battery (common) (Criminal Justice Act 1988 s.39)
- Assault occasioning actual bodily harm (Offences against the Person Act 1861 s.47)
- Wounding or inflicting grievous bodily harm (Offences against the Person Act 1861 s.20)
- Wounding or causing grievous bodily harm with intent (Offences against the Person Act 1861 s.18)
- Making threats to kill (Offences against the Person Act 1861 s.16)
- Racially aggravated assaults (Crime and Disorder Act 1998 s.29(1))
- Assault on constable in execution of duty (Police Act 1996 s.89)
- Resisting or wilfully obstructing constable (Police Act 1996 s.89)
- Assault with intention to resist arrest (Offences against the Person Act 1861 s.38)
- Attempting to choke, suffocate, strangle etc. (Offences against the Person Act 1861 s.21)
- Endangering the safety of railway passengers (Offences against the Person Act 1861 s.32, 33, 34)
- Causing bodily injury by explosives (Offences against the Person Act 1861 s.28)
- Using gunpowder to explode, or sending to any person an explosive substance, or throwing corrosive fluid on a person, with intent to grievous bodily harm (Offences against the Person Act 1861 s.29)
- Placing explosives etc., with intent to do bodily injury to any person (Offences against the Person Act 1861 s.30)
- Making or having gunpowder etc., with intent to commit or enable any person to commit a felony (Offences against the Person Act 1861 s.64)
- Causing miscarriage by poison, instrument (Offences against the Person Act 1861 s.58)
- Supplying instrument etc. to cause miscarriage (Offences against the Person Act 1861 s.59)
- Concealment of birth (Offences against the Person Act 1861 s.60)
- Administering chloroform, laudanum etc. (Offences against the Person Act 1861 s.22)
- Administering poison etc. so as to endanger life (Offences against the Person 1861 s.23)
- Administering poison with intent to injure etc. (Offences against the Person Act 1961 s.24)
- Circumcision of females (Prohibition of Female Circumcision Act 1985 s.1)

- Kidnapping (common law)
- Hostage taking (Taking of Hostages Act 1982 s.1)
- False imprisonment (common law)
- Torture (Criminal Justice Act 1988 s.134)

Homicide and related grave offences

- Murder (common law)
- Manslaughter (common law)
- Causing death by dangerous driving (Road Traffic Act 1991 s.1)
- Causing death by careless driving while under the influence of drink or drugs (Road Traffic Act 1988 s.3A)
- Aggravated vehicle taking resulting in death (Theft Act 1968 s.12A)
- Killing in pursuance of suicide pact (Homicide Act 1957 s.4)
- Complicity to suicide (Suicide Act 1961 s.2)
- Soliciting to murder (Offences against the Person Act 1861 s.4)
- Child destruction (Infant Life (Preservation) Act 1929 s.1(1))
- Infanticide (Infanticide Act 1938 s.1(1))
- Abortion (Offences against the Person Act 1861 s.58)
- Supplying or procuring means for abortion (Offences against the Person Act 1861 s.59)
- Concealment of birth (Offences against the Person Act 1861 s.60)

Firearms offences

- Possession of firearm without certificate (Firearms Act 1968 s.1)
- Possession or acquisition of shotgun without certificate (Firearms Act 1968 s.2)
- Dealing in firearms (Firearms Act 1968 s.3)
- Shortening of shotgun or possession of shortened shotgun (Firearms Act 1968 s.4)
- Possession or acquisition of certain prohibited weapons etc. (Firearms Act 1968 s.5)
- Possession of firearm with intent to injure/endanger life (Firearms Act 1968 s.16)
- Possession of firearm or imitation firearm with intent to cause fear of violence (Firearms Act 1968 s.16A)
- Use of firearm to resist arrest (Firearms Act 1968 s.17)
- Possession of firearm with criminal intent (Firearms Act 1968 s.18)
- Carrying loaded firearm in public place (Firearms Act 1968 s.19)
- Possession of firearm without certificate (Firearms Act 1968 s.19)
- Trespassing with a firearm (Firearms Act 1968 s.20)
- Possession of firearms by person convicted of crime (Firearms Act 1968 s.21(4))
- Acquisition by or supply of firearms to person denied them (Firearms Act 1968 s.21(5))
- Failure to comply with certificate when transferring firearm (Firearms Act 1968 s.42)
- Shortening of smooth bore gun (Firearms Amendment Act 1988 s.6(1))

Prison offences

- Permitting an escape (common law)
- Rescue (common law)
- Escape (common law)
- Escaping from lawful custody without force (common law)
- Breach of prison (common law)
- Prison mutiny (Prison Security Act 1992 s.1)

- Assaulting prison officer whilst possessing firearm etc. (Criminal Justice Act 1991 s.90)
- Harbouring escaped prisoners (Criminal Justice Act 1961 s.22)
- Assisting prisoners to escape (Prison Act 1952 s.39)

Terrorist offences

- Offences under the Terrorism Act 2000
- Offences against international protection of nuclear material (Nuclear Material (Offences) Act 1983 s.2)
- Offences under the Northern Ireland (Emergency Provisions) Act 1991)

Sexual offences and offences against children

- Offences under the Sexual Offences Act 2003
- Child abduction by connected person (Child Abduction Act 1984 s. 1)
- Child abduction by other person (Child Abduction Act 1984 s.2)
- Keeping brothel and related offences (Sexual Offences Act ss.33, 34, 35, and 36)
- Keeping a disorderly house (common law: Disorderly Houses Act 1751 s.8)
- Soliciting (Street Offences Act 1959 s.1)
- Taking, having etc. indecent photographs of children (Protection of Children Act 1978 s.1)
- Sexual intercourse with patients (Mental Health Act 1959 s.128)
- Ill treatment of persons of unsound mind (Mental Health Act 1983 s.127)
- Bigamy (Offences against the Person Act 1861 s.57)
- Abuse of position of trust (Sexual Offences (Amendment) Act 2000 s.3)
- Abandonment of children under two (Offences against the Person Act 1861 s.27)
- Cruelty to persons under 16 (Children and Young Persons Act 1933 s.1)

Robbery

- Robbery (Theft Act 1968 s.8(1))
- Armed robbery (Theft Act 1968 s.8(1))
- Assault with weapon with intent to rob (Theft Act 1968 s.8(2))

Burglary

- Burglary (domestic) (Theft Act 1968 s.9(3)(a))
- Going equipped to steal (Theft Act 1968 s.25)
- Burglary (non-domestic) (Theft Act 1968 s.9(3)(b))
- Aggravated burglary (Theft Act 1968 s.10)

Criminal damage and arson

- Criminal damage (Criminal Damage Act 1971 s.1(1))
- Destroying or damaging property with the intention or recklessness as to endanger life (Criminal Damage Act 1971 s.1(2))
- Aggravated criminal damage (Criminal Damage Act 1971 s.1(2))
- Threats to destroy or damage property (Criminal Damage Act 1971 s.2)
- Racially aggravated criminal damage (Crime and Disorder Act 1998 s.30)
- Possessing anything with intent to destroy or damage property (Criminal Damage Act 1971 s.3)

- Possessing bladed article/instrument (Criminal Justice Act 1988 s.139)
- Prohibition of the carrying of offensive weapons without lawful authority or reasonable excuse (Prevention of Crime Act 1953 s.1)
- Arson (Criminal Damage Act 1971 s.1(3))
- Aggravated arson (Criminal Damage Act 1971 s.1(2), (3))
- Racially aggravated arson (Crime and Disorder Act 1998 s.30)

Theft (including taking vehicle without consent)

- Theft (Theft Act 1968 s.1)
- Taking conveyance without authority (Theft Act 1968 s.12)
- Taking or riding a pedal cycle without authority (Theft Act 1968 s. 12(5) and s.12(6))
- Aggravated vehicle taking (Theft Act 1968 s.12A)
- Handling stolen goods (Theft Act 1968 s.22)
- Receiving property by another's mistake (Theft Act 1968 s.5(4))
- Removal of articles from places open to the public (Theft Act 1968 s.11)
- Abstraction of electricity (Theft Act 1968 s.13)
- Making off without payment (Theft Act 1978 s.3)

Fraud, forgery and other offences of dishonesty

- Fraud (common law)
- Forgery (Forgery and Counterfeiting Act 1981 s.1)
- Copying a false instrument (Forgery and Counterfeiting Act 1981 s.2)
- Using a false statement (Forgery and Counterfeiting Act 1981 s.3)
- Using a copy of a false instrument (Forgery and Counterfeiting Act 1981 s.4)
- Custody or control of false instruments etc. (Forgery and Counterfeiting Act 1981 s.5)
- Offences relating to money orders, share certificates, passports etc., etc. (Forgery and counterfeiting Act 1981 s.5)
- Counterfeiting notes and coins (Forgery and Counterfeiting Act 1981 s.14)
- Passing, etc. counterfeiting notes and coins (Forgery and Counterfeiting Act 1981 s.15)
- Offences involving the custody/control of counterfeit notes and coins (Forgery and Counterfeiting Act 1981 s.16)
- Making, custody or control of counterfeiting materials etc. (Forgery and Counterfeiting Act 1981 s.175)
- Illegal importation: Counterfeit notes or coins (Customs and Excise Management Act 1979 s.50)
- Offences involving the making/custody/control of counterfeiting materials and implements (Forgery and Counterfeiting Act 1981 s.17)
- Reproducing British currency (Forgery and Counterfeiting Act 1981 s.18)
- Offences in making, etc., imitation of British coins (Forgery and Counterfeiting Act 1981 s.19)
- Prohibition of importation of counterfeit notes and coins (Forgery and Counterfeiting Act 1981 s.20)
- Prohibition of exportation of counterfeit notes and coins (Forgery and Counterfeiting Act 1981 s.21)
- Destruction of registers of births etc. (Forgery Act 1861 s.36)
- Making false entries in copies of registers sent to registrar (Forgery Act 1861 s.37)
- Fraudulent evasion: counterfeit notes or coins (Customs and Excise Management Act 1979 s.170(2)(b), (c))
- Obtaining services by deception (Theft Act 1978 s.1)

- Evasion of liability by deception (Theft Act 1978 s.2)
- Obtaining property by deception (Theft Act 1968 s.15)
- Obtaining a money transfer by deception (Theft Act 1968 s.15A)
- Obtaining pecuniary advantage by deception (Theft Act 1968 s.16)
- False accounting (Theft Act 1968 s.17)
- Liability of company officers for offences of deception committed by the company (Theft Act 1968 s.18)
- False statements by company directors (Theft Act 1968 s.19)
- Suppression, etc. of documents (Theft Act 1968 s.20)
- Procuring execution of a valuable security by deception (Theft Act 1968 s.20)
- Advertising rewards for return of goods stolen or lost (Theft Act 1968 s.23)
- Dishonestly retaining a wrongful credit (Theft Act 1968 s.24A)
- Fraudulent use of telecommunication system (Telecommunications Act 1984 s.42)
- Possession or supply of anything for fraudulent purpose in connection with use of telecommunication system (Telecommunications Act 1984 s.42A)
- Offences under the Companies Act 1985
- Insider dealing (Criminal Justice Act 1993 s.52)
- False declarations of insolvency in voluntary liquidations (Insolvency Act 1986 s.89)
- Concealment of property and failure to account for losses (Insolvency Act 1986 s.354)
- Concealment or falsification of books and papers (Insolvency Act 1986 s.355)
- False statements (Insolvency Act 1986 s.356)
- Fraudulent disposal of property (Insolvency Act 1986 s.357)
- Absconding with property (Insolvency Act 1986 s.358)
- Fraudulent dealing with property obtained on credit (Insolvency Act 1986 s.359)
- Undischarged bankrupt concerned in a company (Insolvency Act 1986 s.360)
- Failure to keep proper business accounts (Insolvency Act 1986 s.361)
- Misleading statements and practices (Financial Services Act 1986 s.47)
- Fraudulent inducement to make a deposit (Banking Act 1987 s.35(1))
- Counterfeiting customs documents (Customs and Excise Management Act 1979 s.168)
- Offences in relation to dies or stamps (Stamp Duties Management Act 1891 s.13)
- Counterfeiting of dies or marks (Hallmarking Act 1973 s.6)
- Fraudulent application of trademark (Trade Marks Act 1938 s.58A)
- False application or use of trademarks (Trade Marks Act 1994 s.92)
- Forgery of driving documents (Road Traffic Act 1960 s.233)
- Forgery and misuse of driving documents (Public Passenger Vehicles Act 1981 s.65)
- Forgery etc. of licences and other documents (Road Traffic Act 1988 s.173)
- Mishandling or falsifying parking documents (Road Traffic Regulations Act 1984 s.115)
- Forgery, alteration etc. of documents etc. (Goods Vehicles (Licensing of Operators) Act 1995 s.38)
- False records or entries relating to driver's hours (Transport Act 1968 s.99)
- Forgery, alteration, fraud of licences etc. (Vehicle (Excise) Act 1971 s.26)
- Forgery, alteration etc. of licences, marks, trade plates etc. (Vehicle Excise and Registration Act 1994 ss.44 and 45)
- Forgery of documents etc.: Motor vehicles (EC Type approval) Regulations 1992, reg.11(1) and Motor cycles etc. (EC Type approval) Regulations 1999, reg.20(1)
- Fraudulent evasion of agricultural levy (Customs and Excise Management Act 1979 s.68A(1) and (2))
- Evasion of duty (Customs and Excise Management Act 1979 s.170)
- Trade description offences (9 offences) (Trade Descriptions Act 1968 ss.1, 8, 9, 12, 13, 14, 18)
- VAT offences (VAT Act 1994)

Public order offences

- Breach of any order made by a court
- Causing explosion likely to endanger life or property (Explosive Substances Act 1883 s.2)
- Attempt to cause explosion, making or keeping explosive etc. (Explosive Substances Act 1883 s.3)
- Making or possession of explosive under suspicious circumstances (Explosive Substances Act 1883 s.4)
- Bomb hoaxes (Criminal Law Act 1977 s.51)
- Contamination of goods with intent (Public Order Act 1986 s.38)
- Placing wood etc. on railway (Malicious Damage Act 1861 s.35)
- Exhibiting false signals etc. (Malicious Damage Act 1861 s.47)
- Perjuries (7 offences) (Perjury Act 1911 s.1–7(2))
- Offences akin to perjury: False testimony of unsworn child witnesses in criminal proceedings (Children and Young Persons Act 1933 s.38)
- Perverting the course of public justice (common law)
- Public nuisance (common law)
- Contempt of court (common law)
- Blackmail (Theft Act 1968 s.21)
- Corrupt transactions with agents (Prevention of Corruption Act 1906 s.1)
- Corruption (common law)
- Corruption in public office (Public Bodies Corrupt Practices Act 1889 s.1)
- Embracery (common law)
- Fabrication of evidence with intent to mislead a tribunal (common law)
- Personation of jurors (common law)
- Concealing an arrestable offence (Criminal Law Act 1967 s.5)
- Assisting offenders (Criminal Law Act 1967 s.4(1))
- False evidence before European Court (European Communities Act 1972 s.11)
- Intimidating a witness, juror etc. (Criminal Justice and Public Order Act 1994 s.51(1))
- Harming, threatening to harm a witness, juror etc. (Criminal Justice and Public Order Act 1994 s.51(2))
- Ticket touts (Criminal Justice and Public Order Act 1994 s.166)
- Prejudicing a drug trafficking investigation (Drug Trafficking Act 1994 s.58(1))
- Giving false statements to procure cremation (Cremation Act 1902 s.8(2))
- False statement tendered under section 9 of the Criminal Justice Act 1967 (Criminal Justice Act 1967 s.89)
- False statement tendered under section 102 of the Magistrates' Courts Act 1980 (Magistrates' Courts Act 1980 s.106)
- Making a false statement to obtain or resist interim possession order (Criminal Justice and Public Order Act 1994 s.75)
- Making false statement to authorised officer (Trade Descriptions Act 1968 s.29(2))
- Riot (Public Order Act 1986 s.1)
- Violent disorder (Public Order Act 1986 s.2)
- Affray (Public Order Act 1986 s.3)
- Fear or provocation of violence (Public Order Act 1986 s.4)
- Intentional harassment, alarm, or distress (Public Order Act 1986 s.4A)
- Harassment, alarm or distress (Public Order Act 1986 s.5)
- Harassment of debtors (Administration of Justice Act 1970 s.40)
- Offence of harassment (Protection from Harassment Act 1997 ss.1 and 2)
- Putting people in fear of violence (Protection from Harassment Act 1997 s.4)
- Breach of restraining order/injunction (Protection from Harassment Act 1997 ss.3 and 5)

- Racially aggravated public order offences (Crime and Disorder Act 1998 s.31)
- Racially aggravated harassment etc. (Crime and Disorder Act 1998 s.32)
- Using words or behaviour or displaying written material stirring up racial hatred (Public Order Act 1986 s.18)
- Publishing or distributing written material stirring up racial hatred (Public Order Act 1986 s.19)
- Public performance of play stirring up racial hatred (Public Order Act 1986 s.20)
- Distributing, showing or playing a recording stirring up racial hatred (Public Order Act 1986 s.21)
- Broadcasting programme stirring up racial hatred (Public Order Act 1986 s.22)
- Possession of written material or recording stirring up racial hatred (Public Order Act 1986 s.23)
- Possession of offensive weapon (Prevention of Crime Act 1953 s.1)
- Possession of bladed article (Criminal Justice Act 1988 s.139)
- Criminal libel (common law)
- Blasphemy and blasphemous libel (common law)
- Sedition
- Indecent display (Indecent Displays (Control) Act 1981 s.1)
- Presentation of obscene performance (Theatres Act 1968 s.2)
- Obstructing railway or carriage on railway (Malicious Damage Act 1861 s.36)
- Obscene articles intended for publication for gain (Obscene Publications Act 1964 s.1)
- Offences of publication of obscene matter (Obscene Publications Act 1959 s.2)
- Agreeing to indemnify sureties (Bail Act 1976 s.9(1))
- Absconding by person released on bail (Bail Act 1976 s.6(1), (2))
- Personating for purposes of bail etc. (Forgery Act 1861 s.34)
- Sending prohibited articles by post (Post Office Act 1953 s.11)
- Impersonating Customs officer (Customs and Excise Management Act 1979 s.3)
- Obstructing Customs officer (Customs and Excise Management Act 1979 s.16)
- Penalty on keepers of refreshment houses permitting drunkenness, disorderly conduct, or gaming, etc., therein (Metropolitan Police Act 1839 s.44)
- Penalty on persons found drunk (Licensing Act 1872 s.12)
- Drunkenness in a public place (Criminal Justice Act 1967 s.91)
- Drunk in a late night refreshment house (Late Night Refreshment Houses Act 1969 s.9(4)) [this provision was repealed by Licensing Act 2003]
- Drunk while in charge of a child (Licensing Act 1902 s.2(1))
- Drunk on an aircraft (Air Navigation Order 2000 and Civil Aviation Act (SI 2000 No. 1562), art.65(1))
- Intimidation or annoyance by violence or otherwise (Trade Union and Labour Relations (Consolidation) Act 1992 s.241)

Offences affecting security

- Offences under the Official Secrets Acts 1911, 1920 and 1989
- Unlawful interception of communications by public and private systems (Regulation of Investigatory Powers Act 2000 s.1)
- Disclosure of telecommunication messages (Telecommunications Act 1984 s.45)
- Incitement to disaffection (Incitement to Disaffection Act 1934 ss.1 and 2)

Drug offences

- Restriction of importation and exportation of controlled drugs (Misuse of Drugs Act s.3)

- Producing or supplying a Class A, B or C drug (Misuse of Drugs Act 1971 s.4)
- Possession of controlled drugs (Misuse of Drugs Act 1971 s.5(2))
- Possession of a Class A, B or C drug with intent to supply (Misuse of Drugs Act 1971 s.5(3))
- Cultivation of cannabis plant (Misuse of Drugs Act 1971 s.6)
- Occupier knowingly permitting drugs offences etc. (Misuse of Drugs Act 1971 s.8)
- Activities relating to opium (Misuse of Drugs Act 1971 s.9)
- Prohibition of supply etc., of articles for administering or preparing controlled drugs (Misuse of Drugs Act 1971 s.9A)
- Offences relating to the safe custody of controlled drugs (Misuse of Drugs Act 1971 s.11)
- Practitioner contravening drug supply regulations (Misuse of Drugs Act 1971 ss.12 and 13)
- Incitement (Misuse of Drugs Act 1971 s.19)
- Assisting in or inducing commission outside United Kingdom of offence punishable under a corresponding law (Misuse of Drugs Act 1971 s.20)
- Powers of entry, search and seizure (Misuse of Drugs Act 1971 s.23)
- Illegal importation of Class A, B or C drugs (Customs and Excise Management Act 1979 s.50)
- Fraudulent evasion of controls on Class A, B or C drugs (Customs and Excise Management Act 1979 s.170(2)(b)(c))
- Failure to disclose knowledge or suspicion of money laundering (Drug Trafficking Offences Act 1986 s.26B)
- Tipping-off in relation to money laundering investigations (Drug Trafficking Offences Act 1986 s.26C)
- Offences in relation to proceeds of drug trafficking (Drug Trafficking Act 1994 ss.49, 50 and 51)
- Offences in relation to money laundering investigations (Drug Trafficking Act 1994 ss.52 and 53)
- Manufacture and supply of scheduled substances (Criminal Justice (International Co-operation) Act 1990 s.12)
- Drug trafficking offences at sea (Criminal Justice (International Co-operation) Act 1990 s.18)
- Ships used for illicit traffic (Criminal Justice (International Cooperation) Act 1990 s.19)
- Making and preserving records of production and supply of certain scheduled substances (Controlled Drugs (Substances Useful for Manufacture) Regulations 1991)
- Supply of intoxicating substance (Intoxicating Substances (Supply) Act 1985 s.1)

Driving and motor vehicle offences (other than those covered by codes 1, 6 & 7)

- Dangerous driving (Road Traffic Act 1988 s.2)
- Careless, and inconsiderate driving (Road Traffic Act 1988 s.3)
- Driving, or being in charge, when under the influence of drink or drugs (Road Traffic Act 1988 s.4)
- Driving or being in charge of a motor vehicle with excess alcohol (Road Traffic Act 1988 s.5)
- Breath tests (Road Traffic Act 1988 s.6)
- Provision of specimens for analysis (Road Traffic Act 1988 s.7)
- Motor racing on highways (Road Traffic Act 1988 s.12)
- Leaving vehicle in dangerous position (Road Traffic Act 1988 s.22)
- Causing danger to road users (Road Traffic Act 1988 s.22A)

- Restriction of carriage of persons on motor cycles (Road Traffic Act 1988 s.23)
- Failing to stop at school gate (Road Traffic Act 1988 s.28)
- Failure to comply with indication given by traffic sign (Road Traffic Act 1988 s.36)
- Directions to pedestrians (Road Traffic Act 1988 s.37)
- Using vehicles in dangerous condition (Road Traffic Act 1988 s.40A)
- Contravention of construction and use regulations (Road Traffic Act 1988 s.41A)
- Using etc. motor vehicle without test certificate (Road Traffic Act 1988 s.47)
- Driving otherwise than in accordance with a licence (Road Traffic Act 1988 s.87)
- Driving after refusal or revocation of licence (Road Traffic Act 1988 s.94A)
- False declaration as to physical fitness (Road Traffic Act 1988 s.92)
- Failure to notify disability (Road Traffic Act 1988 s.94)
- Driving with uncorrected defective eyesight (Road Traffic Act 1988 s.96)
- Driving while disqualified (Road Traffic Act 1988 s.103)
- Using etc. motor vehicle without insurance (Road Traffic Act 1988 s.143)
- Failure to produce driving licence, insurance etc. (Road Traffic Offenders Act 1988 s.27)
- Failure to give, or giving false, name and address in case of dangerous or careless or inconsiderate driving or cycling (Road Traffic Act 1988 s.168)
- Pedestrian contravening constable's direction to stop to give name and address (Road Traffic Act 1988 s.169)
- Failing to stop and failing to report accident (Road Traffic Act 1988 s.170)
- Duty of owner of motor vehicle to give information for verifying compliance with requirement of compulsory insurance or security (Road Traffic Act 1988 s.171)
- Duty to give information as to identity of driver etc., in certain circumstances (Road Traffic Act 1988 s.172)
- Pedestrian crossing regulations (Road Traffic Regulation Act 1984 s.25)
- Street playgrounds (Road Traffic Regulation Act 1984 s.29)
- Speeding (Road Traffic Regulation Act 1984 s.89)
- Wanton or furious driving (Offences against the Person Act 1861 s.35)
- Interference with vehicles (Criminal Attempts Act 1981 s.9)
- Other road traffic offences (including policing etc.)

Other

- Proceedings for the making of anti-social behaviour orders, sex offender orders etc.
- Failing to keep dogs under proper control resulting in injury and other dog offences (Dangerous Dogs Act 1991 s.3)
- Failing to keep dogs under proper control resulting in injury and other dog offences (Dangerous Dogs Act 1991 s.3)
- Hijacking of aircraft (Aviation Security Act 1982 s.1)
- Destroying, damaging or endangering safety of aircraft (Aviation Security Act 1982 s.2)
- Other acts endangering or likely to endanger safety of aircraft (Aviation Security Act 1982 s.3)
- Offences in relation to certain dangerous articles (Aviation Security Act 1982 s.4)
- Endangering safety at aerodromes (Aviation and Maritime Security Act 1990 s.1)
- Hijacking of ships (Aviation and Maritime Security Act 1990 s.9)
- Other offences under the Aviation and Maritime Security Act 1990 (Aviation and Maritime Security Act 1990 ss.10, 11, 12, and 13)
- Piracy (Piracy Act 1837 s.2)
- Offences under the Football Spectators Act 1989

- Throwing of missiles (Football (Offences) Act 1991 s.2)
- Indecent or racialist chanting (Football (Offences) Act 1991 s.3)
- Going onto the playing area (Football (Offences) Act 1991 s.4)
- Offences in connection with alcohol on coaches and trains (Sporting Events (Control of Alcohol etc.) Act 1985 s.1)
- Offences in connection with alcohol, containers etc., at sports grounds (Sporting Events (Control of Alcohol etc.) Act 1985 s.2)
- Offences of cruelty (Protection of Animals Act 1911 s.1)
- Penalties for abandonment of animals (Abandonment of Animals Act 1960 s.1)
- Offences (Wild Mammals (Protection) Act 1996 s.1)
- Raves (Criminal Justice and Public Order Act 1994 s.63)
- Offences affecting enjoyment of premises
- Unlawful eviction and harassment of occupier (Protection of Eviction Act 1977 s.1)
- Use or threat of violence for purpose of securing entry to premises (Criminal Law Act 1977 s.6(1))
- Adverse occupation of residential premises (Criminal Law Act 1977 s.7)
- Trespassing during the currency of an interim possession order (Criminal Justice and Public Order Act 1994 s.76)
- Interim possession orders: false or misleading statements (Criminal Justice and Public Order Act 1994 s.75)
- Aggravated trespass (Criminal Justice and Public Order Act 1994 s.68)
- Failure to leave or re-entry to land after police direction to leave (Criminal Justice and Public Order Act 1994 s.61)
- Unauthorised campers (Criminal Justice and Public Order Act 1994 s.77)

Guidance for Reporting Work on Form CDS6 and CDS7 and Case Referral to DSCC form

[LSC, March 2008]

SECTION 1   TRANSITIONAL ARRANGEMENTS

Use of this new CDS6 is mandatory for all work reported after 1 August 2008. Before that date the pre-August arrangements will apply and VAT information will not be required.

From this date our systems will be set up to only pay VAT on your claim where you have requested this, and all outcomes reported must adhere to the new VAT reporting arrangements regardless of when the work was started, completed or the submission month it is included in.

Requirements for reporting the police station scheme identifier introduced in the October 2007 CDS6 will remain. This is to enable the fixed fee to be derived at the scheme level and paid in place of profit, travel and waiting costs. These actual costs must still be reported (except travel – see below).

We will not substitute the actual claim value with the fixed fee unless the start date of the case reported (derived from the UFN) is on or after the date of implementation of the fixed fees on 14 January 2008.

SECTION 2   VAT

We are asking your to change the way you report your Criminal costs to make them VAT exclusive. We are also changing the way we publish Fees and Hourly rates to make them also VAT exclusive.

This will bring Crime Reporting into line with Civil Reporting and allow for circumstances where the addition of VAT is not appropriate.

The CDS6 has been changed to reflect this move and you will note the addition of the two new VAT fields, one for Profit Costs and the other for Disbursements. You are asked to report all costs exclusive of VAT and to indicate for each case line reported whether VAT should be added to Profit, Travel and Waiting Costs and also to enter the amount of VAT which you wish to claim on any disbursements.

The total Page Value at the foot of the form is for all costs including VAT.

You should use the new CDS6 (Version 7 July 2008) for all Cases completed from the 1st July 08, which you will then report to us in August 08.

1.   POLICE STATION FEES

The Fixed Fee has been designed to cover the supplier's profit costs, travel and waiting. The overall value of an outcome is therefore the fixed fee for the scheme the police station is in, plus any disbursements. The fixed fee as published in the Contract is exclusive of VAT. If VAT needs to be claimed and added to the fixed fee, this should be indicated by clicking on the VAT indicator field and also by entering the VAT amount relevant to any disbursements as a separate amount.

2. REVISED MAGISTRATES FEES

The fee that is claimed must be entered in the profit cost field exclusive of VAT. If VAT is to be claimed against the costs this should be indicated by clicking on the VAT indicator field and also by entering the VAT amount relevant to disbursements as a separate amount.

SECTION 3   REPORTING YOUR CDS6 WORK

As of 1 August 2008 your CDS6 submissions should be made electronically. In exceptional circumstances paper forms may be submitted.

The guidance relates to completing an electronic submission or a CDS6 paper form. Note: additional guidance, including completion of the CDS7, is detailed in Volume 4 of the Legal Services Commission manual.

We produce separate guidance (available on our website: www.legalservices.gov.uk/lsconline.asp) on both civil and criminal online reporting which also may assist you further with submitting claims electronically. Note that when claiming online the new codes (implemented in April 07) are available only, but you can use our online search tool (which can be found on the same web page when filling in the CDS6 online) to find the new code.

Electronic Submissions

Submission Data should be either bulk loaded into LSC Online or entered line by line directly into the LSC Online system.

However due to the current modifications being made to our LSC Online service you should submit claims using the bulk load spreadsheet by file transfer.

Detailed instructions are on our website: http://www.legalservices.gov.uk/lsconline/howitworks.asp

LSC Online is being relaunched in a wave approach. You will be advised of the date when you can start using LSC Online to make your submissions.

Field	Use	Format/examples
Client surname and initial	Surname and first-name initial of the client receiving legal aid	e.g. Jones, T.
Equal opportunities monitoring	Refers to the ethnic origin, gender and disability of your client. Equal opportunity codes should be inputted. The codes are listed in section 3 of this document	e.g. 01/M/N
UFN	Unique file number. Made up of the start date (with only yy for the year) and 3 digit case ID. This will uniquely identify a legal aid case (when combined with supplier account number)	ddmmyy/000 e.g. 010607/004

Stage reached	The stage the case has reached at the end. A claim code is entered under this field. Claim codes are listed in section 2 of this document	e.g. INVA
Outcome code	The outcome for the client at the end of the stage or case	e.g. CN01
Matter type	The entry for matter type is the offence code for the case. Guidance and codes are listed in section 2 of this document	Numeric e.g. for offences against the person enter code '1'.
Profit costs	Police Station: Total cost of hourly rate for profit costs (excluding VAT).	Numeric
	Note: the relevant fixed fee will be substituted for the amount of profit costs, travel and waiting claimed.	
	Magistrates' Court: Standard Fee Claimed (excluding VAT)	
Disbursements	Total amount of disbursements (including VAT)	Numeric
Travel	There is no requirement under the July 2008 Unified Contract to record travel costs.	Numeric
	If you do record these costs (for example for Exceptional Cases or Non-urban Magistrates' Court Fees) they should be the total cost of hourly rate for travel (excluding VAT)	
	Note: Police Station: the relevant fixed fee will be substituted for the amount of profit costs, travel and waiting claimed.	
	Magistrates' Court: Travel will be paid for non-urban court claims	
Waiting	Total cost of hourly rate for waiting (excluding VAT)	Numeric
	Note: Police Station: the relevant fixed fee will be substituted for the amount of profit costs, travel and waiting claimed.	
	Magistrate's Court: Waiting will be paid for non-urban court claims	
Date class of work concluded	The date you concluded the case	dd mm yyyy e.g. 03 08 2007

Number of suspects/ defendants	How many suspects or defendants in the case	Numerical e.g. 2
Number of police/ court attendances	How many times you have attended the police station or court for this case	Numerical e.g. 4
Police station/court identifier	A unique code should be entered for the specific police station or court. **The code must be for the Police Station or Court where *the first attendance* took place.**	Alphanumeric e.g. NE001
	Police Station codes and Court codes are listed in a separate document in the forms and codes section of our website	
Police station scheme identifier	A unique code should be entered for the specific police station scheme. Instructing scheme code to be used (i.e. the scheme on which the solicitor was on duty when instructed), not necessarily the scheme in which the police station is located. **This identifier is only required for Duty Solicitor Matters**	Numeric e.g. 1001
Duty solicitor	Add 'Y' (Yes) or 'N' (No) depending on whether you were acting as the duty solicitor or not	Initial used e.g. Y
Youth Court	Add 'Y' (Yes) or 'N' (No) depending on whether the case is being dealt with at the Youth Court or not	Initial used e.g. N
VAT indicator (Profit Costs, Travel and Waiting)	When selected applies VAT to the outcome value (excluding disbursements (please see below)).	Initial used e.g. Y
	Where deriving value it will apply VAT to the fee and any other additional payments. If the fixed fee does not apply it should apply VAT to the NET profit costs, travel & waiting costs fields	
VAT disbursement	This numeric field will allow the input of the amount of VAT that should properly be added to the value contained in the Disbursement Amount Excluding VAT field. The VAT amount can only be greater than zero if a value has been input to the disbursement amount field	Numeric

Entering Costs

For Police Station claims providers are asked to record actual profit costs in this field as well as actual waiting costs in the appropriate separate field. This will allow us to monitor the sensitivity of the Fixed Fees and take account of any significant changes on the ground that impact on provider delivery costs as well as identifying when a case has exceeded the Exceptional Case threshold. The relevant fixed fee will be substituted for the amount of profit costs, and also the amount of waiting claimed.

For Magistrates' Court Work providers are asked to continue the practice of entering the relevant Standard Fee in the Profit Costs field, and to record actual waiting in the appropriate separate field.

Travel Costs

Whilst the requirement to record the actual cost of waiting remains for both Police Station and Magistrates' Court Fixed and Standard Fees, the new Unified Contract (Crime) July 2008 removes the requirement to record travel costs, although providers may continue to report these costs if so desired. When submitting online or through bulk load transfer, if you do not wish to report travel costs, you will be required to enter £0 in the relevant field to prevent the claim being rejected by our system.

We will continue to pay the costs of travel where included in claims for standard fees in non-urban courts and Police Station Exceptional Case Claims.

Claiming for Exceptional Cases

Providers must report the actual profit costs incurred when making any claim on the CDS6. The system will automatically calculate whether the case meets the Exceptional Case criteria (i.e. whether the profit costs plus travel and waiting exceed three times the value of the appropriate fixed fee).

As detailed above, the requirement to record travel for fixed cases has been removed from the Unified Contract. If you want these costs to contribute towards meeting the Exceptional Case criteria you must record them as part of your claim on the CDS6.

Providers should also complete an Exceptional Case Claim Form (EC-Claim1) and forward all such cases to the relevant Exceptional Case teams for costs assessment.

SECTION 4   CRIMINAL DEFENCE SERVICE – CODE GUIDANCE

This guidance covers the description and use of the Criminal Matter Types, Claim/Stage Reached and Outcome Codes that are required to complete forms CDS6 and CDS7.

Throughout this guidance UCC means the Unified Criminal Contract.

1.   CRIMINAL MATTER TYPES

Criminal Matter Type Code Guidance

1. There are a total of 16 Criminal Matter Type codes. They are numbered 1 to 16.
2. Criminal Matter Types are only recorded for the Criminal Investigations Class of Work and those Matters and Cases in the Criminal Proceedings Class of Work where a Representation Order was issued.
3. You must not record a Criminal Matter Type when making a consolidated standby or Court Duty Solicitor claim or for any claim made in relation to the Appeals and Reviews, Prison Law, Associated CLS Classes of Work or Other – LSC internal use only.

4. A Criminal Matter Type is not required for a claim made under Claim/Stage Reached Codes INVH and INVI.

Recording Criminal Matter Type for Criminal Investigations

5. Where your client has been charged or warned, you should determine which heading the principal offence or charge that your client faces is listed under. A list of offences falling under a matter type can be found in LSC Manual Volume 4 – Part E.
6. Where you cannot locate the appropriate charge, you should select Code 12. Where your client has been released without charge, you must record the heading that covers the Criminal Matter Type that he or she was interviewed in relation to (if an interview took place).
7. Where you have given freestanding Advice and Assistance (INVA) only, you must record the heading that covers the Criminal Matter Type that advice was given in relation to.
8. Where you have only given Police Station Telephone Advice, you must record the heading that covers the Criminal Matter Type that advice was given in relation to. If you do not know what the nature of the matter was, you must record the Code 12.

Recording Criminal Matter Types for Criminal Proceedings

9. If you advise a witness or any other person who is not subject to an investigation or proceedings then record Code 12.
10. Where your client has been charged or summonsed, you must record the final charge that your client faces. Where your client is facing multiple charges, you should identify the most serious charge.
11. You should only record the original charge laid by the police / if this has not altered during the course of the proceedings. In cases where the charge does alter it is the final charge that must be recorded.

Criminal Matter Type Code Table

Code	Description
1	Offences against the person
2	Homicide and related grave offences
3	Sexual offences and associated offences against children
4	Robbery
5	Burglary
6	Criminal damage
7	Theft (including taking vehicle without consent)
8	Fraud and forgery and other offences of dishonesty
9	Public order offences
10	Drug offences
11	Driving and motor vehicle offences (other than those covered by codes 1, 6 & 7)
12	Other offences
13	Terrorism
14	Anti-social behaviour orders
15	Sexual offender orders
16	Other prescribed proceedings

2. CLAIM/STAGE REACHED CODE GUIDANCE

1. The claim code/stage reached is made up of four characters. The first three characters record the Class of Work that is being claimed for: Criminal Investigation (INV-), Criminal Proceedings (PRO-), Appeals and Reviews (APP-), Prison Law (PRI-) and Associated CLS work (ASS-). The fourth character is a letter that records the unit of work within the Class of Work.

Table of Claim/Stage Reached Codes

Code	Description
Criminal investigation	
INVA	Advice and assistance (not at the police station)
INVB	Police station: telephone advice only
INVC	Police station: attendance
INVD	Police station: attendance (armed forces)
INVE	Warrant of further detention (including Terrorism Act 2000, advice & assistance and other police station advice where given)
INVF	Warrant of further detention (armed forces) (including Terrorism Act 2000, advice & assistance and other police station advice where given)
INVG	Duty solicitor standby
INVH	Police station: post-charge attendance – breach of bail/arrest on warrant
INVI	Police station: post-charge attendance – post-charge identification procedure/recharge/referral back for caution, reprimand, warning
INVJ	Immigration matter
Criminal proceedings	
PROC	Magistrates' court advocacy assistance
PROD	Court duty solicitor session
PROE	Representation order – lower standard fee
PROF	Representation order – higher standard fee
PROG	Representation order – non-standard fee
PROH	Crown Court advocacy assistance
PROI	High court representation
PROJ	Second claim for deferred sentence
PROK	Revised standard fee (designated areas): lower standard fee
PROL	Revised standard fee (designated areas): higher standard fee
PROM	Revised standard fee (designated areas): non-standard fee
PROP	Pre-order cover
PROT	Early cover
PROU	Refused means test – form completion fee
Appeals & reviews	
APPA	Advice and assistance in relation to an appeal (except CCRC)
APPB	Advice and assistance in relation to CCRC application
APPC	Representation on an appeal by way of case stated
Prison law	
PRIA	Free standing advice and assistance
PRIB	Advocacy assistance at prison discipline hearings
PRIC	Advocacy assistance at parole board hearings

Associated CLS work	
ASSA	Legal help and CLS associated work

Other – LSC internal use only	
FRVA	File review

3. OUTCOME CODE GUIDANCE

Purpose

1. The Outcome Code indicates the furthest point to which the Case or Matter progressed and the outcome achieved.
2. The appropriate Outcome Code can only be determined once the Case or Matter has reached the end of the relevant Class of Work (thereby triggering a claim) or has been disposed of finally.
3. Outcome Codes only apply to Matters and Cases in the Criminal Investigations Class of Work (INVA to INVF and INVJ) and magistrates' court representation under a Representation Order in the Criminal Proceedings Class of Work (PROE to PROG and PROK to PROM).
4. Outcome Codes are not required for Claim Code/Stage Reached, INVG to INVI, PROC and PROD, (Court Duty Solicitor session), PROH to PROJ, PROP to PROU or for work in the Appeals and Reviews, Prison Law and Associated CLS Classes of Work.

Format

5. The code consists of 4 characters. The first two letters indicate the specific class of work and the following two digits determine the individual outcome within the Class of Work.
6. The letter key is as follows:

    CN = Criminal Investigations CP = Criminal Proceedings

7. It is important to note that the Outcome Codes are not interchangeable between Classes of Work, e.g. CP cannot be used for a Criminal Investigations claim and CN cannot be used for a Criminal Proceedings claim.

Table of Outcome Codes

Code	Description
Criminal investigation	
CN01	No further instructions
CN02	Change of solicitor
CN03	Client not a suspect
CN04	No further action
CN05	Simple caution, reprimand, warning
CN06	Charge, summons or reported for summons
CN07	Conditional caution
CN08	Fixed penalty notice

Criminal proceedings

CP01	Arrest warrant issued/adjourned indefinitely
CP02	Change of solicitor
CP03	Representation order withdrawn
CP04	Trial: acquitted
CP05	Trial: mixed verdicts
CP06	Trial: convicted
CP07	Discontinued (before any pleas entered)
CP08	Discontinued (after pleas entered)
CP09	Guilty plea to all charges put – not listed for trial
CP10	Guilty plea to all charges put after case listed for trial
CP11	Guilty plea to substitute charges put – after case listed for trial
CP12	Mix of guilty plea(s) and discontinuance – not listed for trial
CP13	Mix of guilty plea(s) and discontinuance – listed for trial
CP14	Committal: election
CP15	Committal/transfer: direction
CP16	Committal: discharged
CP17	Extradition
CP18	Case remitted from Crown to magistrates' court for sentencing
CP19	Deferred sentence
CP20	Granted anti-social behaviour order/sexual offences order/other order
CP21	Part-granted anti-social behaviour order/sexual offences order/other order
CP22	Refused anti-social behaviour order/sexual offences order/other order
CP23	Varied anti-social behaviour order/sexual offences order/other order
CP24	Discharged anti-social behaviour order/sexual offences order/other order

Application of Specific Codes

Criminal Investigations

CN01   NO FURTHER INSTRUCTIONS

8. This code must be used when you are claiming because your client has not made any further contact with you even though the Matter has not concluded and you are not aware that their instructions have been transferred.

9. The UCC Specification stipulates that one month must pass since the last contact with the client before any claim can be made (Part A, paragraph 24.1(h)).

10. This code can only be used when claiming in accordance with 24.1(h), i.e. where you have had no contact from your client for at least a month. It must not be used in relation to a claim where it is known that no further work will be undertaken for the client in the same matter, (Part A, paragraph 24.1(g)).

CN02   CHANGE OF SOLICITOR

11. This code must be used when you have been advised by your client(s) that they no longer wish to instruct you and the Matter has not been disposed of.

CN03   CLIENT NOT A SUSPECT

12. This code must only be used when free standing Advice and Assistance or Police Station Advice and Assistance has been given to a client who is not directly the subject of a criminal investigation but qualifies for Advice and Assistance e.g. a witness at risk of self incrimination.

CN04   NO FURTHER ACTION

13. This code should only be used when the client(s) has been released without a reprimand, warning, summons or charge.

CN05   SIMPLE CAUTION, REPRIMAND, WARNING

14. This code should only be used when the client(s) has been released following a reprimand, warning or simple caution. Any level of assistance can have been given, namely Advice and Assistance, Police Station Telephone Advice, Police Station Attendance, Warrants of Further Detention and armed forces custody hearings.

CN06   CHARGE, SUMMONS OR REPORTED FOR SUMMONS

15. This code should only be used when the client(s) has been charged with or summoned for a criminal offence. Any level of assistance can have been given.

CN07   CONDITIONAL CAUTION

16. This code should only be used when the client(s) has received a conditional caution.

CN08   FIXED PENALTY NOTICE

17. This code should only be used when the client(s) has received a fixed penalty notice.

Criminal Proceedings

General Guidance

18. The Outcome Codes for criminal proceedings have been revised to give us more information on the actual outcome achieved for the client and the stage at which that outcome was reached.
19. Matters that are **committed to the Crown Court for sentence** or end with a **Newton Hearing** should be given the Outcome Code that represents the actual outcome of the Matter in the magistrates' court. For instance, a client who was convicted of some Matters but acquitted of others, before a committal for sentence or Newton Hearing, should have the Outcome Code CP05 – Trial: mixed matters.
20. Matters that are **remitted back from the Crown Court** should be given the Outcome Code that represents the final outcome of the Matter in the magistrates' court.
21. When **deciding whether or not a case has been listed for trial**, (Outcome Codes CP07 to CP13), the definition used for standard fee purposes should be used. CRIMLA 41 provides that a case is to be treated as listed for trial whenever it is adjourned following a not guilty plea, irrespective of whether the court actually lists the trial date at that point or simply adjourns to a pre-trial review date.

CP01   ARREST WARRANT ISSUED/ADJOURNED INDEFINITELY

22. This code must be used when you are claiming because an arrest warrant has been issued or the court has adjourned the Matter, without a decision, indefinitely. Note: where an arrest warrant has been issued, UCC Part C, Rule 1.2–1.5 states that a claim for costs shall be made not earlier than six weeks from the date of issue of the warrant.

23. This code can only be used when claiming in accordance with UCC Part A, paragraph 24.1(h). It must not be used in relation to a claim where it is known that no further work will be undertaken for the client in the same matter or case (UCC Part A, paragraph 3.4.4(g)).

CP02   CHANGE OF SOLICITOR

24. This code must be used when you have been advised by your client(s) that they no longer wish to instruct you and the representation order is transferred to another provider.

CP03   REPRESENTATION ORDER WITHDRAWN

25. This code must be used when the representation order has been withdrawn or revoked before a conclusion to the case is reached.

CP04   TRIAL: ACQUITTED

26. This code must be used when the client is acquitted at trial of all contested Matters (whether or not there are other guilty pleas). This code also includes contested breach proceedings.

CP05   TRIAL: MIXED VERDICT

27. This code must be used when the client is convicted at trial of some contested Matters but is acquitted of other contested Matters (whether or not there are other guilty pleas). This code also includes contested breach proceedings where the client is convicted of some breaches and acquitted of others in a separate information or charge.

CP06   TRIAL: CONVICTED

28. This code must be used when the client is convicted at trial of all contested Matters (whether or not there are other guilty pleas). This code also includes contested breach proceedings. It should not be used for any other outcome.

CP07   DISCONTINUED (BEFORE ANY PLEAS ENTERED)

29. This code must be used when the proceedings have been discontinued and the Matter has not been listed for trial. This code also includes breach proceedings.

CP08   DISCONTINUED (AFTER PLEAS ENTERED)

30. This code must be used when the proceedings have been discontinued after the Matter has been listed for trial. This code also includes breach proceedings.

CP09   GUILTY PLEA TO ALL CHARGES PUT – NOT LISTED FOR TRIAL

31. This code must be used when guilty pleas have been entered to all Matters put where the Matter has not been listed for trial. This code also includes breach proceedings.

CP10   GUILTY PLEA TO ALL CHARGES PUT AFTER CASE LISTED FOR TRIAL

32. This code must be used when guilty pleas have been entered to all Matters put where the Matter has been listed for trial. This code also includes breach proceedings.

CP11   GUILTY PLEA TO SUBSTITUTE CHARGES PUT – AFTER CASE LISTED FOR TRIAL

33. This code must be used when guilty pleas are entered to substitute charges where the matter has been listed for trial. This code includes breach proceedings.

CP12   MIX OF GUILTY PLEA(S) AND DISCONTINUANCE – NOT LISTED FOR TRIAL

34. This code must be used when a guilty plea has been entered to one or more Matters, one or more other Matters have been discontinued, or the Crown accepted a not guilty plea and formally offered no evidence, and the Matter has not been listed for trial. This code also includes breach proceedings.

CP13   MIX OF GUILTY PLEA(S) AND DISCONTINUANCE – LISTED FOR TRIAL

35. This code must be used when a guilty plea has been entered to one or more Matters, one or more other Matters have been discontinued, and the Matter has been listed for trial. This code also includes breach proceedings.

CP14   COMMITTAL: ELECTION

36. This code must be used when the client has elected on at least one Matter to have the Matter tried at the Crown Court.

CP15   COMMITTAL/TRANSFER: DIRECTION

37. This code must be used when the court has declined jurisdiction to deal with the Matter and committed it to the Crown Court for trial.
38. This code does not include Committals to Crown Court for sentence. Cases that are committed for sentence should be given the outcome that relates to the actual outcome of the Matter in the magistrates' court. For example, if the client was convicted at trial of all contested Matters and was then committed to the Crown Court for sentence, the CP06 Outcome Code 'Trial: convicted' would be used.

CP16   COMMITTAL: DISCHARGED

39. This code must be used when committal proceedings (however those arose) have been discharged.

CP17   EXTRADITION

40. This code must be used for extradition hearings.

CP18   CASE REMITTED FROM CROWN COURT TO MAGISTRATES' COURT FOR SENTENCING

41. This code must be used when the matter has been passed back to the magistrates' court for sentencing.

CP19   DEFERRED SENTENCE

42. This code must be used where a sentence has been deferred.

CP20   GRANTED ANTI-SOCIAL BEHAVIOUR ORDER/SEXUAL OFFENCES ORDER/ OTHER ORDER

43. This code must be used where an application for an anti social behaviour or other order has been contested and the conditions proposed by the applicant agency are granted in full.

CP21   PART GRANTED ANTI SOCIAL BEHAVIOUR ORDER/SEXUAL OFFENCES ORDER/ OTHER ORDER

44. This code must be used where an application for an anti social behaviour or other order has been contested and the conditions proposed by the applicant agency are only granted in part.

CP22   REFUSED ANTI SOCIAL BEHAVIOUR ORDER/SEXUAL OFFENCES/OTHER ORDER

45. This code must be used where an application for an anti social behaviour or other order has been contested and the application is refused in full.

CP23   VARIED ANTI SOCIAL BEHAVIOUR ORDER/SEXUAL OFFENCE ORDER/OTHER ORDER

46. This code must be used where an application has been made to vary an anti social behaviour or other order whether the application was granted or not.

CP24   DISCHARGED ANTI SOCIAL BEHAVIOUR ORDER/SEXUAL OFFENCES ORDER/ OTHER ORDER

47. This code must be used where an application has been made to discharge an anti social behaviour or other order whether the application was granted or not.

Breach of anti social behaviour order/sexual offences order/other order

48. If the matter type is a breach of an anti social behaviour or other order then the matter type will be 14, 15 or 16 (see Matter code Type table below), but the Outcome Code will be one most suitable from the Outcome Code Table above, e.g. CP04, CP06, (but not CP020 to CP024).

Issue of anti social behaviour order/sexual offences order/other order following a Criminal Matter

49. If an anti social behaviour order is issued following a criminal matter then the Matter Type will be the substantive charge from the Matter Code table below (but not 14, 15, or 16), and the Outcome Code will be the most appropriate from CP01 to CP19 in the Outcome Code Table above.

SECTION 5   EQUAL OPPORTUNITIES MONITORING

Completion of the ethnic origin and disability fields is voluntary. However, where the client is willing to provide this information it is compulsory to report this and the information will greatly assist us in monitoring and researching access to LSC funded services in line with our commitment to promote equal opportunities, set out in our Equality Scheme (available on our website). This information will be treated in the strictest confidence and will be used purely for statistical monitoring and research.

Where a client does not wish to provide this information, please use code '99' for unknown.

Field	Use	Format
Ethnicity	Ethnicity of client The Commission for Racial Equality recommended categories to be used In this field are coded as follows:	00 Other 01 White British 02 White Irish 03 Black or Black British African 04 Black or Black British Caribbean 05 Black or Black British Other 06 Asian or Asian British Indian 07 Asian or Asian British Pakistani 08 Asian or Asian British Bangladeshi 09 Chinese 10 Mixed White & Black Caribbean 11 Mixed White & Black African 12 Mixed White & Asian 13 Mixed Other 14 White Other 15 Asian or Asian British Other 99 Unknown
Gender	Gender of client	Single letter: F – Female M – Male U – Unknown

[LSC, DSCC case referral form, January 2008]

CASE REFERRAL TO DEFENCE SOLICITOR CALL CENTRE

Please send this form to the Defence Solicitor Call Centre (DSCC) by:

- emailing it to: casereferrals.dscc@firstassist.co.uk
- faxing to: 0208 763 3191
- telephoning the details through to: 08457 500 620

Solicitor name:

Solicitor pin number:

Firm name:

Police station name:

Officer's name (if known):

Telephone number (if known):

Detainee surname:

Detainee forename:

Custody number (if known):

Male or female:

Adult or juvenile:

Date & time of advice given:

Offence 1:

Offence 2:

Offence 3:

Other offence:

Additional comments:

APPENDIX 4

Police station advice and assistance fixed fees*

[Editor's note:
  1. For each area a 'non-police station' code is available. If the interview is with a 'constable' at a prison or military establishment the area in which the establishment is placed should be used, and the fixed fee claimed for that area.
  2. Military cases outside England and Wales fall outside this scheme.
  3. For each claim it is the fee for the first police station actually attended that is used.

*All fees are displayed exclusive of VAT.

Regional Office 1: Newcastle

CJS Area	Schemes	Fixed Fee	Escape	Code
Cleveland	Hartlepool	£148.09	£444.27	1001
	Teeside	£152.34	£457.02	1002
Durham	Darlington	£169.36	£508.08	1003
	South Durham	£171.06	£513.18	1004
	Durham	£202.55	£607.65	1005
	Derwentside	£188.09	£564.27	1006
	Easington	£187.23	£561.69	1007
Northumbria	South East Northumberland	£162.55	£487.65	1008
	Newcastle	£154.89	£464.67	1009
	Gateshead	£156.60	£469.80	1010
	North Tyneside	£157.45	£472.35	1011
	South Tyneside	£149.79	£449.37	1012
	Sunderland/Houghton Le Spring	£173.62	£520.86	1013
	Berwick & Alnwick	£199.15	£597.45	1014
	Tynedale & Hexham	£173.62	£520.86	1015

96

Regional Office 2: Bristol

CJS Area	Schemes	Fixed Fee	Escape	Code
Avon & Somerset	North Avon & Thornbury	£205.11	£615.33	2001
	Bath & Wansdyke	£211.91	£635.73	2002
	Mendip/Yeovil & South Somerset	£237.45	£712.35	2003
	Bristol	£175.32	£525.96	2004
	Sedgemoor/Taunton Deane	£224.68	£674.04	2005
	Weston Super Mare	£198.30	£594.90	2006
Dorset	Central Dorset	£200.00	£600.00	2007
	Bournemouth & Christchurch	£159.15	£477.45	2008
	Poole East Dorset	£171.91	£515.73	2009
	Bridport West Dorset/Weymouth & Dorchester	£160.00	£480.00	2010
Wiltshire	Salisbury	£195.74	£587.22	2011
	Chippenham/ Trowbridge	£205.96	£617.88	2012
	Swindon	£193.19	£579.57	2013
Gloucestershire	Cheltenham	£177.87	£533.61	2014
	Gloucester	£174.47	£523.41	2015
	Stroud	£200.00	£600.00	2016
Devon & Cornwall	Barnstaple	£190.64	£571.92	2017
	Exeter	£169.36	£508.08	2018
	Plymouth	£196.60	£589.80	2019
	East Cornwall	£246.81	£740.43	2020
	Carrick/Kerrier (Camborne)/Penwith	£205.96	£617.88	2021
	Teignbridge/Torbay	£178.72	£536.16	2022

Regional Office 3: Birmingham

CJS Area	Schemes	Fixed Fee	Escape	Code
Staffordshire	Stoke On Trent/Leek	£205.96	£617.88	3001
	Stafford/Cannock & Rugeley	£200.00	£600.00	3002
	Lichfield & Tamworth/ Burton Upon Trent/ Uttoxeter	£194.04	£582.12	3003

Warwickshire	Leamington/Nuneaton/ Rugby	£195.74	£587.22	3004
West Mercia	Hereford/Leominster	£170.21	£510.63	3005
	Kidderminster/ Redditch	£217.87	£653.61	3006
	Shrewsbury	£186.38	£559.14	3007
	Telford	£194.04	£582.12	3008
	Worcester	£198.30	£594.90	3009
West Midlands	Sandwell	£197.45	£592.35	3010
	Wolverhampton & Seisdon	£197.45	£592.35	3011
	Dudley & Halesowen	£189.79	£569.37	3012
	Walsall	£200.85	£602.55	3013
	Birmingham	£206.81	£620.43	3014
	Solihull	£205.11	£615.33	3015
	Coventry	£168.51	£505.53	3016

Regional Office 4: Cardiff

CJS Area	Schemes	Fixed Fee	Escape	Code
Dyfed Powys	Amman Valley	£208.51	£625.53	4001
	Carmarthen East Dyfed	£221.28	£663.84	4002
	Llanelli	£155.74	£467.22	4003
	Brecon & Radnor	£222.98	£668.94	4004
	Mid Wales	£170.21	£510.63	4005
	North Ceredigion/South Ceredigion	£223.83	£671.49	4006
	Pembrokeshire	£188.09	£564.27	4007
Gwent	East Gwent	£190.64	£571.92	4008
	Newport	£187.23	£561.69	4009
	Lower Rhymney Valley/ North Bedwellty/South Bedwellty	£203.40	£610.20	4010
North Wales	Bangor & Caernarfon	£207.66	£622.98	4011
	Colwyn Bay	£194.89	£584.67	4012
	Denbighshire	£206.81	£620.43	4013
	Dolgellau	£206.81	£620.43	4014
	Mold & Hawarden	£202.55	£607.65	4015
	North Anglesey	£216.17	£648.51	4016
	Pwllheli	£146.38	£439.14	4017
	Wrexham	£177.02	£531.06	4018

South Wales	Cardiff	£214.47	£643.41	4019
	Vale Of Glamorgan	£228.09	£684.27	4020
	Cynon Valley	£205.96	£617.88	4021
	Miskin	£214.47	£643.41	4022
	Merthyr Tydfil	£212.77	£638.31	4023
	Port Talbot	£270.64	£811.92	4024
	Newcastle & Ogmore	£217.87	£653.61	4025
	Neath	£223.83	£671.49	4026
	Swansea	£193.19	£579.57	4027

Regional Office 5: Liverpool

CJS Area	Schemes	Fixed Fee	Escape	Code
Merseyside	Bootle & Crosby	£182.13	£546.39	5001
	Southport	£148.94	£446.82	5002
	Liverpool	£196.60	£589.80	5003
	St Helens	£172.77	£518.31	5004
	Knowsley	£185.53	£556.59	5005
	Wirral	£177.02	£531.06	5006

Regional Office 6: Manchester

CJS Area	Schemes	Fixed Fee	Escape	Code
Cheshire	Crewe & Nantwich/ Sandbach & Congleton/ Macclesfield	£197.45	£592.35	6001
	Warrington/Halton	£169.36	£508.08	6002
	Chester/Vale Royal (Northwich)	£176.17	£528.51	6003
Cumbria	Barrow In Furness	£168.51	£505.53	6004
	Kendall & Windermere	£200.85	£602.55	6005
	Carlisle/Penrith	£189.79	£569.37	6006
	Whitehaven/Workington	£157.45	£472.35	6007
Greater Manchester	Manchester	£214.47	£643.41	6008
	Stockport	£183.83	£551.49	6009
	Trafford	£204.26	£612.78	6010
	Salford	£208.51	£625.53	6011
	Bolton	£180.43	£541.29	6012
	Bury	£175.32	£525.96	6013
	Wigan	£186.38	£559.14	6014
	Rochdale/Middleton	£185.53	£556.59	6015
	Tameside	£175.32	£525.96	6016

Lancashire	Oldham	£150.64	£451.92	6017
	Burnley/Rossendale	£177.87	£533.61	6018
	Accrington/Blackburn/ Ribble Valley	£211.91	£635.73	6019
	Blackpool	£138.72	£416.16	6020
	Fleetwood	£142.13	£426.39	6021
	Lancaster	£174.47	£523.41	6022
	Chorley/Ormskirk/South Ribble & Leyland	£191.49	£574.47	6023
	Preston	£156.60	£469.80	6024

Regional Office 7: Brighton

CJS Area	Schemes	Fixed Fee	Escape	Code
Kent	Dartford & Gravesend	£255.32	£765.96	7001
	Ashford & Tenterden/ Dover /Folkestone	£254.47	£763.41	7002
	Medway	£224.68	£674.04	7003
	Swale	£266.38	£799.14	7004
	Maidstone & West Malling	£237.45	£712.35	7005
	Canterbury/Thanet	£220.43	£661.29	7006
	West Kent (Tonbridge)	£228.09	£684.27	7007
Surrey	Guildford & Farnham	£222.98	£668.94	7008
	North West Surrey (Woking)	£243.40	£730.20	7009
	South East Surrey	£257.02	£771.06	7010
	Epsom	£260.43	£781.29	7011
	Staines	£297.87	£893.61	7012
Sussex	Brighton & Hove & Lewes	£227.23	£681.69	7013
	Chichester & District	£182.13	£546.39	7014
	Crawley/Horsham	£250.21	£750.63	7015
	Hastings	£160.00	£480.00	7016
	Worthing	£184.68	£554.04	7017
	Eastbourne	£189.79	£569.37	7018

Regional Office 8: Nottingham

CJS Area	Schemes	Fixed Fee	Escape	Code
Derbyshire	East Derbyshire (Ripley)/Ilkeston	£226.38	£679.14	8001
	Ashbourne/Matlock/ High Peak (Buxton)	£208.51	£625.53	8002
	Chesterfield	£194.89	£584.67	8003
	Derby/Swadlincote	£208.51	£625.53	8004
Leicestershire	Ashby & Coalville/ Loughborough/ Melton Mowbray	£199.15	£597.45	8005
	Leicester	£201.70	£605.10	8006
	Hinckley/ Market Harborough	£221.28	£663.84	8007
Lincolnshire	Boston, Bourne, Stamford	£194.89	£584.67	8008
	Skegness	£171.06	£513.18	8009
	Lincoln/ Gainsborough	£177.02	£531.06	8010
	Grantham & Sleaford	£179.57	£538.71	8011
Nottinghamshire	Mansfield	£180.43	£541.29	8012
	Newark	£197.45	£592.35	8013
	Nottingham	£196.60	£589.80	8014
	Worksop & East Retford	£191.49	£574.47	8015
Northamptonshire	Corby (Kettering)/ Wellingborough	£172.77	£518.31	8016
	Northampton	£187.23	£561.69	8017

Regional Office 9: Cambridge

CJS Area	Schemes	Fixed Fee	Escape	Code
Bedfordshire	Bedford	£188.94	£566.82	9001
	Luton	£219.57	£658.71	9002
Cambridgeshire	Cambridge	£182.98	£548.94	9003
	Ely	£210.21	£630.63	9004
	Huntingdon	£189.79	£569.37	9005
	March & Wisbech	£188.09	£564.27	9006
	Peterborough	£156.60	£469.80	9007
Essex	Basildon	£200.85	£602.55	9008
	Brentwood	£308.94	£926.82	9009
	Braintree	£245.96	£737.88	9010

	Clacton & Harwich/ Colchester	£205.96	£617.88	9011
	Grays	£288.51	£865.53	9012
	Harlow/ Loughton	£288.51	£865.53	9013
	Stansted	£319.15	£957.45	9014
	Rayleigh/ Southend On Sea	£182.98	£548.94	9015
	Chelmsford/Witham	£198.30	£594.90	9016
Hertfordshire	Dacorum (Hemel Hempstead)	£259.57	£778.71	9017
	Bishop's Stortford/East Hertfordshire	£315.74	£947.22	9018
	Stevenage & North Herts	£292.77	£878.31	9019
	St Albans	£265.53	£796.59	9020
	Watford	£261.28	£783.84	9021
Norfolk	Cromer & North Walsham	£228.09	£684.27	9022
	Great Yarmouth	£184.68	£554.04	9023
	Kings Lynn & West Norfolk	£180.43	£541.29	9024
	Norwich & District	£185.53	£556.59	9025
	Diss/Thetford	£196.60	£589.80	9026
	Dereham	£245.11	£735.33	9027
Suffolk	Lowestoft, Beccles & Halesworth/Aldeburgh	£185.53	£556.59	9028
	Woodbridge/Felixstowe/ Ipswich & District	£188.94	£566.82	9029
	Newmarket/Bury St Edmunds/Haverhill/ Sudbury	£201.70	£605.10	9030

Regional Office 10: Reading

CJS Area	Schemes	Fixed Fee	Escape	Code
Thames Valley	Abingdon, Didcot & Witney (South Oxfordshire)	£258.72	£776.16	1131
	Aylesbury	£217.87	£653.61	1132
	High Wycombe & Amersham	£236.60	£709.80	1133
	Milton Keynes	£185.53	£556.59	1134

	Banbury/Bicester (North Oxon)	£240.85	£722.55	1135
	Oxford	£240.85	£722.55	1136
	Reading	£206.81	£620.43	1137
	Slough (East Berkshire)	£258.72	£776.16	1138
	West Berks (Newbury)	£191.49	£574.47	1139
Hampshire	Aldershot/Petersfield (North East Hampshire)	£256.17	£768.51	1140
	Andover/Basingstoke/ Winchester (NW Hants)	£230.64	£691.92	1141
	Isle Of Wight	£188.09	£564.27	1142
	Portsmouth/ Waterlooville (South East Hampshire)	£193.19	£579.57	1143
	Gosport & Fareham	£235.74	£707.22	1144
	South West Hants (Southampton)	£217.87	£653.61	1145

Regional Office 11: Leeds

CJS Area	Schemes	Fixed Fee	Escape	Code
Humberside	Grimsby & Cleethorpes	£147.23	£441.69	1201
	Scunthorpe	£162.55	£487.65	1202
	Hull	£171.91	£515.73	1203
	Beverley/Bridlington	£214.47	£643.41	1204
	Goole	£225.53	£676.59	1205
North Yorkshire	Northallerton & Richmond	£210.21	£630.63	1206
	Harrogate & Ripon	£201.70	£605.10	1207
	Skipton, Settle & Ingleton	£200.00	£600.00	1208
	Scarborough/Whitby	£171.06	£513.18	1209
	Malton & Rydale	£160.85	£482.55	1210
	York/Selby	£179.57	£538.71	1211
South Yorkshire	Barnsley	£178.72	£536.16	1212
	Doncaster	£171.91	£515.73	1213
	Rotherham	£182.98	£548.94	1214
	Sheffield	£188.09	£564.27	1215
West Yorkshire	Halifax	£190.64	£571.92	1216
	Huddersfield	£160.55	£482.55	1217
	Dewsbury	£174.47	£523.41	1218
	Bradford	£153.19	£459.57	1219
	Keighley & Bingley	£171.91	£515.73	1220
	Leeds	£161.70	£485.10	1221
	Pontefract & Castleford	£154.89	£464.67	1222
	Wakefield	£156.60	£469.80	1223

Regional Office 12: London

CJS Area	Schemes	Fixed Fee	Escape	Code
London	Barking	£278.30	£834.90	1301
	Bexley	£248.51	£745.53	1302
	Bishopsgate	£290.21	£870.63	1303
	Brent	£270.64	£811.92	1304
	Brentford	£275.74	£827.22	1305
	Bromley	£262.13	£786.39	1306
	Camberwell Green	£271.49	£814.47	1307
	Central London	£293.62	£880.86	1308
	Clerkenwell/ Hampstead	£274.04	£822.12	1309
	Croydon	£267.23	£801.69	1310
	Ealing	£285.11	£855.33	1311
	Enfield	£269.79	£809.37	1312
	Greenwich/Woolwich	£258.72	£776.16	1313
	Haringey	£279.15	£837.45	1314
	Harrow	£271.49	£814.47	1315
	Havering	£252.77	£758.31	1316
	Heathrow	£340.43	£1,021.29	1317
	Hendon/Barnet	£273.19	£819.57	1318
	Highbury Corner	£284.26	£852.78	1319
	Kingston-Upon- Thames	£282.55	£847.65	1320
	Newham	£272.34	£817.02	1321
	Old Street	£271.49	£814.47	1322
	Redbridge	£279.15	£837.45	1323
	Richmond-Upon- Thames	£297.87	£893.61	1324
	South London	£284.26	£852.78	1325
	Sutton	£269.79	£809.37	1326
	Thames	£269.79	£809.37	1327
	Tower Bridge	£288.51	£865.53	1328
	Uxbridge	£261.28	£783.84	1329
	Waltham Forest	£253.62	£760.86	1330
	West London	£291.91	£875.73	1331
	Wimbledon	£276.60	£829.80	1332

APPENDIX 5

Police station fixed fees: scenarios

[LSC, Police Station Advice and Assistance Fixed Fee Scheme Questions and Answers For Service Providers working under the Unified Contract (Crime) from 14 July 2008]

Scenario	Fees payable	Notes	Unified Contract ref
One client arrested on one Matter	**One fee**	One fee will be paid per client per Matter.	Part B1.1.21(1)
Two clients arrested at the same time and advised by firm	**Two fees**	One fee will per paid per client per Matter. Note that both must be advised at the police station to trigger the fixed fee. If one is advised by telephone only the telephone advice fixed fee will be paid for that client.	Part A19
Conflicts of Interest: e.g. Two clients arrested at the same time, but there is a conflict so the firm can only act for one	**Two fees**	As above, one fee will be paid per client per Matter. Note that both must be advised at the police station to trigger the fixed fee. If one is advised by telephone only the telephone advice fixed fee will be paid for that client.	Part A19
Client arrested for multiple offences - irrespective of whether they are linked or not e.g. Arrested for burglary committed on 20 January 2008 and rape committed on 10 August 1983	**The starting point is that this will be one fee. In order for more than one fee to be paid there must be separate Matters**	Separate Matters arise where the Client has **genuinely separate legal problems requiring separate advice.** Note: Where two or more Matters require advice **on one occasion only** they should be treated as the same Matter.	Part A19 contains guidance on Separate Matters and Boundaries between Classes of Work

		Where two or more Matters arise from **the same set of circumstances**, the chances of them being separate Matters diminish.	
		Charges laid at the same time which are **likely to be dealt with under one Representation Order or are likely to be heard together, or are likely to form part of the same Case**, should [be] dealt with as one Matter.	
		Advice given on related issues which could be considered a '**series of offences**' should be dealt with as a single Matter.	
Two Matters in total. No Further Action on one Matter, the other Matter charged	**One fee**	Advice provided on separate Matters on one occasion only should be treated as a single Matter.	Part A19
Two Matters in total. One of those Matters charged, the other bailed to return	**Two fees**	Two Matters advised on and advice continued on one of the Matters after first occasion. Two fees will be paid.	Part A19
Three Matters in total. One of those Matters charged and two bailed to return but to different dates	**Three fees**	As above	Part A19
Any number of Matters. All Matters charged to same date	**One fee**	Charges laid at the same time which are **likely to be dealt with under one Representation Order or are likely to be heard together, or are likely to form part of the same Case**, should dealt with as one Matter.	Part A19
Any number of Matters. All Matters charged but to different courts/dates	**One fee for each Matter charged to different dates/courts**	As above	Part A19

Arrested on one offence; at police station arrested on further offences(s)	**One fee, unless they become separate Matters**	See above for guidance on separate Matters.	Part A19 contains guidance on separate Matters and boundaries between classes of work
Post-charge ID procedure	**Paid at hourly rates**	Post-charge work and Advocacy Assistance on Warrants for Further Detention are paid at hourly rates.	Part A2.4.3–4

APPENDIX 6

CDS police station codes

[LSC, Guidance for reporting work on form CDS6, section 4, March 2008]

Regional Office: Newcastle

CJS Area	Police Station ID	Police Station Name	PS Scheme ID	PS Scheme Name
Cleveland	NE001	HARTLEPOOL	1001	Hartlepool
	NE900	HARTLEPOOL NON-POLICE STATION	1001	Hartlepool
	NE002	GUISBOROUGH	1002	Teeside
	NE003	SOUTH BANK	1002	Teeside
	NE004	REDCAR	1002	Teeside
	NE005	NORTH ORMESBY	1002	Teeside
	NE006	BILLINGHAM	1002	Teeside
	NE007	STOCKTON-ON-TEES	1002	Teeside
	NE008	MIDDLESBOROUGH	1002	Teeside
	NE009	COULBY NEWHAM	1002	Teeside
	NE901	TEESIDE NON-POLICE STATION	1002	Teeside
Durham	NE010	DARLINGTON	1003	Darlington
	NE011	DARLINGTON RAIL STATION, BTP	1003	Darlington
	NE012	TEESIDE AIRPORT	1003	Darlington
	NE902	DARLINGTON NON-POLICE STATION	1003	Darlington
	NE013	SPENNYMOOR	1004	South Durham
	NE014	NEWTON AYCLIFFE	1004	South Durham
	NE015	CROOK	1004	South Durham
	NE016	BISHOP AU[C]KLAND	1004	South Durham
	NE017	BARNARD CASTLE	1004	South Durham
	NE903	SOUTH DURHAM NON-POLICE STATION	1004	South Durham
	NE018	DURHAM	1005	Durham
	NE019	CHESTER LE STREET	1005	Durham
	NE904	DURHAM NON-POLICE STATION	1005	Durham
	NE020	STANLEY	1006	Derwentside

	NE021	CONSETT	1006	Derwentside
	NE905	DERWENTSIDE NON-POLICE STATION	1006	Derwentside
	NE022	SEAHAM	1007	Easington
	NE023	PETERLEE	1007	Easington
	NE024	EASINGTON	1007	Easington
	NE906	EASINGTON NON-POLICE STATION	1007	Easington
Northumbria	NE025	PONTELAND	1008	South East Northumberland
	NE026	MORPETH	1008	South East Northumberland
	NE027	CRAMLINGTON	1008	South East Northumberland
	NE028	BLYTH	1008	South East Northumberland
	NE029	ASHINGTON	1008	South East Northumberland
	NE030	BEDLINGTON	1008	South East Northumberland
	NE907	SOUTH EAST NORTHUMBERLAND NON-POLICE STATION	1008	South East Northumberland
	NE031	BTP NEVILLE ST NEWCASTLE	1009	Newcastle Upon Tyne
	NE032	NEWCASTLE WEST (WESTGATE ROAD)	1009	Newcastle Upon Tyne
	NE033	NEWCASTLE EAST	1009	Newcastle Upon Tyne
	NE034	NEWCASTLE CENTRAL	1009	Newcastle Upon Tyne
	NE035	NEWBURN (CLOSED)	1009	Newcastle Upon Tyne
	NE036	NEWCASTLE NORTH, ETAL LANE (GOSFORTH)	1009	Newcastle Upon Tyne
	NE037	NEWCASTLE AIRPORT/ HM CUSTOMS	1009	Newcastle Upon Tyne
	NE908	NEWCASTLE-UPON-TYNE NON-POLICE STATION	1009	Newcastle Upon Tyne
	NE038	WHICKHAM	1010	Gateshead
	NE039	GATESHEAD	1010	Gateshead
	NE040	FELLING	1010	Gateshead
	NE909	GATESHEAD NON-POLICE STATION	1010	Gateshead
	NE041	WHITLEY BAY	1011	North Tyneside
	NE042	WALLSEND	1011	North Tyneside
	NE043	NORTH SHIELDS	1011	North Tyneside
	NE044	FOREST HALL	1011	North Tyneside
	NE910	NORTH TYNESIDE NON-POLICE STATION	1011	North Tyneside
	NE045	SOUTH SHIELDS	1012	South Tyneside
	NE046	JARROW	1012	South Tyneside

NE914	SOUTH TYNESIDE NON-POLICE STATION	1012	South Tyneside
NE047	SUNDERLAND WEST	1013	Sunderland/Houghton Le Spring
NE048	SUNDERLAND NORTH	1013	Sunderland/Houghton Le Spring
NE049	SUNDERLAND CENTRAL	1013	Sunderland/Houghton Le Spring
NE050	WASHINGTON	1013	Sunderland/Houghton Le Spring
NE051	HOUGHTON-LE-SPRING	1013	Sunderland/Houghton Le Spring
NE911	SUNDERLAND/ HOUGHTON LE SPRING NON-POLICE STATION	1013	Sunderland/Houghton Le Spring
NE052	SEAHOUSES	1014	Berwick & Alnwick
NE053	AMBLE	1014	Berwick & Alnwick
NE054	ALNWICK	1014	Berwick & Alnwick
NE055	BERWICK	1014	Berwick & Alnwick
NE056	RAF BOULMER	1014	Berwick & Alnwick
NE912	BERWICK & ALNWICK NON-POLICE STATION	1014	Berwick & Alnwick
NE057	PRUDHOE	1015	Tynedale & Hexham
NE058	HEXHAM	1015	Tynedale & Hexham
NE059	HALTWHISTLE	1015	Tynedale & Hexham
NE060	CORBRIDGE	1015	Tynedale & Hexham
NE061	BELLINGHAM	1015	Tynedale & Hexham
NE913	TYNEDALE & HEXHAM NON-POLICE STATION	1015	Tynedale & Hexham

Regional Office: Bristol

CJS Area	Police Station ID	Police Station Name	PS Scheme ID	PS Scheme Name
Avon & Somerset	BR001	THORNBURY	2001	Avon North & Thornbury
	BR002	STAPLE HILL	2001	Avon North & Thornbury
	BR003	KINGSWOOD	2001	Avon North & Thornbury
	BR004	FILTON	2001	Avon North & Thornbury
	BR005	CHIPPING SODBURY	2001	Avon North & Thornbury
	BR006	CRIBBS CAUSEWAY (BRISTOL)	2001	Avon North & Thornbury

BR900	AVON NORTH & THORNBURY NON-POLICE STATION	2001	Avon North & Thornbury
BR007	RADSTOCK	2002	Bath & Wansdyke
BR008	KEYNSHAM	2002	Bath & Wansdyke
BR009	BATH	2002	Bath & Wansdyke
BR902	BATH & WANSDYKE NON-POLICE STATION	2002	Bath & Wansdyke
BR010	WELLS, AVON & SOMERSET	2003	Mendip/Yeovil & South Somerset
BR011	SHEPTON MALLET	2003	Mendip/Yeovil & South Somerset
BR012	FROME	2003	Mendip/Yeovil & South Somerset
BR013	WINCANTON	2003	Mendip/Yeovil & South Somerset
BR014	SOMERTON	2003	Mendip/Yeovil & South Somerset
BR015	ILMINSTER	2003	Mendip/Yeovil & South Somerset
BR016	CREWKERNE	2003	Mendip/Yeovil & South Somerset
BR017	CHARD	2003	Mendip/Yeovil & South Somerset
BR018	RNAS YEOVILTON	2003	Mendip/Yeovil & South Somerset
BR019	YEOVIL	2003	Mendip/Yeovil & South Somerset
BR922	MENDIP/YEOVIL & SOUTH SOMERSET NON-POLICE STATION	2003	Mendip/Yeovil & South Somerset
BR020	CLEVEDON	2004	Bristol
BR021	LOCKLEAZE	2004	Bristol
BR022	TRINITY ROAD	2004	Bristol
BR023	ST GEORGE	2004	Bristol
BR024	SOUTHMEAD	2004	Bristol
BR025	REDLAND	2004	Bristol
BR026	BROADBURY ROAD	2004	Bristol
BR027	BRISTOL CENTRAL (BRIDEWELL)	2004	Bristol
BR028	BISHOPSWORTH	2004	Bristol
BR029	PORTISHEAD	2004	Bristol
BR030	NAILSEA	2004	Bristol
BR031	HM CUSTOMS BRISTOL AIRPORT	2004	Bristol
BR032	AVONMOUTH	2004	Bristol
BR033	BRISLINGTON	2004	Bristol
BR903	BRISTOL NON-POLICE STATION	2004	Bristol
BR034	CHEDDAR	2005	Sedgemore/Taunton D[e]ane

	BR035	BURNHAM-ON-SEA	2005	Sedgemore/Taunton D[e]ane
	BR036	BRIDGEWATER	2005	Sedgemore/Taunton D[e]ane
	BR037	WILLITON	2005	Sedgemore/Taunton D[e]ane
	BR038	MINEHEAD	2005	Sedgemore/Taunton D[e]ane
	BR039	DULVERTON	2005	Sedgemore/Taunton D[e]ane
	BR040	WELLINGTON, TAUNTON	2005	Sedgemore/Taunton D[e]ane
	BR041	TAUNTON	2005	Sedgemore/Taunton D[e]ane
	BR904	SEDGEMORE/ TAUNTON DEANE NON-POLICE STATION	2005	Sedgemore/Taunton D[e]ane
	BR043	WESTON-SUPER-MARE	2006	Weston-Super-Mare
	BR905	WESTON-SUPER-MARE NON-POLICE STATION	2006	Weston-Super-Mare
Dorset	BR044	WAREHAM	2007	Central Dorset
	BR045	SWANAGE	2007	Central Dorset
	BR046	STURMINSTER NEWTON	2007	Central Dorset
	BR047	SHERBORNE	2007	Central Dorset
	BR048	SHAFTESBURY	2007	Central Dorset
	BR049	BLANDFORD	2007	Central Dorset
	BR050	ROYAL SIGNALS, BLANDFORD	2007	Central Dorset
	BR051	RMP BOVINGTON CAMP	2007	Central Dorset
	BR906	CENTRAL DORSET NON-POLICE STATION	2007	Central Dorset
	BR052	WINTON	2008	Bournemouth & Christchurch
	BR053	KINSON	2008	Bournemouth & Christchurch
	BR054	BOURNEMOUTH	2008	Bournemouth & Christchurch
	BR055	BOSCOMBE	2008	Bournemouth & Christchurch
	BR056	HIGHCLIFFE	2008	Bournemouth & Christchurch
	BR057	CHRISTCHURCH	2008	Bournemouth & Christchurch
	BR907	BOURNEMOUTH & CHRISTCHURCH NON-POLICE STATION	2008	Bournemouth & Christchurch
	BR058	POOLE	2009	Poole East Dorset
	BR059	GRAVEL HILL	2009	Poole East Dorset
	BR060	WIMBORNE	2009	Poole East Dorset
	BR061	FERNDOWN	2009	Poole East Dorset

	BR063	VERWOOD	2009	Poole East Dorset
	BR908	POOLE EAST DORSET NON-POLICE STATION	2009	Poole East Dorset
	BR064	LYME REGIS	2010	Bridport West Dorset/Weymouth & Dorchester
	BR065	BRIDPORT	2010	Bridport West Dorset/Weymouth & Dorchester
	BR066	DORCHESTER	2010	Bridport West Dorset/Weymouth & Dorchester
	BR067	WEYMOUTH	2010	Bridport West Dorset/Weymouth & Dorchester
	BR909	BRIDPORT WEST DORSET/WEYMOUTH & DORCHESTER NON-POLICE STATION	2010	Bridport West Dorset/Weymouth & Dorchester
Wiltshire	BR068	ARMY 158 PROVOST PSU	2011	Salisbury
	BR069	MOD LARKHILL	2011	Salisbury
	BR070	SALISBURY	2011	Salisbury
	BR071	AMESBURY	2011	Salisbury
	BR072	ALDERBURY	2011	Salisbury
	BR073	BULFORD MILITARY CAMP	2011	Salisbury
	BR910	SALISBURY NON-POLICE STATION	2011	Salisbury
	BR074	TIDWORTH	2012	Chippenham/Trowbridge
	BR075	MALMESBURY	2012	Chippenham/Trowbridge
	BR076	CORSHAM	2012	Chippenham/Trowbridge
	BR077	CHIPPENHAM	2012	Chippenham/Trowbridge
	BR078	CALNE	2012	Chippenham/Trowbridge
	BR079	RMP UPAVON	2012	Chippenham/Trowbridge
	BR080	WESTBURY	2012	Chippenham/Trowbridge
	BR081	WARMINSTER	2012	Chippenham/Trowbridge
	BR082	MELKSHAM	2012	Chippenham/Trowbridge
	BR083	DEVIZES	2012	Chippenham/Trowbridge
	BR084	BRADFORD ON AVON	2012	Chippenham/Trowbridge

	BR085	PEWSEY	2012	Chippenham/ Trowbridge
	BR086	LUDGERSHALL	2012	Chippenham/ Trowbridge
	BR087	TROWBRIDGE (WILTSHIRE)	2012	Chippenham/ Trowbridge
	BR911	CHIPPENHAM/ TROWBRIDGE NON-POLICE STATION	2012	Chippenham/ Trowbridge
	BR088	MARLBOROUGH	2013	Swindon
	BR089	HIGHWORTH	2013	Swindon
	BR091	RAF LYNEHAM PSU	2013	Swindon
	BR092	WOOTON BASSETT	2013	Swindon
	BR093	SWINDON CENTRAL	2013	Swindon
	BR094	SWINDON WESTLEA (CLOSED)	2013	Swindon
	BR095	GABLECROSS	2013	Swindon
	BR912	SWINDON NON-POLICE STATION	2013	Swindon
Gloucestershire	BR097	STOW ON THE WOLD [DESIGNATED]	2014	Cheltenham
	BR098	TEWKESBURY	2014	Cheltenham
	BR099	CHELTENHAM	2014	Cheltenham
	BR913	CHELTENHAM NON-POLICE STATION	2014	Cheltenham
	BR100	GLOUCESTER CENTRAL	2015	Gloucester
	BR101	COLEFORD	2015	Gloucester
	BR102	CINDERFORD	2015	Gloucester
	BR914	GLOUCESTER NON-POLICE STATION	2015	Gloucester
	BR103	NAILSWORTH	2016	Stroud
	BR104	DURSLEY	2016	Stroud
	BR105	FAIRFORD	2016	Stroud
	BR106	CIRENCESTER	2016	Stroud
	BR107	STROUD	2016	Stroud
	BR915	STROUD NON-POLICE STATION	2016	Stroud
Devon & Cornwall	BR108	SOUTH MOLTON	2017	Barnstaple
	BR109	BIDEFORD	2017	Barnstaple
	BR110	WOOLACOMBE	2017	Barnstaple
	BR111	LYNTON	2017	Barnstaple
	BR112	ILFRACOMBE	2017	Barnstaple
	BR113	COMBE MARTIN	2017	Barnstaple
	BR114	BRAUNTON	2017	Barnstaple
	BR115	BARNSTAPLE	2017	Barnstaple
	BR116	CHULMLEIGH	2017	Barnstaple
	BR117	CLOVELLY	2017	Barnstaple
	BR118	GREAT TORRINGTON	2017	Barnstaple
	BR119	HOLSWORTH	2017	Barnstaple
	BR916	BARNSTAPLE NON-POLICE STATION	2017	Barnstaple

BR120	COLYTON (EXMOUTH)	2018	Exeter
BR121	BEER (EXETER)	2018	Exeter
BR122	TIVERTON	2018	Exeter
BR123	SIDMOUTH	2018	Exeter
BR124	SEATON	2018	Exeter
BR125	HONITON	2018	Exeter
BR126	EXMOUTH	2018	Exeter
BR127	EXETER	2018	Exeter
BR128	CULLOMPTON	2018	Exeter
BR129	CREDITON	2018	Exeter
BR130	AXMINSTER	2018	Exeter
BR131	ROYAL MARINE POLICE, LYMPSTONE	2018	Exeter
BR917	EXETER NON-POLICE STATION	2018	Exeter
BR132	PRINCETOWN (USE DARTMOOR PRISON)	2019	Plymouth
BR133	IVYBRIDGE (CHARLES CROSS)	2019	Plymouth
BR134	TAVISTOCK	2019	Plymouth
BR135	HMS DRAKE	2019	Plymouth
BR136	PLYMSTOCK	2019	Plymouth
BR137	PLYMPTON	2019	Plymouth
BR138	PLYMOUTH DEVENPORT	2019	Plymouth
BR139	PLYMOUTH CROWNHILL	2019	Plymouth
BR140	PLYMOUTH CHARLES CROSS	2019	Plymouth
BR141	OKEHAMPTON	2019	Plymouth
BR142	MOD ALBERT GATE (PLYMOUTH)	2019	Plymouth
BR143	ROYAL MARINES, STONE HOUSE PLYMOUTH	2019	Plymouth
BR144	MOD NAVAL BASE, DEVENPORT	2019	Plymouth
BR145	DARTMOOR PRISON	2019	Plymouth
BR918	PLYMOUTH NON-POLICE STATION	2019	Plymouth
BR146	TORPOINT	2020	East Cornwall
BR147	KINGSAND	2020	East Cornwall
BR148	LOOE	2020	East Cornwall
BR149	MEVAGISSEY	2020	East Cornwall
BR150	FOWEY	2020	East Cornwall
BR151	LOSTWITHIEL	2020	East Cornwall
BR152	GUNNISLAKE	2020	East Cornwall
BR153	CALLINGTON	2020	East Cornwall
BR154	BUDE	2020	East Cornwall
BR155	WADEBRIDGE	2020	East Cornwall
BR156	CAMELFORD	2020	East Cornwall

BR157	ST AUSTELL	2020	East Cornwall
BR158	LISKEARD	2020	East Cornwall
BR159	LAUNCESTON	2020	East Cornwall
BR160	BODMIN	2020	East Cornwall
BR161	HMS RALEIGH	2020	East Cornwall
BR162	SALTASH	2020	East Cornwall
BR170	NEWQUAY	2020	East Cornwall
BR919	EAST CORNWALL NON-POLICE STATION	2020	East Cornwall
BR163	ST IVES (PENZANCE)	2021	Carrick/Kerrier (Camborne)/Penwith
BR164	ISLES OF SCILLY (PENZANCE)	2021	Carrick/Kerrier (Camborne)/Penwith
BR165	HAYLE (PENZANCE)	2021	Carrick/Kerrier (Camborne)/Penwith
BR166	PENZANCE	2021	Carrick/Kerrier (Camborne)/Penwith
BR167	HELSTON	2021	Carrick/Kerrier (Camborne)/Penwith
BR168	PENRYN	2021	Carrick/Kerrier (Camborne)/Penwith
BR169	FALMOUTH	2021	Carrick/Kerrier (Camborne)/Penwith
BR171	ST COLUMB (NEWQUAY)	2021	Carrick/Kerrier (Camborne)/Penwith
BR172	ST AGNES (NEWQUAY)	2021	Carrick/Kerrier (Camborne)/Penwith
BR173	RAF ST MAWGAN	2021	Carrick/Kerrier (Camborne)/Penwith
BR174	REDRUTH (CAMBORNE)	2021	Carrick/Kerrier (Camborne)/Penwith
BR175	CAMBORNE	2021	Carrick/Kerrier (Camborne)/Penwith
BR176	ST MAWES (CAMBORNE)	2021	Carrick/Kerrier (Camborne)/Penwith
BR177	TRURO	2021	Carrick/Kerrier (Camborne)/Penwith
BR178	PERRANPORTH	2021	Carrick/Kerrier (Camborne)/Penwith
BR920	CARRICK/KERRIER/ (CAMBOURNE)/ PENWITH NON-POLICE STATION	2021	Carrick/Kerrier (Camborne)/Penwith
BR179	TEIGNBRIDGE	2022	Teignbridge/Torbay
BR180	MORETONHAMPSTEAD	2022	Teignbridge/Torbay
BR181	KINGSTEIGNTON	2022	Teignbridge/Torbay
BR182	TORQUAY	2022	Teignbridge/Torbay
BR183	TEIGNMOUTH	2022	Teignbridge/Torbay
BR184	NEWTON ABBOT	2022	Teignbridge/Torbay
BR185	KINGSKERSWELL	2022	Teignbridge/Torbay
BR186	DAWLISH WARREN	2022	Teignbridge/Torbay

BR187	CHUDLEIGH	2022	Teignbridge/Torbay
BR188	BUCKFASTLEIGH	2022	Teignbridge/Torbay
BR189	BOVEY TRACEY	2022	Teignbridge/Torbay
BR190	ASHBURTON	2022	Teignbridge/Torbay
BR191	BRIXHAM	2022	Teignbridge/Torbay
BR192	PAIGNTON, TORBAY	2022	Teignbridge/Torbay
BR193	TORQUAY (TORBAY) (NOT FOUND)	2022	Teignbridge/Torbay
BR194	TOTNES	2022	Teignbridge/Torbay
BR195	TORQUAY (SOUTH HAMS)	2022	Teignbridge/Torbay
BR196	SOUTH BRENT	2022	Teignbridge/Torbay
BR197	KINGSBRIDGE	2022	Teignbridge/Torbay
BR198	DARTMOUTH	2022	Teignbridge/Torbay
BR921	TEIGNBRIDGE/ TORBAY NON-POLICE STATION	2022	Teignbridge/Torbay

Regional Office: Birmingham

CJS Area	Police Station ID	Police Station Name	PS Scheme ID	PS Scheme Name
Staffordshire	BM001	NEWCASTLE UNDER LYME	3001	Stoke On Trent/Leek
	BM002	TRENTHAM	3001	Stoke On Trent/Leek
	BM003	NORTON GREEN	3001	Stoke On Trent/Leek
	BM004	BUCKNALL	3001	Stoke On Trent/Leek
	BM005	BRITISH RAIL (NOT FOUND)	3001	Stoke On Trent/Leek
	BM006	TUNSTALL	3001	Stoke On Trent/Leek
	BM007	STOKE	3001	Stoke On Trent/Leek
	BM008	LONGTON	3001	Stoke On Trent/Leek
	BM009	KIDSGROVE	3001	Stoke On Trent/Leek
	BM010	HANLEY	3001	Stoke On Trent/Leek
	BM011	BURSLEM	3001	Stoke On Trent/Leek
	BM012	LEEK	3001	Stoke On Trent/Leek
	BM013	CHEADLE	3001	Stoke On Trent/Leek
	BM014	BIDDULPH	3001	Stoke On Trent/Leek
	BM015	BTP STOKE-ON-TRENT	3001	Stoke On Trent/Leek
	BM029	NORTHERN AREA CUSTODY FACILITY	3001	Stoke On Trent/Leek
	BM256	WERRINGTON	3001	Stoke On Trent/Leek
	BM257	WATERHOUSES	3001	Stoke On Trent/Leek
	BM258	WARSLOW	3001	Stoke On Trent/Leek
	BM259	ENDON	3001	Stoke On Trent/Leek
	BM283	KEELE	3001	Stoke On Trent/Leek
	BM284	MEIR	3001	Stoke On Trent/Leek
	BM285	ABBEY HULTON	3001	Stoke On Trent/Leek

BM900	STOKE-ON-TRENT/ LEEK NON-POLICE STATION	3001	Stoke On Trent/Leek
BM016	MADELEY	3002	Stafford/Cannock & Rugeley
BM017	STONE	3002	Stafford/Cannock & Rugeley
BM018	STAFFORD	3002	Stafford/Cannock & Rugeley
BM019	M6 MOTORWAY (DOXEY)	3002	Stafford/Cannock & Rugeley
BM020	ECCLESHALL	3002	Stafford/Cannock & Rugeley
BM021	RUGELEY	3002	Stafford/Cannock & Rugeley
BM022	HILTON	3002	Stafford/Cannock & Rugeley
BM023	HEDNESFORD	3002	Stafford/Cannock & Rugeley
BM024	CHESLYN HAY	3002	Stafford/Cannock & Rugeley
BM025	CANNOCK	3002	Stafford/Cannock & Rugeley
BM026	BREWOOD	3002	Stafford/Cannock & Rugeley
BM028	RAF STAFFORD	3002	Stafford/Cannock & Rugeley
BM223	PENKRIDGE	3002	Stafford/Cannock & Rugeley
BM224	ARMITAGE	3002	Stafford/Cannock & Rugeley
BM282	AUDLEY	3002	Stafford/Cannock & Rugeley
BM901	STAFFORD/CANNOCK & RUGELEY NON-POLICE STATION	3002	Stafford/Cannock & Rugeley
BM030	BURTON-UPON-TRENT	3003	Lichfield & Tamworth/ Burton Upon Trent/ Uttoxeter
BM031	BARTON-UNDER-NEEDWOOD	3003	Lichfield & Tamworth/ Burton Upon Trent/ Uttoxeter
BM032	UTTOXETER	3003	Lichfield & Tamworth/ Burton Upon Trent/ Uttoxeter
BM033	ALREWAS	3003	Lichfield & Tamworth/ Burton Upon Trent/ Uttoxeter
BM034	∗ CHASETOWN	3003	Lichfield & Tamworth/ Burton Upon Trent/ Uttoxeter

	BM035	TAMWORTH	3003	Lichfield & Tamworth/ Burton Upon Trent/ Uttoxeter
	BM036	LICHFIELD	3003	Lichfield & Tamworth/ Burton Upon Trent/ Uttoxeter
	BM221	SHENSTONE	3003	Lichfield & Tamworth/ Burton Upon Trent/ Uttoxeter
	BM902	LICHFIELD & TAMWORTH/BURTON-UPON-TRENT/ UTTOXETER NON-POLICE STATION	3003	Lichfield & Tamworth/ Burton Upon Trent/ Uttoxeter
Warwickshire	BM037	STOCKTON	3004	Leamington/ Nuneaton/Rugby
	BM038	WOLSTON	3004	Leamington/ Nuneaton/Rugby
	BM039	SOUTHAM	3004	Leamington/ Nuneaton/Rugby
	BM040	RUGBY	3004	Leamington/ Nuneaton/Rugby
	BM041	NUNEATON	3004	Leamington/ Nuneaton/Rugby
	BM042	BEDWORTH	3004	Leamington/ Nuneaton/Rugby
	BM043	HM CUSTOMS COVENTRY AIRPORT	3004	Leamington/ Nuneaton/Rugby
	BM044	BAGINTON	3004	Leamington/ Nuneaton/Rugby
	BM045	BISHOPS ITCHINGTON	3004	Leamington/ Nuneaton/Rugby
	BM046	WESTON UNDER WETHERLEY	3004	Leamington/ Nuneaton/Rugby
	BM047	KINETON	3004	Leamington/ Nuneaton/Rugby
	BM048	WARWICK	3004	Leamington/ Nuneaton/Rugby
	BM049	LEAMINGTON SPA	3004	Leamington/ Nuneaton/Rugby
	BM050	KENILWORTH	3004	Leamington/ Nuneaton/Rugby
	BM051	ATHERSTONE	3004	Leamington/ Nuneaton/Rugby
	BM052	LONG COMPTON	3004	Leamington/ Nuneaton/Rugby
	BM053	GREAT ALNE	3004	Leamington/ Nuneaton/Rugby
	BM054	ILMINGTON	3004	Leamington/ Nuneaton/Rugby
	BM055	SNITTERFIELD	3004	Leamington/ Nuneaton/Rugby

BM056	STRATFORD-UPON-AVON	3004	Leamington/Nuneaton/Rugby
BM057	SHIPSTON ON STOUR	3004	Leamington/Nuneaton/Rugby
BM058	HENLEY IN ARDEN	3004	Leamington/Nuneaton/Rugby
BM059	ALCESTER (CLOSED)	3004	Leamington/Nuneaton/Rugby
BM060	COLESHILL	3004	Leamington/Nuneaton/Rugby
BM061	RAF FARNBOROUGH (CLOSED)	3004	Leamington/Nuneaton/Rugby
BM062	STOCKINGFORD	3004	Leamington/Nuneaton/Rugby
BM238	CLAVERDON	3004	Leamington/Nuneaton/Rugby
BM239	WELLESBOURNE	3004	Leamington/Nuneaton/Rugby
BM240	STONELEIGH	3004	Leamington/Nuneaton/Rugby
BM241	LONG ITCHINGTON	3004	Leamington/Nuneaton/Rugby
BM242	HATTON	3004	Leamington/Nuneaton/Rugby
BM243	HARBURY	3004	Leamington/Nuneaton/Rugby
BM244	GAYDON	3004	Leamington/Nuneaton/Rugby
BM245	BARFORD	3004	Leamington/Nuneaton/Rugby
BM246	WOTTON WAWEN	3004	Leamington/Nuneaton/Rugby
BM247	TREDINGTON	3004	Leamington/Nuneaton/Rugby
BM248	STUDLEY	3004	Leamington/Nuneaton/Rugby
BM249	LONG MARSTON	3004	Leamington/Nuneaton/Rugby
BM250	ETTINGTON	3004	Leamington/Nuneaton/Rugby
BM251	ALDERMINSTER	3004	Leamington/Nuneaton/Rugby
BM252	TANWORTH IN ARDEN	3004	Leamington/Nuneaton/Rugby
BM253	BRAILES	3004	Leamington/Nuneaton/Rugby
BM254	BIDFORD-ON-AVON	3004	Leamington/Nuneaton/Rugby
BM255	MIDDLE TYSOE	3004	Leamington/Nuneaton/Rugby

	BM903	LEAMINGTON/ NUNEATON/RUGBY NON-POLICE STATION	3004	Leamington/ Nuneaton/Rugby
West Mercia	BM063	CHURCH STRETTON	3005	Hereford/Leominster
	BM065	TENBURY WELLS	3005	Hereford/Leominster
	BM066	LEOMINSTER	3005	Hereford/Leominster
	BM067	BROMYARD	3005	Hereford/Leominster
	BM068	CRAVEN ARMS (LEOMINSTER)	3005	Hereford/Leominster
	BM069	CHURCH STRETTON (LEOMINSTER)	3005	Hereford/Leominster
	BM070	PETERCHURCH	3005	Hereford/Leominster
	BM071	KINGTON	3005	Hereford/Leominster
	BM072	KINGSTONE	3005	Hereford/Leominster
	BM073	HM CUSTOMS HEREFORD	3005	Hereford/Leominster
	BM074	HEREFORD	3005	Hereford/Leominster
	BM075	ROSS ON WYE	3005	Hereford/Leominster
	BM076	CLEOBURY MORTIMER	3005	Hereford/Leominster
	BM077	ST WEONARDS	3005	Hereford/Leominster
	BM130	LEDBURY	3005	Hereford/Leominster
	BM226	DORE	3005	Hereford/Leominster
	BM227	MADLEY	3005	Hereford/Leominster
	BM228	BREDWARDINE	3005	Hereford/Leominster
	BM904	HEREFORD/ LEOMINSTER/NON- POLICE STATION	3005	Hereford/Leominster
	BM079	WYTHALL	3006	Kidderminster/ Redditch
	BM080	REDDITCH	3006	Kidderminster/ Redditch
	BM081	INKBERROW	3006	Kidderminster/ Redditch
	BM082	HOPWOOD	3006	Kidderminster/ Redditch
	BM083	ALVECHURCH	3006	Kidderminster/ Redditch
	BM084	STOKE WORKS	3006	Kidderminster/ Redditch
	BM085	RUBERY	3006	Kidderminster/ Redditch
	BM086	ROMSLEY	3006	Kidderminster/ Redditch
	BM087	BROMSGROVE	3006	Kidderminster/ Redditch
	BM088	HAGLEY	3006	Kidderminster/ Redditch
	BM089	STOURPORT ON SEVERN	3006	Kidderminster/ Redditch
	BM090	KIDDERMINSTER	3006	Kidderminster/ Redditch

BM091	BEWDLEY	3006	Kidderminster/Redditch
BM093	GREAT WITLEY	3006	Kidderminster/Redditch
BM094	CRABBS CROSS	3006	Kidderminster/Redditch
BM095	HEADLESS CROSS	3006	Kidderminster/Redditch
BM096	WINYATES	3006	Kidderminster/Redditch
BM102	ASTLEY	3006	Kidderminster/Redditch
BM196	FRANKLEY	3006	Kidderminster/Redditch
BM230	ROCK	3006	Kidderminster/Redditch
BM231	MARTLEY	3006	Kidderminster/Redditch
BM232	BURLISH	3006	Kidderminster/Redditch
BM233	WOLVERLY	3006	Kidderminster/Redditch
BM234	CHADDESLEY	3006	Kidderminster/Redditch
BM235	CORBETT	3006	Kidderminster/Redditch
BM236	CLIFTON-ON-TEME	3006	Kidderminster/Redditch
BM237	HARTLEBURY	3006	Kidderminster/Redditch
BM266	ASTWOOD BANK	3006	Kidderminster/Redditch
BM267	BARNT GREEN	3006	Kidderminster/Redditch
BM905	KIDDERMINSTER/REDDITCH NON-POLICE STATION	3006	Kidderminster/Redditch
BM078	BISHOPS CASTLE	3007	Shrewsbury
BM097	BTP SHREWSBURY RAILWAY STATION	3007	Shrewsbury
BM098	OSWESTRY	3007	Shrewsbury
BM099	GOBOWEN (SHREWSBURY)	3007	Shrewsbury
BM100	BAYSTON HILL (SHREWSBURY)	3007	Shrewsbury
BM101	SHREWSBURY	3007	Shrewsbury
BM064	LUDLOW	3007	Shrewsbury
BM112	RAF SHAWBURY	3007	Shrewsbury
BM103	WEM	3007	Shrewsbury
BM104	MARKET DRAYTON	3007	Shrewsbury
BM113	RAF COSFORD	3007	Shrewsbury

BM270	WHITCHURCH, CHESHIRE	3007	Shrewsbury
BM906	SHREWSBURY NON-POLICE STATION	3007	Shrewsbury
BM105	BRIDGNORTH	3008	Telford
BM106	SHIFNAL	3008	Telford
BM107	MUCH WENLOCK	3008	Telford
BM108	OAKENGATES	3008	Telford
BM109	DONNINGTON	3008	Telford
BM110	WELLINGTON	3008	Telford
BM111	MALLINSGATE (TELFORD)	3008	Telford
BM286	RMP DONNINGTON	3008	Telford
BM907	TELFORD NON-POLICE STATION	3008	Telford
BM092	HARVINGTON	3009	Worcester
BM114	WELLAND	3009	Worcester
BM115	MALVERN	3009	Worcester
BM116	CRADLEY	3009	Worcester
BM117	ALFRICK	3009	Worcester
BM118	DROITWICH	3009	Worcester
BM119	WORCESTER	3009	Worcester
BM120	KEMPSEY	3009	Worcester
BM121	CROWLE	3009	Worcester
BM122	BROADWAS	3009	Worcester
BM123	PERSHORE	3009	Worcester
BM124	LITTLETON	3009	Worcester
BM125	EVESHAM	3009	Worcester
BM126	CROPTHORNE	3009	Worcester
BM127	BROADWAY	3009	Worcester
BM128	BREDON	3009	Worcester
BM129	BECKFORD	3009	Worcester
BM131	WORCESTER, HINDLIP HALL	3009	Worcester
BM132	STRENSHAM	3009	Worcester
BM292	WHITTINGTON	3009	Worcester
BM293	WARNDON	3009	Worcester
BM294	POWICK	3009	Worcester
BM295	HALLOW	3009	Worcester
BM296	FERNHILL HEATH	3009	Worcester
BM297	BROADHEATH (WORCESTER)	3009	Worcester
BM298	UPTON-ON-SEVERN	3009	Worcester
BM299	LEIGH SYNTON	3009	Worcester
BM300	ASHPERTON	3009	Worcester
BM301	OFFENHAM	3009	Worcester
BM302	LOWER MOOR	3009	Worcester
BM303	DRAKES BROUGHTON	3009	Worcester
BM304	BRETFORTON	3009	Worcester
BM305	BADSEY	3009	Worcester
BM306	HM CUSTOMS DROITWICH	3009	Worcester

	BM307	OMBERSLEY	3009	Worcester
	BM908	WORCESTER NON-POLICE STATION	3009	Worcester
West	BM133	WEST BROMWICH	3010	Sandwell
Midlands	BM134	WEDNESBURY	3010	Sandwell
	BM135	TIPTON	3010	Sandwell
	BM136	SMETHWICK	3010	Sandwell
	BM137	SANDWELL	3010	Sandwell
	BM138	OLDBURY	3010	Sandwell
	BM139	OLD HILL	3010	Sandwell
	BM909	SANDWELL NON-POLICE STATION	3010	Sandwell
	BM027	WOMBOURNE	3011	Wolverhampton & Seisdon
	BM140	BTP WOLVERHAMPTON RAILWAY STATION	3011	Wolverhampton & Seisdon
	BM141	DUNSTALL ROAD	3011	Wolverhampton & Seisdon
	BM142	BIRMINGHAM ROAD	3011	Wolverhampton & Seisdon
	BM143	RED LION STREET	3011	Wolverhampton & Seisdon
	BM144	WEDNESFIELD	3011	Wolverhampton & Seisdon
	BM145	TETTENHALL	3011	Wolverhampton & Seisdon
	BM146	BILSTON (NOT FOUND)	3011	Wolverhampton & Seisdon
	BM147	WOLVERHAMPTON CENTRAL	3011	Wolverhampton & Seisdon
	BM289	KINVER	3011	Wolverhampton & Seisdon
	BM290	CODSALL	3011	Wolverhampton & Seisdon
	BM291	SEISDON	3011	Wolverhampton & Seisdon
	BM910	WOLVERHAMPTON & SEISDON NON-POLICE STATION	3011	Wolverhampton & Seisdon
	BM148	STOURBRIDGE	3012	Dudley & Halesowen
	BM149	HALESOWEN	3012	Dudley & Halesowen
	BM150	SEDGELEY	3012	Dudley & Halesowen
	BM151	KINGSWINFORD	3012	Dudley & Halesowen
	BM152	DUDLEY	3012	Dudley & Halesowen
	BM153	BRIERLEY HILL	3012	Dudley & Halesowen
	BM225	HM CUSTOMS DUDLEY	3012	Dudley & Halesowen
	BM911	DUDLEY & HALESOWEN NON-POLICE STATION	3012	Dudley & Halesowen
	BM154	ALDRIDGE	3013	Walsall
	BM155	WILLENHALL	3013	Walsall

BM156	WALSALL	3013	Walsall
BM157	DARLASTON	3013	Walsall
BM158	BROWNHILLS	3013	Walsall
BM159	BLOXWICH	3013	Walsall
BM912	WALSALL NON-POLICE STATION	3013	Walsall
BM160	HM CUSTOMS ALPHA TOWER B'HAM	3014	Birmingham
BM161	BTP BIRMINGHAM NEW STREET STATION	3014	Birmingham
BM162	WOODBRIDGE ROAD	3014	Birmingham
BM163	WALSALL ROAD	3014	Birmingham
BM164	VYSE STREET	3014	Birmingham
BM165	THORNHILL ROAD	3014	Birmingham
BM166	THORNBRIDGE AVENUE (MOTORWAY)	3014	Birmingham
BM167	SUTTON COLDFIELD	3014	Birmingham
BM168	HARBORNE ROSE ROAD	3014	Birmingham
BM169	STEELHOUSE LANE	3014	Birmingham
BM170	STECHFORD, STATION ROAD	3014	Birmingham
BM171	SPARKHILL, STRATFORD ROAD	3014	Birmingham
BM172	SHELDON	3014	Birmingham
BM173	QUINTON ROAD WEST	3014	Birmingham
BM174	NECHELLS GREEN, FOWLER STREET	3014	Birmingham
BM175	LONGBRIDGE	3014	Birmingham
BM176	LADYWOOD	3014	Birmingham
BM177	KINGSTANDING ROAD	3014	Birmingham
BM178	KINGS NORTON, WHARF ROAD	3014	Birmingham
BM179	KINGS HEATH HIGH STREET	3014	Birmingham
BM180	HOLYHEAD ROAD	3014	Birmingham
BM181	HARBOURNE HIGH STREET	3014	Birmingham
BM182	ERDINGTON, WITTON ROAD	3014	Birmingham
BM183	EDWARD ROAD	3014	Birmingham
BM184	DUDLEY ROAD	3014	Birmingham
BM185	DIGBETH	3014	Birmingham
BM186	COVENTRY ROAD, SMALL HEATH	3014	Birmingham
BM187	CANTERBURY ROAD	3014	Birmingham
BM188	BRIDGE STREET WEST	3014	Birmingham
BM189	BRADFORD STREET	3014	Birmingham
BM190	BOURNEVILLE LANE	3014	Birmingham
BM191	BORDESLEY GREEN	3014	Birmingham

BM192	BILLESLEY, YARDLEY WOOD ROAD	3014	Birmingham
BM193	BELGRAVE ROAD	3014	Birmingham
BM194	ASTON, QUEENS ROAD	3014	Birmingham
BM195	ACOCKS GREEN	3014	Birmingham
BM197	BIRMINGHAM HQ (LLOYDS HOUSE)	3014	Birmingham
BM211	BROMFORD LANE	3014	Birmingham
BM214	DUKE STREET (TRAFFIC)	3014	Birmingham
BM215	HM CUSTOMS CONTAINERBASE BIRMINGHAM	3014	Birmingham
BM216	HM CUSTOMS ST JAMES HOUSE	3014	Birmingham
BM217	HM CUSTOMS SUTTON COLDFIELD	3014	Birmingham
BM218	HM CUSTOMS TWO BROADWAY	3014	Birmingham
BM219	MOSELEY, WOODBRIDGE ROAD	3014	Birmingham
BM220	SHARD END, PACKINGTON AVENUE	3014	Birmingham
BM913	BIRMINGHAM NON-POLICE STATION	3014	Birmingham
BM198	SOLIHULL	3015	Solihull
BM199	HM CUSTOMS BIRMINGHAM AIRPORT	3015	Solihull
BM200	CASTLE BROMWICH	3015	Solihull
BM201	SHIRLEY, WEST MIDS	3015	Solihull
BM202	BIRMINGHAM INT AIRPORT	3015	Solihull
BM203	CHELMSLEY WOOD	3015	Solihull
BM204	SOLIHULL NORTH	3015	Solihull
BM279	HM CUSTOMS PARK HOUSE	3015	Solihull
BM280	HOCKLEY HEATH	3015	Solihull
BM281	CHADWICK END	3015	Solihull
BM914	SOLIHULL NON-POLICE STATION	3015	Solihull
BM205	CHACE AVENUE	3016	Coventry
BM206	HM CUSTOMS COVENTRY	3016	Coventry
BM207	COVENTRY BTP	3016	Coventry
BM208	FLETCHAMSTEAD HIGHWAY	3016	Coventry
BM209	STONEY STANTON ROAD	3016	Coventry
BM210	LITTLE PARK STREET	3016	Coventry
BM915	COVENTRY NON-POLICE STATION	3016	Coventry

Regional Office: Cardiff

CJS Area	Police Station ID	Police Station Name	PS Scheme ID	PS Scheme Name
Dyfed-Powys	WA001	LLANDOVERY	4001	Amman Valley
	WA002	AMMANFORD	4001	Amman Valley
	WA900	AMMAN VALLEY NON-POLICE STATION	4001	Amman Valley
	WA003	NEWCASTLE EMLYN	4002	Carmarthen East Dyfed
	WA004	CARMARTHEN	4002	Carmarthen East Dyfed
	WA901	CARMARTHEN EAST DYFED NON-POLICE STATION	4002	Carmarthen East Dyfed
	WA005	LLANELLI	4003	Llanelli
	WA006	KIDWELLY	4003	Llanelli
	WA007	CROSSHANDS	4003	Llanelli
	WA008	BURRYPORT	4003	Llanelli
	WA902	LLANELLI NON-POLICE STATION	4003	Llanelli
	WA009	LLANDRINDOD WELLS	4004	Brecon & Radnor
	WA010	HAY-ON-WYE	4004	Brecon & Radnor
	WA011	CRICKHOWELL	4004	Brecon & Radnor
	WA012	BUILTH WELLS	4004	Brecon & Radnor
	WA013	BRECON	4004	Brecon & Radnor
	WA903	BRECON & RADNOR NON-POLICE STATION	4004	Brecon & Radnor
	WA014	LLANIDLOES (NEWTOWN)	4005	Mid Wales
	WA015	WELSHPOOL	4005	Mid Wales
	WA016	NEWTOWN	4005	Mid Wales
	WA904	MID WALES NON-POLICE STATION	4005	Mid Wales
	WA017	MACHYNLLETH	4006	North Ceredigion/ South Ceredigion
	WA018	ABERYSTWYTH	4006	North Ceredigion/ South Ceredigion
	WA019	ABERAERON	4006	North Ceredigion/ South Ceredigion
	WA020	CARDIGAN	4006	North Ceredigion/ South Ceredigion
	WA905	NORTH CEREDIGION/ SOUTH CEREDIGION NON-POLICE STATION	4006	North Ceredigion/ South Ceredigion
	WA021	NEYLAND	4007	Pembrokeshire
	WA022	TENBY	4007	Pembrokeshire
	WA023	PEMBROKE DOCK	4007	Pembrokeshire
	WA024	HAVERFORD WEST	4007	Pembrokeshire
	WA025	SAUNDERSFOOT	4007	Pembrokeshire

	WA026	NARBERTH	4007	Pembrokeshire
	WA027	FISHGUARD	4007	Pembrokeshire
	WA906	PEMBROKESHIRE NON-POLICE STATION	4007	Pembrokeshire
Gwent	WA028	PONTYPOOL	4008	East Gwent
	WA029	MONMOUTH	4008	East Gwent
	WA030	CWMBRAN	4008	East Gwent
	WA031	CHEPSTOW	4008	East Gwent
	WA032	CALDICOT	4008	East Gwent
	WA033	ABERGAVENNY	4008	East Gwent
	WA907	EAST GWENT NON-POLICE STATION	4008	East Gwent
	WA034	NEWPORT CENTRAL	4009	Newport
	WA035	MAINDEE	4009	Newport
	WA908	NEWPORT NON-POLICE STATION	4009	Newport
	WA036	TREDEGAR	4010	Lower Rhymney Valley/North Bedwellty/South Bedwellty
	WA037	EBBW VALE	4010	Lower Rhymney Valley/North Bedwellty/South Bedwellty
	WA038	BRYNMAWR	4010	Lower Rhymney Valley/North Bedwellty/South Bedwellty
	WA039	BLACKWOOD	4010	Lower Rhymney Valley/North Bedwellty/South Bedwellty
	WA040	YSTRAD MYNACH	4010	Lower Rhymney Valley/North Bedwellty/South Bedwellty
	WA041	RHYMNEY	4010	Lower Rhymney Valley/North Bedwellty/South Bedwellty
	WA042	CAERPHILLY	4010	Lower Rhymney Valley/North Bedwellty/South Bedwellty
	WA043	BEDWAS	4010	Lower Rhymney Valley/North Bedwellty/South Bedwellty

	WA044	BARGOED	4010	Lower Rhymney Valley/North Bedwellty/South Bedwellty
	WA045	RISCA	4010	Lower Rhymney Valley/North Bedwellty/South Bedwellty
	WA046	BLACKWOOD, SOUTH BEDWELLTY (NOT FOUND)	4010	Lower Rhymney Valley/North Bedwellty/South Bedwellty
	WA047	ABERTILLERY	4010	Lower Rhymney Valley/North Bedwellty/South Bedwellty
	WA909	LOWER RHYMNEY VALLEY/NORTH BEDWELLTY/SOUTH BEDWELLTY NON-POLICE STATION	4010	Lower Rhymney Valley/North Bedwellty/South Bedwellty
North Wales	WA048	PENYGROES	4011	Bangor & Caernarfon
	WA049	CAERNARFON	4011	Bangor & Caernarfon
	WA050	LLANBERIS	4011	Bangor & Caernarfon
	WA051	BANGOR	4011	Bangor & Caernarfon
	WA910	BANGOR & CAERNARFON NON-POLICE STATION	4011	Bangor & Caernarfon
	WA052	LLANWRST	4012	Colwyn Bay
	WA053	LLANDUDNO	4012	Colwyn Bay
	WA054	CONWY	4012	Colwyn Bay
	WA055	COLWYN BAY	4012	Colwyn Bay
	WA056	ABERGELE	4012	Colwyn Bay
	WA911	COLWYN BAY NON-POLICE STATION	4012	Colwyn Bay
	WA057	ST ASAPH	4013	Denbighshire
	WA058	RUTHIN	4013	Denbighshire
	WA059	RHYL	4013	Denbighshire
	WA060	DENBIGH	4013	Denbighshire
	WA061	ST ASAPH CUSTODY SUITE	4013	Denbighshire
	WA912	DENBIGHSHIRE NON-POLICE STATION	4013	Denbighshire
	WA062	DOLGELLAU	4014	Dolgellau
	WA913	DOLGELLAU NON-POLICE STATION	4014	Dolgellau
	WA063	SALTNEY	4015	Mold & Hawarden
	WA064	CAERGWRLE	4015	Mold & Hawarden
	WA065	BUCKLEY	4015	Mold & Hawarden
	WA066	HAWARDEN	4015	Mold & Hawarden
	WA067	MOLD	4015	Mold & Hawarden

	WA068	HOLYWELL	4015	Mold & Hawarden
	WA069	FLINT	4015	Mold & Hawarden
	WA070	DEESIDE	4015	Mold & Hawarden
	WA914	MOLD & HAWARDEN NON-POLICE STATION	4015	Mold & Hawarden
	WA071	LLANGEFNI	4016	North Anglesey
	WA072	HOLYHEAD	4016	North Anglesey
	WA073	ALMWCH	4016	North Anglesey
	WA915	NORTH ANGLESEY NON-POLICE STATION	4016	North Anglesey
	WA074	BLAENAU FFESTINIOG	4017	Pwllheli
	WA075	PWLLHELI	4017	Pwllheli
	WA076	PORTHMADOG	4017	Pwllheli
	WA916	PWLLHELI NON-POLICE STATION	4017	Pwllheli
	WA077	WREXHAM	4018	Wrexham
	WA078	RUABON	4018	Wrexham
	WA079	RHOSLLANERCHROGOG	4018	Wrexham
	WA080	OVERTON	4018	Wrexham
	WA081	LLANGOLLEN	4018	Wrexham
	WA082	CORWEN	4018	Wrexham
	WA917	WREXHAM NON-POLICE STATION	4018	Wrexham
South Wales	WA083	FAIRWATER	4019	Cardiff
	WA084	RAILWAY STATION (CENTRAL)	4019	Cardiff
	WA085	DOCKS (BUTE TOWN)	4019	Cardiff
	WA086	WHITCHURCH, SOUTH WALES	4019	Cardiff
	WA087	TROWBRIDGE	4019	Cardiff
	WA088	RUMNEY	4019	Cardiff
	WA089	ROATH	4019	Cardiff
	WA090	LLANISHEN	4019	Cardiff
	WA091	LLANEDEYRN	4019	Cardiff
	WA092	ELY, S WALES	4019	Cardiff
	WA093	CATHAYS	4019	Cardiff
	WA094	CARDIFF CENTRAL	4019	Cardiff
	WA095	CANTON	4019	Cardiff
	WA918	CARDIFF NON-POLICE STATION	4019	Cardiff
	WA096	PENARTH	4020	Vale of Glamorgan
	WA097	COWBRIDGE	4020	Vale of Glamorgan
	WA098	BARRY	4020	Vale of Glamorgan
	WA099	CARDIFF AIRPORT	4020	Vale of Glamorgan
	WA100	RAF ST ATHAN	4020	Vale of Glamorgan
	WA919	VALE OF GLAMORGAN NON-POLICE STATION	4020	Vale of Glamorgan
	WA101	TRECYNON	4021	Cynon Valley
	WA102	MOUNTAIN ASH	4021	Cynon Valley
	WA103	CWMBACH	4021	Cynon Valley
	WA104	ABERDARE	4021	Cynon Valley

WA105	ABERCYNON	4021	Cynon Valley
WA920	CYNON VALLEY NON-POLICE STATION	4021	Cynon Valley
WA106	TALBOT GREEN	4022	Mid Glamorgan & Miskin
WA107	TONYREFAIL	4022	Mid Glamorgan & Miskin
WA108	TONYPANDY	4022	Mid Glamorgan & Miskin
WA109	TON PENTRE	4022	Mid Glamorgan & Miskin
WA110	TAFFS WELL	4022	Mid Glamorgan & Miskin
WA111	PORTH	4022	Mid Glamorgan & Miskin
WA112	PONTYPRIDD	4022	Mid Glamorgan & Miskin
WA113	LLANTRISANT	4022	Mid Glamorgan & Miskin
WA114	FERNDALE	4022	Mid Glamorgan & Miskin
WA921	MID GLAMORGAN NON-POLICE STATION	4022	Mid Glamorgan & Miskin
WA115	TREHARRIS	4023	Merthyr Tydfil
WA116	MERTHYR TYDFIL	4023	Merthyr Tydfil
WA117	DOWLAIS	4023	Merthyr Tydfil
WA922	MERTHYR TYDFIL NON-POLICE STATION	4023	Merthyr Tydfil
WA118	PORT TALBOT	4024	Port Talbot
WA119	CYMMER	4024	Port Talbot
WA923	PORT TALBOT NON-POLICE STATION	4024	Port Talbot
WA120	PORTHCAWL	4025	Newcastle & Ogmore
WA121	OGMORE VALE	4025	Newcastle & Ogmore
WA122	MAESTEG	4025	Newcastle & Ogmore
WA123	BRIDGEND	4025	Newcastle & Ogmore
WA124	ABERKENFIG	4025	Newcastle & Ogmore
WA924	NEWCASTLE & OGMORE NON-POLICE STATION	4025	Newcastle & Ogmore
WA125	YSTRAD GYNLAIS	4026	Neath
WA126	SKEWEN	4026	Neath
WA127	SEVEN SISTERS	4026	Neath
WA128	NEATH	4026	Neath
WA925	NEATH NON-POLICE STATION	4026	Neath
WA129	REYNOLDSTONE	4027	Swansea
WA130	PONTARDAWE	4027	Swansea
WA131	SWANSEA CENTRAL	4027	Swansea
WA132	MUMBLES	4027	Swansea
WA133	SKETTY	4027	Swansea
WA134	MORRISTON	4027	Swansea

WA135	GORSEINON	4027	Swansea
WA136	COCKETT	4027	Swansea
WA137	CLYDACH	4027	Swansea
WA926	SWANSEA NON-POLICE STATION	4027	Swansea

Regional Office: Liverpool

CJS Area	Police Station ID	Police Station Name	PS Scheme ID	PS Scheme Name
Merseyside	LV001	GLADSTONE DOCK (NOT FOUND)	5001	Bootle & Crosby
	LV002	MARSH LANE (BOOTLE)	5001	Bootle & Crosby
	LV003	FORMBY	5001	Bootle & Crosby
	LV004	CROSBY (ALEXANDER ROAD)	5001	Bootle & Crosby
	LV005	COPY LANE (BOOTLE)	5001	Bootle & Crosby
	LV006	PORT OF LIVERPOOL	5001	Bootle & Crosby
	LV900	BOOTLE & CROSBY NON-POLICE STATION	5001	Bootle & Crosby
	LV007	PRESCOT	5005	Knowsley
	LV008	KIRKBY	5005	Knowsley
	LV009	HUYTON	5005	Knowsley
	LV010	HALEWOOD	5005	Knowsley
	LV901	KNOWSLEY NON-POLICE STATION	5005	Knowsley
	LV011	HM CUSTOMS SANDON HOUSE (LIVER)	5003	Liverpool
	LV012	BTP LIME STREET RAIL STATION (LIVER)	5003	Liverpool
	LV013	WAVERTREE ROAD	5003	Liverpool
	LV014	WALTON LANE	5003	Liverpool
	LV015	TUEBROOK	5003	Liverpool
	LV016	STANLEY ROAD	5003	Liverpool
	LV017	ST ANNE STREET	5003	Liverpool
	LV018	SPEKE	5003	Liverpool
	LV019	MAIN BRIDEWELL	5003	Liverpool
	LV020	LOWER LANE	5003	Liverpool
	LV021	GARSTON	5003	Liverpool
	LV022	EATON ROAD	5003	Liverpool
	LV023	COPPERAS HILL	5003	Liverpool
	LV024	BELLE VALE	5003	Liverpool
	LV025	ALLERTON	5003	Liverpool
	LV026	ADMIRAL STREET	5003	Liverpool
	LV027	FARNWORTH ST (EATON ROAD)	5003	Liverpool
	LV902	LIVERPOOL NON-POLICE STATION	5003	Liverpool

LV028	SOUTHPORT	5002	Southport
LV029	AINSDALE	5002	Southport
LV903	SOUTHPORT NON-POLICE STATION	5002	Southport
LV030	COLLEGE STREET, ST HELENS	5004	St Helens
LV904	ST HELENS NON-POLICE STATION	5004	St Helens
LV031	LAIRD STREET	5006	Wirral
LV032	MORETON	5006	Wirral
LV033	ROCK FERRY	5006	Wirral
LV034	BROMBOROUGH	5006	Wirral
LV035	WEST FLOAT	5006	Wirral
LV036	WALLASEY	5006	Wirral
LV037	UPTON	5006	Wirral
LV038	HOYLAKE	5006	Wirral
LV039	HESWALL	5006	Wirral
LV040	BIRKENHEAD	5006	Wirral
LV041	BEBINGTON	5006	Wirral
LV905	WIRRAL NON-POLICE STATION	5006	Wirral

Regional Office: Manchester

CJS Area	Police Station ID	Police Station Name	PS Scheme ID	PS Scheme Name
Cheshire	MA001	POYNTON	6001	Crewe & Nantwich/ Sandbach & Congleton/ Macclesfield
	MA002	WILMSLOW	6001	Crewe & Nantwich/ Sandbach & Congleton/ Macclesfield
	MA003	MACCLESFIELD	6001	Crewe & Nantwich/ Sandbach & Congleton/ Macclesfield
	MA004	M6 MOTORWAY POST (KNUTSFORD)	6001	Crewe & Nantwich/ Sandbach & Congleton/ Macclesfield
	MA005	KNUTSFORD	6001	Crewe & Nantwich/ Sandbach & Congleton/ Macclesfield

133

MA006	CONGLETON, MACCLESFIELD	6001	Crewe & Nantwich/ Sandbach & Congleton/ Macclesfield
MA007	ALSAGER	6001	Crewe & Nantwich/ Sandbach & Congleton/ Macclesfield
MA008	NANTWICH	6001	Crewe & Nantwich/ Sandbach & Congleton/ Macclesfield
MA009	CREWE	6001	Crewe & Nantwich/ Sandbach & Congleton/ Macclesfield
MA010	CONGLETON	6001	Crewe & Nantwich/ Sandbach & Congleton/ Macclesfield
MA011	SANDBACH	6001	Crewe & Nantwich/ Sandbach & Congleton/ Macclesfield
MA020	MIDDLEWICH	6001	Crewe & Nantwich/ Sandbach & Congleton/ Macclesfield
MA032	EASTERN AREA (MIDDLEWICH)	6001	Crewe & Nantwich/ Sandbach & Congleton/ Macclesfield
MA900	CREWE & NANTWICH/ SANDBACH & CONGLETON/ MACCLESFIELD NON-POLICE STATION	6001	Crewe & Nantwich/ Sandbach & Congleton/ Macclesfield
MA013	WIDNES (CLOSED)	6002	Warrington/Halton
MA014	RUNCORN (CLOSED)	6002	Warrington/Halton
MA015	WARRINGTON (CLOSED)	6002	Warrington/Halton
MA016	STOCKTON HEATH	6002	Warrington/Halton
MA017	SANKEY	6002	Warrington/Halton
MA018	RISLEY (WARRINGTON)	6002	Warrington/Halton
MA019	NORTHERN AREA (RUNCORN)	6002	Warrington/Halton
MA901	WARRINGTON/ HALTON/NON-POLICE STATION	6002	Warrington/Halton
MA021	HOLMES CHAPEL	6003	Chester/Vale Royal (Northwich)

MA022	WINSFORD	6003	Chester/Vale Royal (Northwich)
MA023	TARPORLEY	6003	Chester/Vale Royal (Northwich)
MA024	NORTHWICH	6003	Chester/Vale Royal (Northwich)
MA025	FRODSHAM	6003	Chester/Vale Royal (Northwich)
MA026	WHITCHURCH, CHESHIRE	6003	Chester/Vale Royal (Northwich)
MA027	CHESTER, NUNNS ROAD	6003	Chester/Vale Royal (Northwich)
MA028	BLACON	6003	Chester/Vale Royal (Northwich)
MA029	NESTON	6003	Chester/Vale Royal (Northwich)
MA030	ELLESMERE PORT (CLOSED)	6003	Chester/Vale Royal (Northwich)
MA031	MALPAS	6003	Chester/Vale Royal (Northwich)
MA033	WESTERN AREA (BLACON)	6003	Chester/Vale Royal (Northwich)
MA229	ELLESMERE	6003	Chester/Vale Royal (Northwich)
MA902	CHESTER/VALE ROYAL (NORTHWICH) NON-POLICE STATION	6003	Chester/Vale Royal (Northwich)
Cumbria	MA034	RAVENGLASS	6004	Barrow In Furness
	MA035	SILECROFT	6004	Barrow In Furness
	MA036	BOOTLE	6004	Barrow In Furness
	MA037	ASKAM	6004	Barrow In Furness
	MA038	ULVERSTON	6004	Barrow In Furness
	MA039	MILLOM	6004	Barrow In Furness
	MA040	DALTON	6004	Barrow In Furness
	MA041	BARROW IN FURNESS	6004	Barrow In Furness
	MA903	BARROW IN FURNESS NON-POLICE STATION	6004	Barrow In Furness
	MA042	TEBAY	6005	Kendal & Windermere
	MA043	SEDBERGH	6005	Kendal & Windermere
	MA044	LINDALE	6005	Kendal & Windermere
	MA045	CARTMEL	6005	Kendal & Windermere
	MA046	BURTON IN KENDAL	6005	Kendal & Windermere
	MA047	BURNSIDE	6005	Kendal & Windermere
	MA048	WINDERMERE	6005	Kendal & Windermere

135

MA049	MILNTHORPE	6005	Kendal & Windermere
MA050	KENDAL	6005	Kendal & Windermere
MA051	AMBLESIDE	6005	Kendal & Windermere
MA904	KENDAL & WINDERMERE NON-POLICE STATION	6005	Kendal & Windermere
MA052	SMITHFIELD	6006	Penrith/Carlisle
MA053	ROCKCLIFFE	6006	Penrith/Carlisle
MA054	ROAD HEAD	6006	Penrith/Carlisle
MA055	LOW HESKET	6006	Penrith/Carlisle
MA056	LONGTOWN	6006	Penrith/Carlisle
MA057	KIRKBRIDE	6006	Penrith/Carlisle
MA058	IRTHINGTON	6006	Penrith/Carlisle
MA059	IREBY	6006	Penrith/Carlisle
MA060	DURDAR	6006	Penrith/Carlisle
MA061	DALSTON, CUMBRIA	6006	Penrith/Carlisle
MA062	COTE HILL	6006	Penrith/Carlisle
MA063	CORBY HILL	6006	Penrith/Carlisle
MA064	BURGH BY SANDS	6006	Penrith/Carlisle
MA065	BRAMPTON	6006	Penrith/Carlisle
MA066	WIGTON	6006	Penrith/Carlisle
MA067	CARLISLE	6006	Penrith/Carlisle
MA068	SKELTON	6006	Penrith/Carlisle
MA069	MELMERBY	6006	Penrith/Carlisle
MA070	KIRKOSWALD	6006	Penrith/Carlisle
MA071	CALDBECK	6006	Penrith/Carlisle
MA072	PENRITH	6006	Penrith/Carlisle
MA073	APPLEBY	6006	Penrith/Carlisle
MA074	ALSTON	6006	Penrith/Carlisle
MA905	PENRITH/CARLISLE NON-POLICE STATION	6006	Penrith/Carlisle
MA075	MEALSGATE	6007	Whitehaven/ Workington
MA076	CLEATOR MOOR	6007	Whitehaven/ Workington
MA077	EGREMONT	6007	Whitehaven/ Workington
MA078	THORNHILL	6007	Whitehaven/ Workington
MA079	ST BEES	6007	Whitehaven/ Workington
MA080	SEASCALE	6007	Whitehaven/ Workington
MA081	PARTON	6007	Whitehaven/ Workington
MA082	DISTINGTON	6007	Whitehaven/ Workington

	MA083	WHITEHAVEN	6007	Whitehaven/ Workington
	MA084	SIDDICK	6007	Whitehaven/ Workington
	MA085	SEATON, CUMBRIA	6007	Whitehaven/ Workington
	MA086	GT CLIFTON	6007	Whitehaven/ Workington
	MA088	FLIMBY	6007	Whitehaven/ Workington
	MA089	DEARHAM	6007	Whitehaven/ Workington
	MA090	CROSBY	6007	Whitehaven/ Workington
	MA091	BROUGHTON MOOR	6007	Whitehaven/ Workington
	MA092	BRIGHAM	6007	Whitehaven/ Workington
	MA093	BOTHEL	6007	Whitehaven/ Workington
	MA094	ALLONBY	6007	Whitehaven/ Workington
	MA095	ABBEYTOWN	6007	Whitehaven/ Workington
	MA096	WORKINGTON	6007	Whitehaven/ Workington
	MA097	MARYPORT	6007	Whitehaven/ Workington
	MA098	COCKERMOUTH	6007	Whitehaven/ Workington
	MA099	KESWICK	6007	Whitehaven/ Workington
	MA100	GREAT BROUGHTON	6007	Whitehaven/ Workington
	MA101	GREAT CLIFTON	6007	Whitehaven/ Workington
	MA906	WHITEHAVEN/ WORKINGTON NON-POLICE STATION	6007	Whitehaven/ Workington
Greater Manchester	MA102	PLANT HILL RD	6008	Manchester
	MA103	NEWTON ST	6008	Manchester
	MA104	HARPURHEY	6008	Manchester
	MA105	CHORLTON	6008	Manchester
	MA106	BTP PICADILLY STATION, MANCHESTER	6008	Manchester
	MA107	HM CUSTOMS MANCHESTER AIRPORT	6008	Manchester
	MA108	NEWTON HEATH/ ANCOATS	6008	Manchester

MA109	LONGSIGHT	6008	Manchester
MA110	LEVENSHULME	6008	Manchester
MA111	HALL LANE	6008	Manchester
MA112	GREYMARE LANE	6008	Manchester
MA113	GREENHEYS	6008	Manchester
MA114	GORTON	6008	Manchester
MA115	DIDSBURY	6008	Manchester
MA116	COLLYHURST	6008	Manchester
MA117	CHEETHAM HILL	6008	Manchester
MA118	BOOTLE ST	6008	Manchester
MA119	WYTHENSHAWE	6008	Manchester
MA120	ELIZABETH SLINGER	6008	Manchester
MA121	GARTSIDE STREET	6008	Manchester
MA142	PENDLETON	6008	Manchester
MA907	MANCHESTER NON-POLICE STATION	6008	Manchester
MA122	MANCHESTER AIRPORT	6008	Manchester
MA123	REDDISH	6009	Stockport
MA124	HAZEL GROVE	6009	Stockport
MA125	BREDBURY	6009	Stockport
MA126	STOCKPORT	6009	Stockport
MA127	CHEADLE HULME	6009	Stockport
MA128	CHEADLE HEATH	6009	Stockport
MA212	MARPLE	6009	Stockport
MA908	STOCKPORT NON-POLICE STATION	6009	Stockport
MA122	MANCHESTER AIRPORT	6010	Trafford
MA129	PARTINGTON	6010	Trafford
MA130	URMSTON	6010	Trafford
MA131	STRETFORD	6010	Trafford
MA132	ALTRINCHAM	6010	Trafford
MA133	BROADHEATH (TRAFFORD)	6010	Trafford
MA909	TRAFFORD NON-POLICE STATION	6010	Trafford
MA134	IRLAM	6011	Salford
MA135	LITTLE HULTON	6011	Salford
MA136	TRAFFORD ROAD	6011	Salford
MA137	THE CRESCENT, SALFORD	6011	Salford
MA138	SWINTON	6011	Salford
MA139	HIGHER BROUGHTON (PARK LANE)	6011	Salford
MA140	ECCLES	6011	Salford
MA141	HM CUSTOMS ALDINE HOUSE, SALFORD	6011	Salford
MA910	SALFORD NON-POLICE STATION	6011	Salford
MA143	WESTHOUGHTON	6012	Bolton

MA144	HORWICH	6012	Bolton
MA145	FARNWORTH	6012	Bolton
MA146	BREIGHTMET	6012	Bolton
MA147	BOLTON CENTRAL	6012	Bolton
MA148	BOLTON (ST HELENS ROAD)	6012	Bolton
MA149	BOLTON (ASTLEY BRIDGE)	6012	Bolton
MA911	BOLTON NON-POLICE STATION	6012	Bolton
MA150	RAMSBOTTOM	6013	Bury
MA151	RADCLIFFE	6013	Bury
MA152	PRESTWICH	6013	Bury
MA153	WHITEFIELD	6013	Bury
MA154	BURY	6013	Bury
MA912	BURY NON-POLICE STATION	6013	Bury
MA155	WIGAN (HARROGATE STREET)	6014	Wigan
MA156	STANDISH	6014	Wigan
MA157	PEMBERTON	6014	Wigan
MA158	ORRELL	6014	Wigan
MA159	INCE-IN-MAKERFIELD	6014	Wigan
MA160	HINDLEY	6014	Wigan
MA161	ASHTON-IN-MAKERFIELD	6014	Wigan
MA162	TYLDESLEY	6014	Wigan
MA163	LEIGH, MANCHESTER	6014	Wigan
MA164	GOLBORNE	6014	Wigan
MA913	WIGAN NON-POLICE STATION	6014	Wigan
MA165	ROCHDALE	6015	Rochdale/Middleton
MA166	MILNROW	6015	Rochdale/Middleton
MA167	LITTLEBOROUGH	6015	Rochdale/Middleton
MA168	MIDDLETON	6015	Rochdale/Middleton
MA169	HEYWOOD	6015	Rochdale/Middleton
MA170	BIRCH SERVICE AREA	6015	Rochdale/Middleton
MA171	MOSSLEY	6015	Rochdale/Middleton
MA914	ROCHDALE/ MIDDLETON NON-POLICE STATION	6015	Rochdale/Middleton
MA172	DENTON	6016	Tameside
MA173	STALYBRIDGE	6016	Tameside
MA174	HYDE	6016	Tameside
MA175	ASHTON-UNDER-LYNE	6016	Tameside
MA915	TAMESIDE NON-POLICE STATION	6016	Tameside
MA176	UPPERMILL	6017	Oldham
MA177	SHAW	6017	Oldham
MA178	ROYTON	6017	Oldham
MA179	OLDHAM	6017	Oldham

	MA180	FAILSWORTH	6017	Oldham
	MA181	CHADDERTON	6017	Oldham
	MA916	OLDHAM NON-POLICE STATION	6017	Oldham
Lancashire	MA182	RAWTENSTALL	6018	Burnley/Rossendale
	MA183	HASLINGDEN	6018	Burnley/Rossendale
	MA184	BACUP	6018	Burnley/Rossendale
	MA185	NELSON	6018	Burnley/Rossendale
	MA186	COLNE	6018	Burnley/Rossendale
	MA187	PADIHAM	6018	Burnley/Rossendale
	MA188	BARNOLDSWICK	6018	Burnley/Rossendale
	MA189	BURNLEY	6018	Burnley/Rossendale
	MA917	BURNEY/ ROSSENDALE NON-POLICE STATION	6018	Burnley/Rossendale
	MA190	DARWEN	6019	Blackburn/ Accrington/Ribble Valley
	MA191	BLACKBURN	6019	Blackburn/ Accrington/Ribble Valley
	MA192	GREAT HARWOOD	6019	Blackburn/ Accrington/Ribble Valley
	MA193	CHURCH	6019	Blackburn/ Accrington/Ribble Valley
	MA194	ACCRINGTON	6019	Blackburn/ Accrington/Ribble Valley
	MA195	GISBURN	6019	Blackburn/ Accrington/Ribble Valley
	MA196	LONGRIDGE	6019	Blackburn/ Accrington/Ribble Valley
	MA197	CLITHEROE	6019	Blackburn/ Accrington/Ribble Valley
	MA198	GREENBANK, BLACKBURN	6019	Blackburn/ Accrington/Ribble Valley
	MA918	BLACKBURN/ ACCRINGTON/RIBBLE VALLEY NON-POLICE STATION	6019	Blackburn/ Accrington/Ribble Valley
	MA199	BLACKPOOL SOUTH	6020	Blackpool
	MA200	BLACKPOOL CENTRAL	6020	Blackpool
	MA201	BISPHAM	6020	Blackpool
	MA202	ST ANNES	6020	Blackpool
	MA203	LYTHAM	6020	Blackpool

MA204	KIRKHAM	6020	Blackpool
MA919	BLACKPOOL NON-POLICE STATION	6020	Blackpool
MA205	THORNTON	6021	Fleetwood
MA206	POULTON-LE-FYLDE	6021	Fleetwood
MA207	FLEETWOOD	6021	Fleetwood
MA208	CLEVELEYS	6021	Fleetwood
MA920	FLEETWOOD NON-POLICE STATION	6021	Fleetwood
MA209	HEYSHAM	6022	Lancaster
MA210	MORECAMBE	6022	Lancaster
MA211	LANCASTER	6022	Lancaster
MA921	LANCASTER NON-POLICE STATION	6022	Lancaster
MA213	WHEELTON	6023	Chorley/Ormskirk/ South Ribble & Leyland
MA214	COPPULL	6023	Chorley/Ormskirk/ South Ribble & Leyland
MA215	ADLINGTON	6023	Chorley/Ormskirk/ South Ribble & Leyland
MA216	CHORLEY	6023	Chorley/Ormskirk/ South Ribble & Leyland
MA217	SKELMERSDALE	6023	Chorley/Ormskirk/ South Ribble & Leyland
MA218	ORMSKIRK	6023	Chorley/Ormskirk/ South Ribble & Leyland
MA219	BURSCOUGH	6023	Chorley/Ormskirk/ South Ribble & Leyland
MA220	AUGHTON	6023	Chorley/Ormskirk/ South Ribble & Leyland
MA221	PENWORTHAM	6023	Chorley/Ormskirk/ South Ribble & Leyland
MA222	BAMBERBRIDGE	6023	Chorley/Ormskirk/ South Ribble & Leyland
MA223	LEYLAND	6023	Chorley/Ormskirk/ South Ribble & Leyland
MA922	CHORLEY/ ORMSKIRK/SOUTH RIBBLE & LEYLAND NON-POLICE STATION	6023	Chorley/Ormskirk/ South Ribble & Leyland

MA224	PRESTON	6024	Preston	
MA225	LEA	6024	Preston	
MA226	FULWOOD	6024	Preston	
MA227	RMP FULWOOD BARRACKS, PRESTON	6024	Preston	
MA228	BTP PRESTON STATION	6024	Preston	
MA923	PRESTON NON-POLICE STATION	6024	Preston	

Regional Office: Brighton

CJS Area	Police Station ID	Police Station Name	PS Scheme ID	PS Scheme Name
Kent	BG001	SANDWICH	7002	Ashford & Tenterden/Dover/ Folkestone
	BG002	HMC EASTERN DOCKS, DOVER	7002	Ashford & Tenterden/Dover/ Folkestone
	BG003	DOVER	7002	Ashford & Tenterden/Dover/ Folkestone
	BG004	DEAL	7002	Ashford & Tenterden/Dover/ Folkestone
	BG005	HM CUSTOMS DOVER, PRIORY COURT	7002	Ashford & Tenterden/Dover/ Folkestone
	BG006	LYDD	7002	Ashford & Tenterden/Dover/ Folkestone
	BG007	HM CUSTOMS FOLKESTONE	7002	Ashford & Tenterden/Dover/ Folkestone
	BG008	FOLKESTONE	7002	Ashford & Tenterden/Dover/ Folkestone
	BG009	TENTERDEN	7002	Ashford & Tenterden/Dover/ Folkestone
	BG010	ASHFORD	7002	Ashford & Tenterden/Dover/ Folkestone
	BG012	LONGPORT	7002	Ashford & Tenterden/Dover/ Folkestone

BG900	ASHFORD & TENTERDEN/DOVER/ FOLKESTONE NON- POLICE STATION	7002	Ashford & Tenterden/Dover/ Folkestone
BG013	RAF MANSTON KENT	7006	Canterbury/Thanet
BG014	BROADSTAIRS	7006	Canterbury/Thanet
BG015	RAMSGATE	7006	Canterbury/Thanet
BG016	MARGATE	7006	Canterbury/Thanet
BG017	CANTERBURY	7006	Canterbury/Thanet
BG018	HM CUSTOMS CANTERBURY	7006	Canterbury/Thanet
BG901	CANTERBURY/ THANET NON-POLICE STATION	7006	Canterbury/Thanet
BG019	BLUEWATER SHOPPING CENTRE	7001	Dartford & Gravesend
BG020	HM CUSTOMS GRAVESEND	7001	Dartford & Gravesend
BG021	SWANLEY	7001	Dartford & Gravesend
BG022	GRAVESEND	7001	Dartford & Gravesend
BG023	DARTFORD	7001	Dartford & Gravesend
BG902	DARTFORD & GRAVESEND NON- POLICE STATION	7001	Dartford & Gravesend
BG024	WEST MALLING	7005	Maidstone & West Malling
BG025	MAIDSTONE	7005	Maidstone & West Malling
BG026	BOUGHTON	7005	Maidstone & West Malling
BG903	MAIDSTONE & WEST MALLING NON-POLICE STATION	7005	Maidstone & West Malling
BG027	ROCHESTER	7003	Medway
BG028	GILLINGHAM, KENT	7003	Medway
BG029	BTP CHATHAM RAILWAY STATION	7003	Medway
BG030	CHATHAM	7003	Medway
BG904	MEDWAY NON-POLICE STATION	7003	Medway
BG031	EASTLING (FAVERSHAM)	7004	Swale
BG032	SITTINGBOURNE	7004	Swale
BG033	SHEERNESS	7004	Swale
BG034	HM CUSTOMS SHEERNESS	7004	Swale
BG035	FAVERSHAM	7004	Swale
BG036	SELLING (HERNE BAY)	7004	Swale

	BG905	SWALE NON-POLICE STATION	7004	Swale
	BG037	WESTERHAM (SEVENOAKS)	7007	West Kent (Tonbridge)
	BG038	TUNBRIDGE WELLS	7007	West Kent (Tonbridge)
	BG039	TONBRIDGE	7007	West Kent (Tonbridge)
	BG040	SEVENOAKS	7007	West Kent (Tonbridge)
	BG041	CRANBROOK	7007	West Kent (Tonbridge)
	BG907	WEST KENT (TONBRIDGE) NON-POLICE STATION	7007	West Kent (Tonbridge)
Surrey	BG042	EPSOM	7011	Epsom
	BG043	WALTON ON THAMES	7011	Epsom
	BG908	EPSOM NON-POLICE STATION	7011	Epsom
	BG044	HASLEMERE	7008	Guildford & Farnham
	BG045	FARNHAM	7008	Guildford & Farnham
	BG046	GUILDFORD BTP	7008	Guildford & Farnham
	BG047	GUILDFORD	7008	Guildford & Farnham
	BG048	GODALMING	7008	Guildford & Farnham
	BG909	GUILDFORD & FARNHAM NON-POLICE STATION	7008	Guildford & Farnham
	BG049	CAMBERLEY	7009	North West Surrey (Woking)
	BG050	ADDLESTONE	7009	North West Surrey (Woking)
	BG051	WOKING	7009	North West Surrey (Woking)
	BG052	EGHAM	7009	North West Surrey (Woking)
	BG910	NORTH WEST SURREY (WOKING) NON-POLICE STATION	7009	North West Surrey (Woking)
	BG053	LEATHERHEAD	7010	South East Surrey
	BG054	REIGATE	7010	South East Surrey
	BG055	OXTED	7010	South East Surrey
	BG056	HORLEY	7010	South East Surrey
	BG057	DORKING	7010	South East Surrey
	BG058	CATERHAM	7010	South East Surrey
	BG059	REDHILL	7010	South East Surrey
	BG911	SOUTH EAST SURREY NON-POLICE STATION	7010	South East Surrey

	BG060	SUNBURY	7012	Staines
	BG061	STAINES	7012	Staines
	BG912	STAINES NON-POLICE STATION	7012	Staines
Sussex	BG062	HOVE	7013	Brighton & Hove & Lewes
	BG063	BTP BRIGHTON	7013	Brighton & Hove & Lewes
	BG064	BRIGHTON	7013	Brighton & Hove & Lewes
	BG065	SEAFORD	7013	Brighton & Hove & Lewes
	BG066	NEWHAVEN HARBOUR, BT POLICE (NOT FOUND)	7013	Brighton & Hove & Lewes
	BG067	NEWHAVEN	7013	Brighton & Hove & Lewes
	BG068	LEWES, UCKFIELD	7013	Brighton & Hove & Lewes
	BG069	HM CUSTOMS NEWHAVEN	7013	Brighton & Hove & Lewes
	BG913	BRIGHTON & HOVE & LEWES NON-POLICE STATION	7013	Brighton & Hove & Lewes
	BG070	PETWORTH	7014	Chichester & District
	BG071	MIDHURST	7014	Chichester & District
	BG072	CHICHESTER	7014	Chichester & District
	BG073	BOGNOR REGIS	7014	Chichester & District
	BG914	CHICHESTER & DISTRICT NON-POLICE STATION	7014	Chichester & District
	BG074	GATWICK	7015	Crawley/Horsham
	BG075	CRAWLEY	7015	Crawley/Horsham
	BG076	HORSHAM	7015	Crawley/Horsham
	BG077	HM CUSTOMS GATWICK AIRPORT	7015	Crawley/Horsham
	BG078	BTP GATWICK AIRPORT	7015	Crawley/Horsham
	BG079	HAYWARDS HEATH	7015	Crawley/Horsham
	BG080	BURGESS HILL	7015	Crawley/Horsham
	BG081	EAST GRINSTEAD	7015	Crawley/Horsham
	BG915	CRAWLEY/HORSHAM NON-POLICE STATION	7015	Crawley/Horsham
	BG082	CROWBOROUGH	7018	Eastbourne
	BG083	HAILSHAM	7018	Eastbourne
	BG084	EASTBOURNE	7018	Eastbourne
	BG085	UCKFIELD	7018	Eastbourne

BG916	EASTBOURNE NON-POLICE STATION	7018	Eastbourne
BG086	HASTINGS	7016	Hastings
BG087	BEXHILL	7016	Hastings
BG917	HASTINGS NON-POLICE STATION	7016	Hastings
BG088	WORTHING	7017	Worthing
BG089	STEYNING	7017	Worthing
BG090	SHOREHAM	7017	Worthing
BG091	LITTLEHAMPTON	7017	Worthing
BG092	ARUNDEL	7017	Worthing
BG918	WORTHING NON-POLICE STATION	7017	Worthing

Regional Ofice:Nottingham

CJS Area	Police Station ID	Police Station Name	PS Scheme ID	PS Scheme Name
Derbyshire	NT001	LONG EATON	8001	East Derbyshire (Ripley)/Ilkeston
	NT002	ILKESTON	8001	East Derbyshire (Ripley)/Ilkeston
	NT003	RIPLEY - DIVISIONAL HQ	8001	East Derbyshire (Ripley)/Ilkeston
	NT004	HEANOR	8001	East Derbyshire (Ripley)/Ilkeston
	NT005	ALFRETON	8001	East Derbyshire (Ripley)/Ilkeston
	NT006	BUTTERLEY	8001	East Derbyshire (Ripley)/Ilkeston
	NT007	BELPER	8001	East Derbyshire (Ripley)/Ilkeston
	NT008	ALFRETON – HALL STREET	8001	East Derbyshire (Ripley)/Ilkeston
	NT900	EAST DERBYSHIRE (RIPLEY)/ILKESTON NON-POLICE STATION	8001	East Derbyshire (Ripley)/Ilkeston
	NT009	NEW MILLS	8002	Ashbourne/Matlock/ High Peak (Buxton)
	NT010	CHAPEL-EN-LE-FRITH	8002	Ashbourne/Matlock/ High Peak (Buxton)
	NT011	BUXTON	8002	Ashbourne/Matlock/ High Peak (Buxton)
	NT012	MATLOCK	8002	Ashbourne/Matlock/ High Peak (Buxton)
	NT013	BAKEWELL	8002	Ashbourne/Matlock/ High Peak (Buxton)
	NT014	ASHBOURNE	8002	Ashbourne/Matlock/ High Peak (Buxton)

	NT015	GLOSSOP	8002	Ashbourne/Matlock/ High Peak (Buxton)
	NT901	ASHBOURNE/ MATLOCK/HIGH PEAK (BUXTON) NON- POLICE STATION	8002	Ashbourne/Matlock/ High Peak (Buxton)
	NT016	KILAMARSH	8003	Chesterfield
	NT017	DRONFIELD	8003	Chesterfield
	NT018	STAVELEY	8003	Chesterfield
	NT019	SHIREBROOK	8003	Chesterfield
	NT020	CLAY CROSS	8003	Chesterfield
	NT021	CHESTERFIELD	8003	Chesterfield
	NT022	BOLSOVER	8003	Chesterfield
	NT902	CHESTERFIELD NON- POLICE STATION	8003	Chesterfield
	NT023	ST MARY'S GATE	8004	Derby/Swadlincote
	NT024	PEARTREE	8004	Derby/Swadlincote
	NT025	CHADDESDEN	8004	Derby/Swadlincote
	NT026	FULL STREET (STATION CLOSED)	8004	Derby/Swadlincote
	NT027	DERBY CENTRAL (NOT FOUND)	8004	Derby/Swadlincote
	NT028	COTTON LANE	8004	Derby/Swadlincote
	NT029	ST MARY'S WHARF (DERBY)	8004	Derby/Swadlincote
	NT030	LITTLEOVER	8004	Derby/Swadlincote
	NT032	SWADLINCOTE	8004	Derby/Swadlincote
	NT903	DERBY/ SWADLINCOTE NON- POLICE STATION	8004	Derby/Swadlincote
Leicestershire	NT033	COALVILLE	8005	Ashby & Coalville/ Loughborough/ Melton Mowbray
	NT034	ASHBY-DE-LA ZOUCH	8005	Ashby & Coalville/ Loughborough/ Melton Mowbray
	NT035	EAST MIDLANDS AIRPORT	8005	Ashby & Coalville/ Loughborough/ Melton Mowbray
	NT036	LOUGHBOROUGH	8005	Ashby & Coalville/ Loughborough/ Melton Mowbray
	NT037	RAF COTTESMORE	8005	Ashby & Coalville/ Loughborough/ Melton Mowbray
	NT038	MELTON MOWBRAY [DESIGNATED]	8005	Ashby & Coalville/ Loughborough/ Melton Mowbray
	NT904	ASHBY & COALVILLE/ LOUGHBOROUGH/ MELTON BROWBRAY NON-POLICE STATION	8005	Ashby & Coalville/ Loughborough/ Melton Mowbray

	NT039	BEAUMONT LEYES	8006	Leicester
	NT040	BRAUNSTONE	8006	Leicester
	NT041	HAMILTON	8006	Leicester
	NT042	WIGSTON	8006	Leicester
	NT043	CHARLES STREET	8006	Leicester
	NT044	OAKHAM (SYSTON)	8006	Leicester
	NT045	SYSTON	8006	Leicester
	NT046	WELFORD ROAD (LEICESTER)	8006	Leicester
	NT047	MANSFIELD HOUSE	8006	Leicester
	NT048	SPINNEY HILL	8006	Leicester
	NT049	EUSTON STREET (LEICESTER)	8006	Leicester
	NT905	LEICESTER NON-POLICE STATION	8006	Leicester
	NT050	MARKET BOSWORTH	8007	Hinckley/Market Harborough
	NT051	LUTTERWORTH	8007	Hinckley/Market Harborough
	NT052	HINCKLEY	8007	Hinckley/Market Harborough
	NT053	MARKET HARBOROUGH	8007	Hinckley/Market Harborough
	NT906	HINCKLEY/MARKET HARBOROUGH NON-POLICE STATION	8007	Hinckley/Market Harborough
Lincolnshire	NT054	COLSTERWORTH	8008	Boston/Bourne/Stamford
	NT055	BOURNE	8008	Boston/Bourne/Stamford
	NT056	STAMFORD	8008	Boston/Bourne/Stamford
	NT062	HOLBEACH	8008	Boston/Bourne/Stamford
	NT064	SPALDING	8008	Boston/Bourne/Stamford
	NT065	BOSTON	8008	Boston/Bourne/Stamford
	NT907	BOSTON/BOURNE/STAMFORD NON-POLICE STATION	8008	Boston/Bourne/Stamford
	NT066	MABLETHORPE	8009	Skegness
	NT067	LOUTH	8009	Skegness
	NT068	SKEGNESS	8009	Skegness
	NT069	HORNCASTLE	8009	Skegness
	NT070	ALFORD (SKEGNESS)	8009	Skegness
	NT071	RAF CONINGSBY	8009	Skegness
	NT908	SKEGNESS NON-POLICE STATION	8009	Skegness
	NT072	LINCOLN	8010	Lincoln/Gainsborough

	NT073	MARKET RASEN	8010	Lincoln/ Gainsborough
	NT074	GAINSBOROUGH	8010	Lincoln/ Gainsborough
	NT075	CAISTOR	8010	Lincoln/ Gainsborough
	NT076	RAF SCAMPTON	8010	Lincoln/ Gainsborough
	NT081	RAF WADDINGTON	8010	Lincoln/ Gainsborough
	NT122	RAF DIGBY	8010	Lincoln/ Gainsborough
	NT909	LINCOLN/ GAINSBOROUGH NON-POLICE STATION	8010	Lincoln/ Gainsborough
	NT077	SLEAFORD	8011	Grantham & Sleaford
	NT078	HECKINGTON	8011	Grantham & Sleaford
	NT079	LONG BENNINGTON	8011	Grantham & Sleaford
	NT080	GRANTHAM	8011	Grantham & Sleaford
	NT082	RAF CRANWELL	8011	Grantham & Sleaford
	NT910	GRANTHAM & SLEAFORD NON-POLICE STATION	8011	Grantham & Sleaford
Nottinghamshire	NT083	RAVENSHEAD	8012	Mansfield
	NT084	SELSTON	8012	Mansfield
	NT085	SUTTON-IN-ASHFIELD	8012	Mansfield
	NT086	MANSFIELD	8012	Mansfield
	NT911	MANSFIELD NON-POLICE STATION	8012	Mansfield
	NT087	CAYTHORPE	8013	Newark
	NT088	NEWARK	8013	Newark
	NT912	NEWARK NON-POLICE STATION	8013	Newark
	NT031	CARLTON	8014	Nottingham
	NT089	OXCLOSE LANE	8014	Nottingham
	NT090	BRIDEWELL	8014	Nottingham
	NT091	WEST BRIDGFORD	8014	Nottingham
	NT092	STATION STREET	8014	Nottingham
	NT093	ST ANNS	8014	Nottingham
	NT094	SHERWOOD LODGE	8014	Nottingham
	NT095	RADFORD ROAD	8014	Nottingham
	NT096	NOTTINGHAM CENTRAL	8014	Nottingham
	NT097	KIMBERLEY	8014	Nottingham
	NT098	HUCKNALL	8014	Nottingham
	NT099	EASTWOOD	8014	Nottingham

149

	NT100	CLIFTON	8014	Nottingham
	NT101	CANNING CIRCUS	8014	Nottingham
	NT102	BULWELL	8014	Nottingham
	NT103	BROXTOWE	8014	Nottingham
	NT104	BESTWOOD PARK	8014	Nottingham
	NT105	BEESTON	8014	Nottingham
	NT106	ARNOLD (HIGH STREET)	8014	Nottingham
	NT107	BINGHAM	8014	Nottingham
	NT913	NOTTINGHAM NON-POLICE STATION	8014	Nottingham
	NT108	WORKSOP	8015	Worksop & East Retford
	NT109	RETFORD	8015	Worksop & East Retford
	NT110	HARWORTH	8015	Worksop & East Retford
	NT111	CARLTON IN LINDRICK	8015	Worksop & East Retford
	NT914	WORKSOP & EAST RETFORD NON-POLICE STATION	8015	Worksop & East Retford
Northamptonshire	NT112	CORBY	8016	Corby (Kettering)/ Wellingborough
	NT113	KETTERING	8016	Corby (Kettering)/ Wellingborough
	NT114	RUSHDEN, KETTERING	8016	Corby (Kettering)/ Wellingborough
	NT115	WELLINGBOROUGH	8016	Corby (Kettering)/ Wellingborough
	NT915	CORBY (KETTERING)/ WELLINGBOROUGH NON-POLICE STATION	8016	Corby (Kettering)/ Wellingborough
	NT116	WESTON FAVELL	8017	Northampton
	NT117	NORTHAMPTON (CAMPBELL SQUARE)	8017	Northampton
	NT118	BRACKLEY	8017	Northampton
	NT119	TOWCESTER	8017	Northampton
	NT120	DAVENTRY	8017	Northampton
	NT121	HM CUSTOMS, NORTHAMPTON	8017	Northampton
	NT916	NORTHAMPTON NON-POLICE STATION	8017	Northampton

Regional Office: Cambridge

CJS Area	Police Station ID	Police Station Name	PS Scheme ID	PS Scheme Name
Bedfordshire	EA001	BEDFORD	9001	Bedford
	EA002	AMPTHILL	9001	Bedford
	EA143	BIGGLESWADE	9001	Bedford
	EA144	SANDY	9001	Bedford
	EA900	BEDFORD NON-POLICE STATION	9001	Bedford
	EA003	LEIGHTON BUZZARD (DUNSTABLE)	9002	Luton
	EA004	RAF STANBRIDGE	9002	Luton
	EA005	LUTON AIRPORT	9002	Luton
	EA006	LUTON	9002	Luton
	EA007	HM CUSTOMS, LUTON (NOT FOUND)	9002	Luton
	EA008	HM CUSTOMS LUTON AIRPORT	9002	Luton
	EA009	DUNSTABLE	9002	Luton
	EA901	LUTON NON-POLICE STATION	9002	Luton
Cambridgeshire	EA010	CAMBRIDGE	9003	Cambridge
	EA011	SAWSTON	9003	Cambridge
	EA902	CAMBRIDGE NON-POLICE STATION	9003	Cambridge
	EA012	ELY, CAMBS	9004	Ely
	EA903	ELY NON-POLICE STATION	9004	Ely
	EA013	ST NEOTS	9005	Huntingdon
	EA014	ST IVES	9005	Huntingdon
	EA015	RAMSEY	9005	Huntingdon
	EA016	RAF WYTON	9005	Huntingdon
	EA017	HUNTINGDON	9005	Huntingdon
	EA904	HUNTINGDON NON-POLICE STATION	9005	Huntingdon
	EA018	WHITTLESEY	9006	March & Wisbech
	EA019	MARCH	9006	March & Wisbech
	EA020	WISBECH	9006	March & Wisbech
	EA145	CHATTERIS	9006	March & Wisbech
	EA905	MARCH & WISBECH NON-POLICE STATION	9006	March & Wisbech
	EA021	THORPEWOOD (PETERBOROUGH)	9007	Peterborough
	EA022	RAF WITTERING	9007	Peterborough
	EA023	PETERBOROUGH	9007	Peterborough
	EA024	BTP PETERBOROUGH	9007	Peterborough
	EA906	PETERBOROUGH NON-POLICE STATION	9007	Peterborough

151

Essex	EA025	WICKFORD	9008	Basildon
	EA026	BASILDON	9008	Basildon
	EA027	BILLERICAY	9008	Basildon
	EA907	BASILDON NON-POLICE STATION	9008	Basildon
	EA028	BRENTWOOD	9009	Brentwood
	EA908	BRENTWOOD NON-POLICE STATION	9009	Brentwood
	EA030	HEDINGHAM	9010	Braintree
	EA031	HALSTEAD	9010	Braintree
	EA032	BRAINTREE	9010	Braintree
	EA034	WETHERSFIELD MOD POLICE	9010	Braintree
	EA909	BRAINTREE NON-POLICE STATION	9010	Braintree
	EA035	RMP COLCHESTER GARRISON	9011	Clacton & Harwich/Colchester
	EA036	COLCHESTER	9011	Clacton & Harwich/Colchester
	EA037	CLACTON	9011	Clacton & Harwich/Colchester
	EA038	PARKESTON QUAY	9011	Clacton & Harwich/Colchester
	EA039	HARWICH	9011	Clacton & Harwich/Colchester
	EA040	WEST MERSEA	9011	Clacton & Harwich/Colchester
	EA041	WALTON	9011	Clacton & Harwich/Colchester
	EA042	COPFORD	9011	Clacton & Harwich/Colchester
	EA146	BRIGHTLINGSEA	9011	Clacton & Harwich/Colchester
	EA910	CLACTON & HARWICH/COLCHESTER NON-POLICE STATION	9011	Clacton & Harwich/Colchester
	EA043	TILBURY	9012	Grays
	EA044	SOUTH OCKENDON	9012	Grays
	EA045	GRAYS THURROCK	9012	Grays
	EA046	CORRINGHAM	9012	Grays
	EA911	GRAYS NON-POLICE STATION	9012	Grays
	EA047	HARLOW	9013	Harlow & Loughton
	EA048	EPPING	9013	Harlow & Loughton
	EA049	ONGAR	9013	Harlow & Loughton
	EA050	LOUGHTON	9013	Harlow & Loughton
	EA051	CHIGWELL	9013	Harlow & Loughton
	EA912	HARLOW & LOUGHTON NON-POLICE STATION	9013	Harlow & Loughton
	EA052	HM CUSTOMS STANSTED AIRPORT	9014	Stansted

EA053	SAFFRON WALDEN	9014	Stansted
EA054	STANSTED AIRPORT	9014	Stansted
EA913	STANSTED NON-POLICE	9014	Stansted
EA029	BENFLEET	9015	Rayleigh/Southend On Sea
EA055	LEIGH, ESSEX	9015	Rayleigh/Southend On Sea
EA056	HM CUSTOMS SOUTHEND AIRPORT	9015	Rayleigh/Southend On Sea
EA057	SOUTHEND	9015	Rayleigh/Southend On Sea
EA058	ROCHFORD	9015	Rayleigh/Southend On Sea
EA059	CANVEY ISLAND	9015	Rayleigh/Southend On Sea
EA060	RAYLEIGH	9015	Rayleigh/Southend On Sea
EA061	BTP SOUTHEND	9015	Rayleigh/Southend On Sea
EA147	SHOREBURYNESS	9015	Rayleigh/Southend On Sea
EA148	WESTCLIFF	9015	Rayleigh/Southend On Sea
EA914	RAYLEIGH/ SOUTHEND ON SEA NON-POLICE STATION	9015	Rayleigh/Southend On Sea
EA033	WITHAM	9016	Chelmsford/Witham
EA062	CHELMSFORD	9016	Chelmsford/Witham
EA063	MALDON (CHELMSFORD)	9016	Chelmsford/Witham
EA064	SOUTH WOODHAM FERRERS	9016	Chelmsford/Witham
EA065	SOUTHMINSTER	9016	Chelmsford/Witham
EA915	CHELMSFORD/ WITHAM NON-POLICE STATION	9016	Chelmsford/Witham
Hertfordshire EA066	HEMEL HEMPSTEAD	9017	Dacorum (Hemel Hempstead)
EA067	BERKHAMSTED	9017	Dacorum (Hemel Hempstead)
EA149	TRING	9017	Dacorum (Hemel Hempstead)
EA916	DACORUM (HEMEL HEMPSTEAD NON-POLICE STATION	9017	Dacorum (Hemel Hempstead)
EA068	HODDESDON	9018	Bishop's Stortford/ East Hertfordshire
EA069	HERTFORD	9018	Bishop's Stortford/ East Hertfordshire
EA070	BUNTINGFORD	9018	Bishop's Stortford/ East Hertfordshire

EA071	SAWBRIDGEWORTH	9018	Bishop's Stortford/ East Hertfordshire
EA072	BISHOP'S STORTFORD	9018	Bishop's Stortford/ East Hertfordshire
EA073	CHESHUNT (EDMONTON)	9018	Bishop's Stortford/ East Hertfordshire
EA917	BISHOP'S STORTFORD/EAST HERTFORDSHIRE NON-POLICE STATION	9018	Bishop's Stortford/ East Hertfordshire
EA074	ROYSTON, HERTS	9019	Stevenage & North Hertfordshire
EA075	STEVENAGE	9019	Stevenage & North Hertfordshire
EA076	LETCHWORTH	9019	Stevenage & North Hertfordshire
EA077	HITCHIN	9019	Stevenage & North Hertfordshire
EA150	BALDOCK	9019	Stevenage & North Hertfordshire
EA151	BUSHEY (BARNET)	9019	Stevenage & North Hertfordshire
EA918	STEVENAGE & NORTH HERTFORDSHIRE NON-POLICE STATION	9019	Stevenage & North Hertfordshire
EA078	LONDON COLNEY	9020	St Albans
EA079	HARPENDEN	9020	St Albans
EA080	WELWYN GARDEN CITY	9020	St Albans
EA081	ST ALBANS	9020	St Albans
EA082	HATFIELD	9020	St Albans
EA152	POTTER'S BAR	9020	St Albans
EA919	ST ALBANS NON-POLICE STATION	9020	St Albans
EA083	OXHEY	9021	Watford
EA084	RICKMANSWORTH	9021	Watford
EA085	WATFORD	9021	Watford
EA086	WATFORD CENTRAL (NOT FOUND)	9021	Watford
EA153	BOREHAMWOOD	9021	Watford
EA920	WATFORD NON-POLICE STATION	9021	Watford

Norfolk

EA087	SHERINGHAM	9022	Cromer & North Walsham
EA088	HOLT	9022	Cromer & North Walsham
EA089	CROMER	9022	Cromer & North Walsham
EA090	STALHAM	9022	Cromer & North Walsham
EA091	NORTH WALSHAM	9022	Cromer & North Walsham

EA092	RAF COLTISHALL	9022	Cromer & North Walsham
EA106	AYLSHAM	9022	Cromer & North Walsham
EA921	CROMER & NORTH WALSHAM NON-POLICE STATION	9022	Cromer & North Walsham
EA093	HM CUSTOMS GREAT YARMOUTH	9023	Great Yarmouth
EA094	GREAT YARMOUTH	9023	Great Yarmouth
EA095	GORLESTON ON SEA	9023	Great Yarmouth
EA096	CAISTER ON SEA	9023	Great Yarmouth
EA097	ACLE	9023	Great Yarmouth
EA922	GREAT YARMOUTH NON-POLICE STATION	9023	Great Yarmouth
EA098	SWAFFHAM	9024	Kings Lynn & West Norfolk
EA099	WELLS NEXT THE SEA, NORFOLK	9024	Kings Lynn & West Norfolk
EA100	RAF MARHAM	9024	Kings Lynn & West Norfolk
EA101	KINGS LYNN	9024	Kings Lynn & West Norfolk
EA102	HUNTSTANTON	9024	Kings Lynn & West Norfolk
EA103	FAKENHAM	9024	Kings Lynn & West Norfolk
EA104	DOWNHAM MARKET	9024	Kings Lynn & West Norfolk
EA154	DERSINGHAM	9024	Kings Lynn & West Norfolk
EA923	KINGS LYNN & WEST NORFOLK NON-POLICE STATION	9024	Kings Lynn & West Norfolk
EA107	LONG STRATTON	9025	Norwich & District
EA108	LODDON	9025	Norwich & District
EA109	NORWICH	9025	Norwich & District
EA110	HM CUSTOMS NORWICH AIRPORT	9025	Norwich & District
EA155	REEPHAM	9025	Norwich & District
EA924	NORWICH & DISTRICT NON-POLICE STATION	9025	Norwich & District
EA111	THETFORD	9026	Diss/Thetford
EA112	HARLESTON	9026	Diss/Thetford
EA113	DISS	9026	Diss/Thetford
EA132	EYE	9026	Diss/Thetford
EA925	DISS/THETFORD NON-POLICE STATION	9026	Diss/Thetford
EA105	ATTLEBOROUGH	9027	Dereham
EA114	WYMONDHAM	9027	Dereham
EA115	DEREHAM	9027	Dereham

	EA926	DEREHAM NON-POLICE STATION	9027	Dereham
Suffolk	EA116	SOUTHWOLD	9028	Lowestoft/Beccles & Halesworth/ Aldeburgh
	EA117	HALESWORTH	9028	Lowestoft/Beccles & Halesworth/ Aldeburgh
	EA118	BUNGAY	9028	Lowestoft/Beccles & Halesworth/ Aldeburgh
	EA119	BECCLES	9028	Lowestoft/Beccles & Halesworth/ Aldeburgh
	EA120	LOWESTOFT	9028	Lowestoft/Beccles & Halesworth/ Aldeburgh
	EA121	LEISTON	9028	Lowestoft/Beccles & Halesworth/ Aldeburgh
	EA122	SAXMUNDHAM	9028	Lowestoft/Beccles & Halesworth/ Aldeburgh
	EA927	LOWESTOFT/ BECCLES & HALESWORTH/ ALDEBURGH NON-POLICE STATION	9028	Lowestoft/Beccles & Halesworth/ Aldeburgh
	EA123	WOODBRIDGE	9029	Felixstowe/ Ipswich & District/ Woodbridge
	EA124	IPSWICH	9029	Felixstowe/ Ipswich & District/ Woodbridge
	EA125	HM CUSTOMS FELIXSTOWE	9029	Felixstowe/ Ipswich & District/ Woodbridge
	EA126	FELIXSTOWE	9029	Felixstowe/ Ipswich & District/ Woodbridge
	EA127	CAPEL ST MARY	9029	Felixstowe/ Ipswich & District/ Woodbridge
	EA928	FELIXSTOWE/ IPSWICH & DISTRICT/ WOODBRIDE NON-POLICE STATION	9029	Felixstowe/ Ipswich & District/ Woodbridge
	EA128	NEWMARKET	9030	Sudbury & Hadleigh/Bury St Edmunds/Haverhill/ Newmarket

EA129	MILDENHALL	9030	Sudbury & Hadleigh/Bury St Edmunds/Haverhill/ Newmarket
EA130	BRANDEN	9030	Sudbury & Hadleigh/Bury St Edmunds/Haverhill/ Newmarket
EA131	BRANDON	9030	Sudbury & Hadleigh/Bury St Edmunds/Haverhill/ Newmarket
EA133	CLARE	9030	Sudbury & Hadleigh/Bury St Edmunds/Haverhill/ Newmarket
EA134	SUDBURY	9030	Sudbury & Hadleigh/Bury St Edmunds/Haverhill/ Newmarket
EA135	HADLEIGH	9030	Sudbury & Hadleigh/Bury St Edmunds/Haverhill/ Newmarket
EA136	RAF HONNINGTON	9030	Sudbury & Hadleigh/Bury St Edmunds/Haverhill/ Newmarket
EA137	IXWORTH	9030	Sudbury & Hadleigh/Bury St Edmunds/Haverhill/ Newmarket
EA138	HORINGER	9030	Sudbury & Hadleigh/Bury St Edmunds/Haverhill/ Newmarket
EA139	ELMSWELL	9030	Sudbury & Hadleigh/Bury St Edmunds/Haverhill/ Newmarket
EA140	BURY ST EDMUNDS	9030	Sudbury & Hadleigh/Bury St Edmunds/Haverhill/ Newmarket
EA141	STOWMARKET	9030	Sudbury & Hadleigh/Bury St Edmunds/Haverhill/ Newmarket
EA142	HAVERHILL	9030	Sudbury & Hadleigh/Bury St Edmunds/Haverhill/ Newmarket

	EA929	SUDBURY & HADLEIGH/BURY ST EDMUNDS/ HAVERHILL/ NEWMARKET NON-POLICE STATION	9030	Sudbury & Hadleigh/Bury St Edmunds/Haverhill/ Newmarket

Regional Office: Reading

CJS Area	Police Station ID	Police Station Name	PS Scheme ID	PS Scheme Name
Thames Valley	RD001	RAF BRIZE NORTON	1131	Abingdon, Didcot & Whitney (South Oxfordshire)
	RD002	WITNEY	1131	Abingdon, Didcot & Whitney (South Oxfordshire)
	RD003	ABINGDON	1131	Abingdon, Didcot & Whitney (South Oxfordshire)
	RD900	ABINGDON, DIDCOT & WITNEY (SOUTH OXFORDSHIRE) NON-POLICE STATION	1131	Abingdon, Didcot & Whitney (South Oxfordshire)
	RD008	RAF HALTON	1132	Aylesbury
	RD009	AYLESBURY	1132	Aylesbury
	RD901	AYLESBURY NON-POLICE STATION	1132	Aylesbury
	RD010	GERRARDS CROSS	1133	High Wycombe & Amersham
	RD011	CHESHAM	1133	High Wycombe & Amersham
	RD012	AMERSHAM	1133	High Wycombe & Amersham
	RD013	RAF WALTERS ASH STRIKE CMAND	1133	High Wycombe & Amersham
	RD014	MARLOW	1133	High Wycombe & Amersham
	RD015	HIGH WYCOMBE	1133	High Wycombe & Amersham
	RD902	HIGH WYCOMBE & AMERSHAM NON-POLICE STATION	1133	High Wycombe & Amersham
	RD016	BLETCHLEY	1134	Milton Keynes
	RD017	NEWPORT PAGNELL	1134	Milton Keynes
	RD018	CENTRAL MILTON KEYNES	1134	Milton Keynes
	RD019	BUCKINGHAM	1134	Milton Keynes

	RD903	MILTON KEYNES NON-POLICE STATION	1134	Milton Keynes
	RD021	BICESTER	1135	Bicester/North Oxon (Banbury)
	RD022	BANBURY	1135	Bicester/North Oxon (Banbury)
	RD023	CHIPPING NORTON	1135	Bicester/North Oxon (Banbury)
	RD024	RMP 160 PROVOST, BICESTER	1135	Bicester/North Oxon (Banbury)
	RD904	BICESTER/NORTH OXON (BANBURY) NON-POLICE STATION	1135	Bicester/North Oxon (Banbury)
	RD026	ST ALDATES (OXFORD CENTRAL)	1136	Oxford
	RD905	OXFORD NON-POLICE STATION	1136	Oxford
	RD027	WOKINGHAM	1138	Slough (East Berkshire)
	RD028	WINDSOR	1138	Slough (East Berkshire)
	RD029	SLOUGH	1138	Slough (East Berkshire)
	RD030	MAIDENHEAD	1138	Slough (East Berkshire)
	RD035	BRACKNELL	1138	Slough (East Berkshire)
	RD906	SLOUGH (EAST BERKSHIRE) NON-POLICE STATION	1138	Slough (East Berkshire)
	RD037	READING	1137	Reading
	RD039	LODDEN VALLEY	1137	Reading
	RD907	READING NON-POLICE STATION	1137	Reading
	RD061	THATCHAM	1139	West Berkshire (Newbury Etc.)
	RD062	NEWBURY	1139	West Berkshire (Newbury Etc.)
	RD063	LAMBOURNE	1139	West Berkshire (Newbury Etc.)
	RD064	HUNGERFORD	1139	West Berkshire (Newbury Etc.)
	RD908	WEST BERKSHIRE (NEWBURY ETC.) NON-POLICE STATION	1139	West Berkshire (Newbury Etc.)
Hampshire	RD041	160 PROVST CO ALDERSHOT	1140	Aldershot/ Petersfield (North East Hampshire)
	RD042	RAF ODIHAM	1140	Aldershot/ Petersfield (North East Hampshire)

RD043	YATELEY	1140	Aldershot/ Petersfield (North East Hampshire)
RD046	ALDERSHOT	1140	Aldershot/ Petersfield (North East Hampshire)
RD047	ALTON (PETERSFIELD)	1140	Aldershot/ Petersfield (North East Hampshire)
RD048	PETERSFIELD (ALTON)	1140	Aldershot/ Petersfield (North East Hampshire)
RD050	RMP 31 SECTION SIB, ALDERSHOT	1140	Aldershot/ Petersfield (North East Hampshire)
RD051	RMP 160 PROVOST CO, BORDON	1140	Aldershot/ Petersfield (North East Hampshire)
RD909	ALDERSHOT/ PETERSFIELD (NORTH EAST HAMPSHIRE) NON-POLICE STATION	1140	Aldershot/ Petersfield (North East Hampshire)
RD052	TADLEY	1141	Andover/ Basingstoke/ Winchester (Nw Hants)
RD053	BASINGSTOKE	1141	Andover/ Basingstoke/ Winchester (Nw Hants)
RD054	BASING	1141	Andover/ Basingstoke/ Winchester (Nw Hants)
RD055	WHITCHURCH, HAMPSHIRE	1141	Andover/ Basingstoke/ Winchester (Nw Hants)
RD056	STOCKBRIDGE	1141	Andover/ Basingstoke/ Winchester (Nw Hants)
RD057	ANDOVER	1141	Andover/ Basingstoke/ Winchester (Nw Hants)
RD058	WINCHESTER	1141	Andover/ Basingstoke/ Winchester (Nw Hants)

RD914	ANDOVER/ BASINGSTOKE/ WINCHESTER (NW HANTS) NON-POLICE STATION	1141	Andover/ Basingstoke/ Winchester (Nw Hants)
RD067	RYDE	1142	Isle Of Wight
RD068	NEWPORT	1142	Isle Of Wight
RD910	ISLE OF WIGHT NON-POLICE STATION	1142	Isle Of Wight
RD040	SHIRLEY, HANTS	1145	South West Hants (Southampton)
RD071	WEST END	1145	South West Hants (Southampton)
RD072	TOTTON	1145	South West Hants (Southampton)
RD073	SOUTHAMPTON CENTRAL	1145	South West Hants (Southampton)
RD074	ROMSEY	1145	South West Hants (Southampton)
RD075	RINGWOOD	1145	South West Hants (Southampton)
RD076	PORTSWOOD	1145	South West Hants (Southampton)
RD077	NEW MILTON	1145	South West Hants (Southampton)
RD078	NETLEY	1145	South West Hants (Southampton)
RD079	LYNDHURST	1145	South West Hants (Southampton)
RD080	LYMINGTON	1145	South West Hants (Southampton)
RD081	FORDINGBRIDGE	1145	South West Hants (Southampton)
RD082	EASTLEIGH	1145	South West Hants (Southampton)
RD083	BITTERNE	1145	South West Hants (Southampton)
RD084	MOD MILITARY PORT, MARCHWOOD	1145	South West Hants (Southampton)
RD085	HYTHE (SOUTHAMPTON)	1145	South West Hants (Southampton)
RD911	SOUTH WEST HANTS (SOUTHAMPTON) NON-POLICE STATION	1145	South West Hants (Southampton)
RD087	HAVANT	1143	Portsmouth/ Waterlooville (South East Hampshire)

RD088	HM CUSTOMS PORTSMOUTH	1143	Portsmouth/ Waterlooville (South East Hampshire)
RD089	SOUTHSEA	1143	Portsmouth/ Waterlooville (South East Hampshire)
RD090	PORTSMOUTH CENTRAL	1143	Portsmouth/ Waterlooville (South East Hampshire)
RD091	FRATTON	1143	Portsmouth/ Waterlooville (South East Hampshire)
RD092	COSHAM, HAVANT	1143	Portsmouth/ Waterlooville (South East Hampshire)
RD093	ALSFORD	1143	Portsmouth/ Waterlooville (South East Hampshire)
RD094	PORTSMOUTH ID CENTRE	1143	Portsmouth/ Waterlooville (South East Hampshire)
RD095	WATERLOOVILLE	1143	Portsmouth/ Waterlooville (South East Hampshire)
RD096	MOD RN PORTSMOUTH	1143	Portsmouth/ Waterlooville (South East Hampshire)
RD097	RN PORTSMOUTH (OLD NAVY ACAD)	1143	Portsmouth/ Waterlooville (South East Hampshire)
RD912	PORTSMOUTH/ WATERLOOVILLE (SOUTH EAST HAMPSHIRE) NON-POLICE STATION	1143	Portsmouth/ Waterlooville (South East Hampshire)
RD098	HMS SULTAN	1144	Gosport & Fareham
RD099	PARKGATE	1144	Gosport & Fareham
RD100	GOSPORT	1144	Gosport & Fareham
RD101	FAREHAM	1144	Gosport & Fareham
RD913	GOSPORT & FAREHAM NON-POLICE STATION	1144	Gosport & Fareham

Regional Office: Leeds

CJS Area	Police Station ID	Police Station Name	PS Scheme ID	PS Scheme Name
Humberside	LS001	IMMINGHAM	1201	Grimsby & Cleethorpes
	LS002	GRIMSBY	1201	Grimsby & Cleethorpes
	LS003	CLEETHORPES	1201	Grimsby & Cleethorpes
	LS900	GRIMSBY & CLEETHORPES NON-POLICE STATION	1201	Grimsby & Cleethorpes
	LS004	SCUNTHORPE	1202	Scunthorpe
	LS005	BRIGG	1202	Scunthorpe
	LS006	BARTON UPON HUMBER	1202	Scunthorpe
	LS007	EPWORTH	1202	Scunthorpe
	LS901	SCUNTHORPE NON-POLICE STATION	1202	Scunthorpe
	LS008	BTP HULL RAILWAY STATION	1203	Hull
	LS009	WITHERNSEA	1203	Hull
	LS010	TOWER GRANGE	1203	Hull
	LS012	HULL CENTRAL	1203	Hull
	LS013	HESSLE	1203	Hull
	LS014	HM CUSTOMS KING GEORGE DOCKS	1203	Hull
	LS015	BRANSHOLME	1203	Hull
	LS022	PRIORY ROAD	1203	Hull
	LS902	HULL NON-POLICE STATION	1203	Hull
	LS016	BROUGH	1204	Beverley/ Bridlington
	LS017	HORNSEA	1204	Beverley/ Bridlington
	LS018	DRIFFIELD	1204	Beverley/ Bridlington
	LS019	BRIDLINGTON	1204	Beverley/ Bridlington
	LS020	POCKLINGTON	1204	Beverley/ Bridlington
	LS021	BEVERLEY	1204	Beverley/ Bridlington
	LS023	MARKET WEIGHTON	1204	Beverley/ Bridlington
	LS903	BEVERLEY/ BRIDLINGTON NON-POLICE STATION	1204	Beverley/ Bridlington
North Yorkshire	LS024	GOOLE	1205	Goole

LS904	GOOLE NON-POLICE STATION	1205	Goole
LS025	STOKESLEY	1206	Northallerton & Richmond
LS026	CATTERICK GARRISON	1206	Northallerton & Richmond
LS027	CATTERICK	1206	Northallerton & Richmond
LS028	THIRSK	1206	Northallerton & Richmond
LS029	LEYBURN	1206	Northallerton & Richmond
LS030	NORTHALLERTON	1206	Northallerton & Richmond
LS031	RICHMOND (N. YORKS)	1206	Northallerton & Richmond
LS032	RAF LEEMING	1206	Northallerton & Richmond
LS905	NORTHALLERTON & RICHMOND NON-POLICE STATION	1206	Northallerton & Richmond
LS033	RIPON	1207	Harrogate & Ripon
LS034	PATELEY BRIDGE	1207	Harrogate & Ripon
LS035	BOROUGHBRIDGE	1207	Harrogate & Ripon
LS036	KNARESBOROUGH	1207	Harrogate & Ripon
LS037	HARROGATE	1207	Harrogate & Ripon
LS906	HARROGATE & RIPON NON-POLICE STATION	1207	Harrogate & Ripon
LS038	SKIPTON	1208	Skipton, Settle & Ingleton
LS039	SETTLE	1208	Skipton, Settle & Ingleton
LS040	INGLETON	1208	Skipton, Settle & Ingleton
LS907	SKIPTON, SETTLE & INGLETON NON-POLICE STATION	1208	Skipton, Settle & Ingleton
LS041	SCARBOROUGH	1209	Scarborough/ Whitby
LS042	WHITBY	1209	Scarborough/ Whitby
LS908	SCARBOROUGH/ WHITBY NON-POLICE STATION	1209	Scarborough/ Whitby
LS043	PICKERING	1210	Malton & Rydale
LS044	MALTON	1210	Malton & Rydale
LS045	HELMSLEY	1210	Malton & Rydale
LS909	MALTON & RYEDALE NON-POLICE STATION	1210	Malton & Rydale
LS046	BTP YORK RAILWAY STATION	1211	York/Selby

	LS047	YORK	1211	York/Selby
	LS048	SELBY	1211	York/Selby
	LS910	YORK/SELBY NON-POLICE STATION	1211	York/Selby
South Yorkshire	LS049	WORSBOROUGH	1212	Barnsley
	LS050	WOMBWELL	1212	Barnsley
	LS051	PENISTONE	1212	Barnsley
	LS052	GRIMETHORPE	1212	Barnsley
	LS053	GOLDTHORPE	1212	Barnsley
	LS054	DODWORTH	1212	Barnsley
	LS055	CUDWORTH	1212	Barnsley
	LS056	BARNSLEY	1212	Barnsley
	LS911	BARNSLEY NON-POLICE STATION	1212	Barnsley
	LS057	EDLINGTON	1213	Doncaster
	LS058	STAINFORTH	1213	Doncaster
	LS059	ROSSINGTON	1213	Doncaster
	LS060	CONISBOROUGH	1213	Doncaster
	LS061	ASKERN	1213	Doncaster
	LS062	ADWICK	1213	Doncaster
	LS063	THORNE	1213	Doncaster
	LS064	MEXBOROUGH	1213	Doncaster
	LS065	DONCASTER	1213	Doncaster
	LS066	ARMTHORPE	1213	Doncaster
	LS912	DONCASTER NON-POLICE STATION	1213	Doncaster
	LS067	KIVETON PARK (MALTBY)	1214	Rotherham
	LS068	DINNINGTON (MALTBY)	1214	Rotherham
	LS069	WATH-UPON-DEARNE	1214	Rotherham
	LS070	ROTHERHAM MAIN STREET	1214	Rotherham
	LS072	RAWMARSH	1214	Rotherham
	LS073	MALTBY	1214	Rotherham
	LS913	ROTHERHAM NON-POLICE STATION	1214	Rotherham
	LS074	BTP SHEFFIELD RAILWAY STATION	1215	Sheffield
	LS075	SHEFFIELD BRIDGE STREET	1215	Sheffield
	LS076	DEEPCAR	1215	Sheffield
	LS077	WOODSEATS	1215	Sheffield
	LS078	HAMMERTON ROAD	1215	Sheffield
	LS079	HACKENTHORPE (NOT FOUND)	1215	Sheffield
	LS080	ECCLESFIELD	1215	Sheffield
	LS081	WEST BAR GREEN	1215	Sheffield
	LS082	ATTERCLIFFE	1215	Sheffield
	LS083	MOSS WAY	1215	Sheffield
	LS914	SHEFFIELD NON-POLICE STATION	1215	Sheffield

165

West Yorkshire	LS084	TODMORDEN	1216	Halifax
	LS085	SOWERBY BRIDGE	1216	Halifax
	LS086	HEBDEN BRIDGE	1216	Halifax
	LS087	HALIFAX	1216	Halifax
	LS088	BRIGHOUSE	1216	Halifax
	LS915	HALIFAX NON-POLICE STATION	1216	Halifax
	LS089	HUDDERSFIELD	1217	Huddersfield
	LS090	HOLMFIRTH	1217	Huddersfield
	LS916	HUDDERSFIELD NON-POLICE STATION	1217	Huddersfield
	LS091	HECKMONDWIKE	1218	Dewsbury
	LS092	DEWSBURY	1218	Dewsbury
	LS093	BATLEY	1218	Dewsbury
	LS917	DEWSBURY NON-POLICE STATION	1218	Dewsbury
	LS094	ECCLESHILL	1219	Bradford
	LS095	SHIPLEY	1219	Bradford
	LS096	BRADFORD NORTH/ TOLLER LANE	1219	Bradford
	LS097	ODSAL	1219	Bradford
	LS098	MANNINGHAM	1219	Bradford
	LS099	DUDLEY HILL	1219	Bradford
	LS100	BRADFORD SOUTH	1219	Bradford
	LS918	BRADFORD NON-POLICE STATION	1219	Bradford
	LS103	KEIGHLEY	1220	Keighley & Bingley
	LS104	ILKLEY	1220	Keighley & Bingley
	LS105	BINGLEY	1220	Keighley & Bingley
	LS106	PPOTTINGLEY [COTTINGLEY?] (NOT FOUND)	1220	Keighley & Bingley
	LS919	KEIGHLEY & BINGLEY NON-POLICE STATION	1220	Keighley & Bingley
	LS107	WETHERBY	1221	Leeds
	LS108	WEETWOOD	1221	Leeds
	LS109	PUDSEY	1221	Leeds
	LS110	OTLEY	1221	Leeds
	LS111	MORLEY	1221	Leeds
	LS112	MILLGARTH	1221	Leeds
	LS113	BTP LEEDS RAILWAY STATION	1221	Leeds
	LS114	HORSFORTH	1221	Leeds
	LS115	HOLBECK	1221	Leeds
	LS116	ROTHWELL	1221	Leeds
	LS117	HM CUSTOMS LEEDS	1221	Leeds
	LS118	KILLINGBECK (GIPTON)	1221	Leeds
	LS119	CHAPELTOWN	1221	Leeds

LS120	CENTRAL BRIDEWELL, LEEDS	1221	Leeds
LS920	LEEDS NON-POLICE STATION	1221	Leeds
LS121	SOUTH KIRKBY	1222	Pontefract & Castleford
LS122	PONTEFRACT	1222	Pontefract & Castleford
LS123	CASTLEFORD	1222	Pontefract & Castleford
LS124	KNOTTINGLEY	1222	Pontefract & Castleford
LS125	HEMSWORTH	1222	Pontefract & Castleford
LS921	PONTEFRACT & CASTLEFORD NON-POLICE STATION	1222	Pontefract & Castleford
LS126	WAKEFIELD	1223	Wakefield
LS127	OSSETT	1223	Wakefield
LS128	NORMANTON, WAKEFIELD	1223	Wakefield
LS922	WAKEFIELD NON-POLICE STATION	1223	Wakefield

Regional Office: London

CJS Area	Police Station ID	Police Station Name	PS Scheme ID	PS Scheme Name
London	LN001	BARKING	1301	Barking
	LN002	DAGENHAM	1301	Barking
	LN900	BARKING NON-POLICE STATION	1301	Barking
	LN003	BELVEDERE	1302	Bexley
	LN004	BEXLEYHEATH	1302	Bexley
	LN005	ERITH	1302	Bexley
	LN006	SIDCUP	1302	Bexley
	LN007	WELLING	1302	Bexley
	LN901	BEXLEY NON-POLICE STATION	1302	Bexley
	LN008	BISHOPSGATE	1303	Bishopsgate
	LN009	BTP LIVERPOOL STREET STATION	1303	Bishopsgate
	LN010	HM CUSTOMS FETTER LANE	1303	Bishopsgate
	LN011	HM CUSTOMS LOWER THAMES STREET	1303	Bishopsgate
	LN012	SNOWHILL	1303	Bishopsgate
	LN013	WOOD STREET	1303	Bishopsgate
	LN902	BISHOPSGATE NON-POLICE STATION	1303	Bishopsgate
	LN014	BTP WEMBLEY PARK	1304	Brent

LN015	CAREY WAY (WEMBLEY)	1304	Brent
LN016	HARLESDEN	1304	Brent
LN017	KILBURN	1304	Brent
LN018	WEMBLEY	1304	Brent
LN019	WEMBLEY (STADIUM)	1304	Brent
LN020	WILLESDEN GREEN	1304	Brent
LN903	BRENT NON-POLICE STATION	1304	Brent
LN021	BRENTFORD	1305	Brentford
LN022	CHISWICK	1305	Brentford
LN023	FELTHAM	1305	Brentford
LN024	HOUNSLOW	1305	Brentford
LN025	RMP HOUNSLOW CAVALRY	1305	Brentford
LN904	BRENTFORD NON-POLICE STATION	1305	Brentford
LN026	BECKENHAM	1306	Bromley
LN027	BIGGIN HILL	1306	Bromley
LN028	BROMLEY	1306	Bromley
LN029	CHISLEHURST	1306	Bromley
LN030	ORPINGTON	1306	Bromley
LN031	PENGE	1306	Bromley
LN032	RAF BIGGIN HILL	1306	Bromley
LN033	WEST WICKHAM	1306	Bromley
LN905	BROMLEY NON-POLICE STATION	1306	Bromley
LN034	BRIXTON	1307	Camberwell Green
LN035	BTP STOCKWELL STATION (LONDON)	1307	Camberwell Green
LN036	CARTER ST (CLOSED 1/12/93)	1307	Camberwell Green
LN037	CLAPHAM	1307	Camberwell Green
LN038	EAST DULWICH	1307	Camberwell Green
LN039	GYPSY HILL	1307	Camberwell Green
LN040	HERNEHILL (FAVERSHAM)	1307	Camberwell Green
LN041	SOUTHWARK	1307	Camberwell Green
LN042	STREATHAM	1307	Camberwell Green
LN067	VAUXHALL	1307	Camberwell Green
LN906	CAMBERWELL GREEN NON-POLICE STATION	1307	Camberwell Green
LN043	BELGRAVIA	1308	Central London
LN044	BTP BAKER STREET	1308	Central London
LN045	BTP PADDINGTON	1308	Central London
LN046	BTP TOTTENHAM COURT ROAD	1308	Central London
LN047	BTP VICTORIA STATION	1308	Central London
LN048	BTP WATERLOO STATION	1308	Central London

LN049	CHARING CROSS (EX BOW ST)	1308	Central London
LN050	CHELSEA	1308	Central London
LN051	EBURY BRIDGE, BTP (LONDON SOUTH HQ)	1308	Central London
LN052	GERALD ROAD	1308	Central London
LN053	HARROW ROAD	1308	Central London
LN054	HM CUSTOMS WATERLOO STATION	1308	Central London
LN056	HYDE PARK	1308	Central London
LN058	KENSINGTON	1308	Central London
LN059	MARYLEBONE	1308	Central London
LN060	NOTTING DALE	1308	Central London
LN061	NOTTING HILL	1308	Central London
LN062	PADDINGTON GREEN	1308	Central London
LN063	PALACE OF WESTMINSTER	1308	Central London
LN064	RMP ROCHESTER ROW, LONDON	1308	Central London
LN065	ST JOHNS WOOD	1308	Central London
LN066	TOTTENHAM COURT ROAD	1308	Central London
LN068	VINE STREET	1308	Central London
LN069	WEST END CENTRAL	1308	Central London
LN070	WHITEHALL	1308	Central London
LN075	BTP WHITFIELD STREET	1308	Central London
LN907	CENTRAL LONDON NON-POLICE STATION	1308	Central London
LN071	ALBANY STREET	1309	Clerkenwell/ Hampstead
LN072	BTP EUSTON	1309	Clerkenwell/ Hampstead
LN073	BTP KINGS CROSS	1309	Clerkenwell/ Hampstead
LN074	BTP ST PANCRAS	1309	Clerkenwell/ Hampstead
LN076	HAMPSTEAD	1309	Clerkenwell/ Hampstead
LN077	HM CUSTOMS WOBURN PLACE	1309	Clerkenwell/ Hampstead
LN078	HOLBORN	1309	Clerkenwell/ Hampstead
LN079	KENTISH TOWN	1309	Clerkenwell/ Hampstead
LN080	TAVISTOCK PLACE BTP (NOT FOUND)	1309	Clerkenwell/ Hampstead
LN081	WEST HAMPSTEAD	1309	Clerkenwell/ Hampstead
LN908	CLERKENWELL/ HAMPSTEAD NON-POLICE STATION	1309	Clerkenwell/ Hampstead
LN082	ADDINGTON	1310	Croydon

LN083	CROYDON	1310	Croydon
LN084	KENLEY	1310	Croydon
LN085	NORBURY	1310	Croydon
LN086	SOUTH NORWOOD	1310	Croydon
LN909	CROYDON NON-POLICE STATION	1310	Croydon
LN087	ACTON	1311	Ealing
LN088	EALING	1311	Ealing
LN089	SOUTHALL	1311	Ealing
LN910	EALING NON-POLICE STATION	1311	Ealing
LN090	EDMONTON	1312	Enfield
LN091	ENFIELD	1312	Enfield
LN092	PONDERS END	1312	Enfield
LN093	SOUTHGATE	1312	Enfield
LN094	WINCHMORE HILL	1312	Enfield
LN911	ENFIELD NON-POLICE STATION	1312	Enfield
LN095	BROCKLEY	1313	Greenwich/Woolwich
LN096	CATFORD	1313	Greenwich/Woolwich
LN097	DEPTFORD	1313	Greenwich/Woolwich
LN098	ELTHAM	1313	Greenwich/Woolwich
LN099	GREENWICH	1313	Greenwich/Woolwich
LN100	LEE ROAD	1313	Greenwich/Woolwich
LN101	LEWISHAM	1313	Greenwich/Woolwich
LN102	PLUMSTEAD	1313	Greenwich/Woolwich
LN103	SHOOTERS HILL	1313	Greenwich/Woolwich
LN104	SYDENHAM	1313	Greenwich/Woolwich
LN105	THAMESMEAD	1313	Greenwich/Woolwich
LN106	WESTCOMBE PARK	1313	Greenwich/Woolwich
LN107	WOOLWICH	1313	Greenwich/Woolwich
LN912	GREENWICH/WOOLWICH NON-POLICE STATION	1313	Greenwich/Woolwich
LN108	HIGHGATE	1314	Haringey
LN109	HORNSEY	1314	Haringey
LN110	MUSWELL HILL	1314	Haringey
LN111	ST ANN'S ROAD	1314	Haringey
LN112	TOTTENHAM	1314	Haringey

LN113	WOOD GREEN	1314	Haringey
LN913	HARINGEY NON-POLICE STATION	1314	Haringey
LN114	EDGWARE	1315	Harrow
LN115	HARROW	1315	Harrow
LN116	PINNER	1315	Harrow
LN914	HARROW NON-POLICE STATION	1315	Harrow
LN117	COLLIER ROW	1316	Havering
LN118	HAROLD HILL	1316	Havering
LN119	HORNCHURCH	1316	Havering
LN120	RAINHAM	1316	Havering
LN121	RAINHAM ID SUITE	1316	Havering
LN122	ROMFORD	1316	Havering
LN915	HAVERING NON-POLICE STATION	1316	Havering
LN123	BARNET	1318	Hendon/Barnet
LN124	COLINDALE	1318	Hendon/Barnet
LN125	FINCHLEY	1318	Hendon/Barnet
LN126	GOLDERS GREEN	1318	Hendon/Barnet
LN127	HENDON	1318	Hendon/Barnet
LN128	MILL HILL	1318	Hendon/Barnet
LN129	WEST HENDON	1318	Hendon/Barnet
LN130	WHETSTONE (BARNET)	1318	Hendon/Barnet
LN916	HENDON/BARNET NON-POLICE STATION	1318	Hendon/Barnet
LN131	BTP FINSBURY PARK	1319	Highbury Corner
LN132	CALEDONIAN ROAD	1319	Highbury Corner
LN133	HIGHBURY VALE	1319	Highbury Corner
LN134	HOLLOWAY	1319	Highbury Corner
LN135	ISLINGTON (TOLPUDDLE STREET)	1319	Highbury Corner
LN917	HIGHBURY CORNER NON-POLICE STATION	1319	Highbury Corner
LN136	COBHAM	1320	Kingston-Upon-Thames
LN137	EAST MOLESEY	1320	Kingston-Upon-Thames
LN138	ESHER	1320	Kingston-Upon-Thames
LN139	KINGSTON	1320	Kingston-Upon-Thames
LN140	NEW MALDEN	1320	Kingston-Upon-Thames
LN141	SURBITON	1320	Kingston-Upon-Thames
LN918	KINGSTON-UPON-THAMES NON-POLICE STATION	1320	Kingston-Upon-Thames
LN142	EAST HAM	1321	Newham
LN143	FOREST GATE	1321	Newham

171

LN144	NORTH WOOLWICH	1321	Newham
LN145	PLAISTOW	1321	Newham
LN146	THE CITY AIRPORT	1321	Newham
LN147	STRATFORD POLICE STATION (WEST HAM)	1321	Newham
LN919	NEWHAM NON-POLICE STATION	1321	Newham
LN148	DALSTON, LONDON	1322	Old Street
LN149	HACKNEY	1322	Old Street
LN150	SHOREDITCH (CITY ROAD)	1322	Old Street
LN151	STOKE NEWINGTON	1322	Old Street
LN920	OLD STREET NON-POLICE STATION	1322	Old Street
LN152	BARKINGSIDE	1323	Redbridge
LN153	CHADWELL HEATH	1323	Redbridge
LN154	ILFORD	1323	Redbridge
LN155	WANSTEAD	1323	Redbridge
LN156	WOODFORD	1323	Redbridge
LN921	REDBRIDGE NON-POLICE STATION	1323	Redbridge
LN157	BARNES	1324	Richmond-Upon-Thames
LN158	HAM	1324	Richmond-Upon-Thames
LN159	HAMPTON	1324	Richmond-Upon-Thames
LN160	RICHMOND	1324	Richmond-Upon-Thames
LN161	TEDDINGTON	1324	Richmond-Upon-Thames
LN162	TWICKENHAM	1324	Richmond-Upon-Thames
LN922	RICHMOND-UPON-THAMES NON-POLICE STATION	1324	Richmond-Upon-Thames
LN163	BATTERSEA	1325	South London
LN164	EARLSFIELD	1325	South London
LN165	LAVENDER HILL	1325	South London
LN167	ROEHAMPTON	1325	South London
LN168	TOOTING	1325	South London
LN169	WANDSWORTH	1325	South London
LN923	SOUTH LONDON NON-POLICE STATION	1325	South London
LN170	SUTTON	1326	Sutton
LN171	WALLINGTON	1326	Sutton
LN172	WORCESTER PARK	1326	Sutton
LN924	SUTTON NON-POLICE STATION	1326	Sutton
LN173	ARBOUR SQUARE	1327	Thames
LN174	BETHNAL GREEN	1327	Thames
LN175	BOW	1327	Thames

LN176	BRICK LANE	1327	Thames
LN177	ISLE OF DOGS	1327	Thames
LN178	LEMAN STREET	1327	Thames
LN179	LIMEHOUSE	1327	Thames
LN180	POPLAR	1327	Thames
LN925	THAMES NON-POLICE STATION	1327	Thames
LN181	CAMBERWELL	1328	Tower Bridge
LN182	HM CUSTOMS DORSET HOUSE (LONDON)	1328	Tower Bridge
LN183	PECKHAM	1328	Tower Bridge
LN184	ROTHERHITHE	1328	Tower Bridge
LN185	TOWER BRIDGE	1328	Tower Bridge
LN186	WALWORTH	1328	Tower Bridge
LN926	TOWER BRIDGE NON-POLICE STATION	1328	Tower Bridge
LN187	HAYES	1329	Uxbridge
LN188	NORTHWOOD (RUISLIP)	1329	Uxbridge
LN189	RAF NORTHOLT	1329	Uxbridge
LN190	RAF UXBRIDGE	1329	Uxbridge
LN191	RUISLIP	1329	Uxbridge
LN192	UXBRIDGE	1329	Uxbridge
LN193	WEST DRAYTON	1329	Uxbridge
LN205	HEATHROW AIRPORT, MET	1329	Uxbridge
LN927	UXBRIDGE NON-POLICE STATION	1329	Uxbridge
LN194	CHINGFORD	1330	Waltham Forest
LN195	LEYTON	1330	Waltham Forest
LN196	LEYTONSTONE	1330	Waltham Forest
LN197	WALTHAMSTOW	1330	Waltham Forest
LN928	WALTHAM FOREST NON-POLICE STATION	1330	Waltham Forest
LN198	BTP HAMMERSMITH RAIL STATION	1331	West London
LN199	FULHAM	1331	West London
LN200	HAMMERSMITH	1331	West London
LN201	SHEPHERDS BUSH	1331	West London
LN929	WEST LONDON NON-POLICE STATION	1331	West London
LN202	MITCHAM	1332	Wimbledon
LN203	WIMBLEDON	1332	Wimbledon
LN930	WIMBLEDON NON-POLICE STATION	1332	Wimbledon
LN204	BTP HEATHROW	1317	Heathrow
LN206	HM CUSTOMS HEATHROW TERMS 1-4	1317	Heathrow
LN931	HEATHROW NON-POLICE STATION	1317	Heathrow

APPENDIX 7

CDS court codes

[LSC, October 2007]

1. Avon & Somerset
2. Bedfordshire
3. Cambridgeshire
4. Cheshire
5. Cleveland
6. Cumbria
7. Derbyshire
8. Devon & Cornwall
9. Dorset
10. Durham
11. Dyfed-Powys
12. Essex
13. Gloucestershire
14. Greater Manchester
15. Gwent
16. Hampshire
17. Hertfordshire
18. Humberside
19. Kent
20. Lancashire
21. Leicestershire
22. Lincolnshire
23. London
24. Merseyside
25. Norfolk
26. Northampton
27. Northumbria
28. North Wales
29. North Yorkshire
30. Nottinghamshire
31. South Wales
32. South Yorkshire
33. Staffordshire
34. Suffolk
35. Surrey
36. Sussex
37. Thames Valley
38. West Mercia
39. West Midlands
40. Warwickshire
41. West Yorkshire
42. Wiltshire

Court PSD No	Court Name
Avon & Somerset	
C1013	BRISTOL
C1021	NORTH AVON
C1022	BATH & WANSDYKE
C1023	NORTH SOMERSET (WOODSPRING)
C1023A	LONG ASHTON
C1023B	WESTON-SUPER-MARE
C2706	SEDGEMOOR
C2709	TAUNTON & WEST SOMERSET
C2711	WEST SOMERSET (MINEHEAD)
C2714	SOUTH SOMERSET

C2715	MENDIP PSA
C2715B	WELLS
C2715D	FROME
C2718	DIDCOT AND WANTAGE
C2719A	EAST OXFORDSHIRE

Bedfordshire

C1050	AMPTHILL
C1051	BEDFORD
C1052	BIGGLESWADE
C1053	DUNSTABLE
C1054	LEIGHTON BUZZARD
C1055	LUTON & SOUTH BEDFORDSHIRE

Cambridgeshire

C1162	PETERBOROUGH
C1165	CAMBRIDGE
C1166	EAST CAMBS
C1166A	ELY
C1166B	NEWMARKET (CAMBS)
C1167A	NORTH WITCHFORD
C1167B	WISBECH
C1168	HUNTINGDON DIVISION
C1168A	HUNTINGDON
C1168B	TOSELAND
C5166	EAST CAMBRIDGESHIRE (ELY)

Cheshire

C1173	CHESTER
C1176A	ELLESMERE PORT
C1177A	RUNCORN
C1177B	WIDNES
C1178A	MACCLESFIELD
C1179A	NORTHWICH
C1180A	WARRINGTON (WINMARLEIGH ST)
C1180B	STOCKTON HEATH
C1180C	WARRINGTON (ARPLEY ST)
C1187	SOUTH CHESHIRE
C1187A	CONGLETON
C1187B	CREWE AND NANTWICH
C1188	CHESTER, ELLESMERE PORT & NESTON

Cleveland

C1247	HARTLEPOOL
C1248	LANGBAURGH EAST
C1249	TEESSIDE

Cumbria

C1322	CARLISLE AND DISTRICT
C1323	SOUTH LAKELAND PSA (KENDAL/SOUTH CUMBRIA)

C1324	EDEN PSA (PENRITH)
C1325	WEST ALLERDALE AND KESWICK
C1364	CARLISLE
C1369	KESWICK
C1372	NORTH LONSDALE
C1375	WHITEHAVEN
C1376	WIGTON
C1379	WEST ALLERDALE (WORKINGTON)
C1380	BARROW WITH BOOTLE
C1381	SOUTH LAKES
C1382	KENDAL AND LONSDALE
C1384A	PENRITH (EDEN PSA)
C1384B	ALSTON (COURT CLOSED)
C1398	[FURNESS & DISTRICT PSD]
C1398A	BARROW WITH BOOTLE (FURNESS)
C1398B	NORTH LONSDALE

Derbyshire

C1418	CHESTERFIELD (WEST BARS)
C1418B	CHESTERFIELD (BRIMIMINGTON ROAD)
C1421	GLOSSOP
C1422	HIGH PEAK (BUXTON)
C1427	[DERBY & SOUTH DERBYSHIRE PSD]
C1427A	DERBY (DERWENT STREET)
C1427B	SWADLINCOTE
C1427C	DERBY (BOLD LANE)
C1428A	ASHBOURNE
C1428B	BAKEWELL
C1428C	MATLOCK
C1429A	ILKESTON
C1429B	ALFRETON
C1430	HIGH PEAK PSA
C1431	SOUTHERN DERBYSHIRE PSA
C1432	CHESTERFIELD (TAPTON LANE)

Devon & Cornwall

C1263	EAST PENWITH (CAMBORNE)
C1264	EAST POWDER
C1268	ISLES OF SCILLY
C1272	PENWITH (PENZANCE)
C1274	PYDAR (NEWQUAY)
C1279	BODMIN
C1280	SOUTHEAST CORNWALL
C1282	TRURO & SOUTH POWDER
C1283	FALMOUTH AND KERRIER
C1284	DUNHEVED AND STRATTON
C1288	WEST CORNWALL PSA
C1289	EAST CORNWALL PSA
C1290	PLYMOUTH DISTRICT PSA
C1291	NORTH DEVON PSA
C1292	CENTRAL DEVON PSA

C1293	SOUTH DEVON PSA
C1477	BIDEFORD & GREAT TORRINGTON
C1478	CULLOMPTON
C1480	EXMOUTH
C1484	PLYMOUTH
C1488	TEIGNBRIDGE (NEWTON ABBOT)
C1489	TIVERTON
C1490	TORBAY (TORQUAY)
C1493A	AXMINSTER
C1493B	HONITON
C1494	BARNSTAPLE & SOUTH MOLTON PSD]
C1494A	BARNSTAPLE
C1494B	SOUTH MOLTON
C1495A	OKEHAMPTON
C1495B	TAVISTOCK
C1496A	KINGSBRIDGE
C1496B	IVYBRIDGE
C1496C	SOUTH HAMS (TOTNES)
C1497	EXETER & WONFORD

Dorset

C1501	BOURNEMOUTH
C1502	BRIDPORT
C1503	CHRISTCHURCH
C1504	DORCHESTER
C1505	POOLE
C1507	[NORTH DORSET PSD]
C1507A	SHERBOURNE
C1507B	GILLINGHAM
C1509	WAREHAM
C1510	WEYMOUTH & PORTLAND
C1511	WIMBORNE
C1512	BLANDFORD & STURMINSTER
C1513	SHAFTESBURY
C1514	[BOURNEMOUTH & CHRISTCHURCH]
C1514A	BOURNEMOUTH (B&C DIV)
C1514B	CHRISTCHURCH (B&C DIV)
C1515A	BLANDFORD FORUM (CENTRAL DORSET)
C1515B	GILLINGHAM (CENTRAL DORSET)
C1515C	WAREHAM (DORSET)
C1515D	WIMBORNE (CENTRAL DORSET)
C1516A	BRIDPORT (WEST DORSET)
C1516B	DORCHESTER (WEST DORSET)
C1516C	SHERBORNE (WEST DORSET)
C1522	EAST DORSET PSA
C1523	WEST DORSET PSA

Durham

C1576	CHESTER-LE-STREET
C1577	DARLINGTON
C1578	DERWENTSIDE (CONSETT)

C1579	DURHAM
C1580	EASINGTON (PETERLEE)
C1581	SEDGEFIELD (NEWTON AYCLIFFE)
C1582A	BISHOP AUCKLAND
C1582B	BARNARD CASTLE
C1583	NORTH DURHAM PSA
C1584	SOUTH DURHAM PSA
C1595B	RYE

Dyfed-Powys

C3122	LLANELLI
C3134	CEREDIGION GANOL (PSD DELETED)
C3135	CEREDIGION
C3135A	ABERYSTWYTH
C3135B	CARDIGAN
C3136	DE CEREDIGION (PSD DELETED)
C3138	CARMARTHEN
C3139	NORTH PEMBROKESHIRE
C3140	DINEFWR
C3141	GOGLEDD PRESELI (PSD DELETED)
C3142	SOUTH PEMBROKESHIRE
C3142B	TENBY MAGISTRATES COURT
C3330	MACHYNLLETH (PSD DELETED)
C3340	YSTRADGYNLAIS (PSD DELETED)
C3346	WELSHPOOL
C3350	DE BRYCHEINIOG
C3350A	BRECON
C3350B	YSTRADGYNLAIS
C3351	RADNORSHIRE & NORTH BRECKNOCK
C3352	DE MALDWYN
C3352B	WELSHPOOL
C3352C	LLANDRINDOD WELLS

Essex

C1610	BASILDON (MID-SOUTH ESSEX)
C1611	BRENTWOOD
C1612	CHELMSFORD/WITHAM (MID-NORTH)
C1613	COLCHESTER/HARWICH (NORTHEAST ESSEX)
C1613B	COLCHESTER (TOWN HALL)
C1615	DUNMOW
C1616	EPPING
C1617	[BRAINTREE]
C1619	HARLOW/EPPING (NORTHWEST ESSEX)
C1620	HARWICH
C1623	SAFFRON WALDON
C1625	TENDRING
C1626	GRAYS (SOUTHWEST ESSEX)
C1629	SOUTHEND ON SEA (SOUTHEAST ESSEX)
C1630	MALDON & WITHAM
C1631	BRAINTREE
C1632	DUNMOW AND SAFFRON WALDON

C5610	BASILDON
C5629	ROCHFORD & SOUTHEND-ON-SEA

Gloucestershire

C1672	CHELTENHAM
C1689	CIRENCESTER
C1692	GLOUCESTER
C1693	SOUTH GLOUCESTERSHIRE
C1694	NORTH COTSWOLD
C1695	FOREST OF DEAN (COLEFORD)
C1696	[NORTH GLOUCESTERSHIRE PSD]
C1696A	CHELTENHAM (NORTH GLOS)
C1696B	TEWKESBURY (NORTH GLOS)
C1696C	NORTH COTSWOLD

Greater Manchester

C1731	BOLTON
C1732	BURY
C1733	MANCHESTER
C1734	OLDHAM
C1735	MIDDLETON
C1736	ROCHDALE
C1738	SALFORD
C1739	STOCKPORT
C1742	TRAFFORD (SALE)
C1743	LEIGH
C1746	WIGAN
C1747	[CITY OF SALFORD PSD]
C1747A	ECCLES (CITY OF SALFORD)
C1747B	SALFORD (CITY OF SALFORD)
C1748	[TAMESIDE PSD]
C1748A	ASHTON-UNDER-LYNE (TAMESIDE)
C1748B	SOUTH THAMESIDE
C1749	WIGAN AND LEIGH (ACTIVE 01/01/03 -) 1/0

Gwent

C3205	NEWPORT
C3208	[EAST GWENT PSD]
C3208A	ABERGAVENNY
C3208B	CWMBRAN
C3208C	CHEPSTOW
C3208D	MONMOUTH
C3208E	PONTYPOOL
C3208F	USK
C3209	NORTHWEST GWENT
C3210	GWENT

Hampshire

C1775	SOUTHAMPTON
C1775A	SOUTHAMPTON
C1775B	EASTLEIGH (SOUTHAMPTON)
C1778	ALTON & PETERSFIELD
C1779	NEW FOREST (LYNDHURST)
C1779A	HYTHE
C1779B	LYMINGTON
C1779C	RINGWOOD
C1779E	NEW FOREST
C1780	[NORTHEAST HAMPSHIRE PSD]
C1780A	ALTON
C1780B	PETERSFIELD
C1780C	ALDERSHOT (NORTHEAST HANTS)
C1781	[NORTHWEST HAMPSHIRE PSD]
C1781A	ANDOVER
C1781B	BASINGSTOKE
C1781C	WINCHESTER
C1782	PORTSMOUTH (SOUTHEAST HAMPSHIRE)
C1783	FAREHAM (SOUTH HAMPSHIRE)
C1783A	DROXFORD
C1945	ISLE OF WIGHT

Hertfordshire

C1875	BISHOP'S STORTFORD
C1877	CHESHUNT (EAST HERTFORDSHIRE)
C1878	DACORUM
C1883	MID HERTFORDSHIRE (ST ALBANS)
C1886	WATFORD
C1888	EAST HERTFORDSHIRE PSA
C1888A	CHESHUNT (EAST HERTFORDSHIRE)
C1888B	HERTFORD (EAST HERTFORDSHIRE)
C1889	NORTH HERTFORDSHIRE
C1890	MID-HERTFORDSHIRE
C1892	CENTRAL HERTFORDSHIRE
C1893	WEST HERTFORDSHIRE (WATFORD/DACORUM)

Humberside

C1901A	BROUGH
C1901B	HOWDEN (COURT CLOSED)
C1902A	SOUTH AND MIDDLE HOLDERNESS (WITHERNSEA)
C1902B	SPROATLEY
C1903A	NORTH LINCOLNSHIRE (SCUNTHORPE)
C1904	[DICKERING & NORTH HOLDERN PSD]
C1904A	BRIDLINGTON
C1904B	HORNSEA (COURT CLOSED)
C1905	[BAINTON, WILTON, HOLME BEACON PSD]
C1905A	DRIFFIELD
C1925	BEVERLEY
C1928	GOOLE AND HOWDENSHIRE

C1928A	EPWORTH
C1928B	GOOLE
C1933	KINGSTON UPON HULL
C1940	GRIMSBY & CLEETHORPES
C1941	BRIDLINGTON
C1942	BEVERLEY & THE WOLDS
C1943	HULL & HOLDERNESS (KINGSTON UPON HULL)

Kent

C1952	ASHFORD AND TENTERDEN (PSD DELETED)
C1953	CANTERBURY AND ST AUGUSTINE
C1954	DARTFORD
C1955	DOVER AND EAST KENT (PSD DELETED)
C1957	CHANNEL PSA
C1957A	DOVER (CHANNEL)
C1957B	FOLKESTONE (CHANNEL)
C1957C	ASHFORD (CHANNEL)
C1958	GRAVESHAM
C1959	MID KENT (MAIDSTONE)
C1961	MEDWAY (CHATHAM)
C1963	WEST KENT
C1963A	SEVENOAKS (WEST KENT)
C1965A	WEST MALLING
C1965B	TONBRIDGE
C1966A	TUNBRIDGE WELLS
C1967	FAVERSHAM & SITTINGBOURNE
C1968	[THANET PSD]
C1968A	MARGATE (THANET)
C1968B	RAMSGATE (THANET)
C1969	DARTFORD & GRAVESHAM (GRAVESEND)

Lancashire

C1992	FLYDE COAST PSA (BLACKPOOL/WYRE)
C1995	BLACKBURN
C1996	BLACKPOOL
C1997	BURNLEY
C1998	CHORLEY
C2000	DARWEN
C2001	LYTHAM
C2002	LANCASTER
C2003	ORMSKIRK
C2005	PRESTON
C2006	ROSSENDALE
C2007	SOUTH RIBBLE (LEYLAND)
C2009A	FLEETWOOD
C2010	HYNDBURN
C2011A	BURNLEY (BURNLEY & PENDLE)
C2011B	REEDLEY (BURNLEY & PENDLE)
C2012	[BLACKBURN/DARWEN/RIBBLE VALLEY]
C2012A	BLACKBURN (BLACKBURN/DARWEN/RIBBLE VALLEY)
C2012B	DARWEN (BLACKBURN/DARWEN/RIBBLE VALLEY)

C2012C	RIBBLE VALLEY (BLACKBURN/DARWEN/RIBBLE VALLEY)
C2014	BURNLEY, PENDLE AND ROSSENDALE

Leicestershire

C2045	MELTON, BELVOIR AND RUTLAND
C2046	RUTLAND (PSD DELETED)
C2047	ASHBY-DE-LA-ZOUCH (COALVILLE)
C2048A	LEICESTER
C2049	LOUGHBOROUGH
C2050A	HINCKLEY
C2051	[MARKET HARBOROUGH & LUTTERWORTH]
C2051A	LUTTERWORTH
C2051B	MARKET HARBOROUGH

Lincolnshire

C2056	CAISTOR
C2073	BOSTON
C2074	BOURNE & STAMFORD
C2075	GAINSBOROUGH
C2076	[ELLOES DIV]
C2076A	ELLOES (SPALDING)
C2076B	ELLOES (LONG SUTTON)
C2077	GRANTHAM
C2078A	HORNCASTLE
C2078B	LOUTH
C2079	LINCOLN DISTRICT
C2080	SLEAFORD
C2081	MARKET RASEN
C2082	SKEGNESS

London

C2631	CITY OF LONDON (JUSTICE ROOMS)
C2641	BOW STREET
C2642	CLERKENWELL (COURT CLOSED)
C2643	GREENWICH
C2643B	BELMARSH (GREENWICH PSA)
C2644	MARLBOROUGH STREET
C2646	MARYLEBONE
C2649	SOUTHWESTERN
C2650	THAMES
C2651	TOWER BRIDGE
C2653	WOOLWICH
C2656	CAMBERWELL GREEN
C2657	WALTON STREET
C2658	WEST LONDON MAGISTRATES' COURT
C2660	HORSEFERRY ROAD
C2663	HIGHBURY CORNER (EAST CENTRAL)
C2721	STRATFORD
C2722	STRATFORD YOUTH
C2723	ACTON

C2725	BARNET
C2727	BROMLEY
C2728	BEXLEY
C2732	CROYDON
C2733	SUTTON
C2734	EALING
C2740	HAMPSTEAD
C2741	HENDON
C2742	HIGHGATE (HARINGEY)
C2757	TOTTENHAM (ENFIELD)
C2760	HARROW
C2762	BRENT (WILLESDEN)
C2763	WIMBLEDON
C2766	HILLINGDON
C2768	RICHMOND (SURREY)
C2769	[HOUNSLOW PSD] BRENTFORD
C2769A	BRENTFORD
C2769B	FELTHAM
C2812	KINGSTON
C2813	WALTHAM FOREST
C2814	BARKING
C2815	REDBRIDGE
C6013	INNER LONDON JUVENILE COURTS
C6013A	BALHAM HIGH ROAD YOUTH
C6013B	SOUTHWARK YOUTH
C6013C	GREENWICH & LEWISHAM YOUTH
C6643	GREENWICH & LEWISHAM
C6649	LAMBETH & WANDSWORTH YOUTH COURTS
C6650	NORTH AND NORTHEAST LONDON YOUTH COURTS
C6656	GREENWICH, LEWISHAM & SOUTHWARK YOUTH
C6658	WEST LONDON YOUTH COURT
C6686	BALHAM HIGH ROAD
C6693	SOUTHWARK
C6815	REDBRIDGE YOUTH
C1837	HAVERING

Merseyside

C2266A	HUYTON
C2266B	KIRKBY
C2267	LIVERPOOL
C2268	ST HELENS
C2269A	SOUTHPORT AND CROSBY
C2270	SOUTH SEFTON (BOOTLE)
C2271	WIRRAL
C9000	COMMUNITY JUSTICE CENTRE - MERSEYSIDE

Norfolk

C1442A	SWAFFHAM & DEREHAM
C1442B	THETFORD
C1443	GREAT YARMOUTH

C1444A	NORTH WALSHAM
C1444B	CROMER
C1445	NORWICH
C1446	[SOUTH NORFOLK PSD]
C1446A	DISS
C1447	[WEST NORFOLK PSD]
C1447B	FAKENHAM
C1447C	HUNSTANTON
C1447D	KINGS LYNN

Northampton

C2321	CORBY
C2322	DAVENTRY
C2323	KETTERING
C2325	NORTHAMPTON
C2327	TOWCESTER
C2328	WELLINGBOROUGH

Northumbria

C2346	TYNEDALE
C2347	ALNWICK
C2348	BERWICK-ON-TWEED
C2349	SOUTHEAST NORTHUMBERLAND
C2850	GATESHEAD
C2850A	GATESHEAD
C2850B	BLAYDON
C2851	[NEWCASTLE UPON TYNE PSD]
C2851A	MARKET STREET
C2851B	GOSFORTH
C2852	[NORTH TYNESIDE PSD]
C2852A	NORTH SHIELDS
C2852C	WHITLEY BAY
C2853	[SOUTH TYNESIDE PSD]
C2853A	SOUTH SHIELDS
C2853B	HEBBURN
C2854A	HOUGHTON-LE-SPRING
C2854B	WASHINGTON
C2855	SUNDERLAND
C6851	GOSFORTH YOUTH (NEWCASTLE UPON TYNE)

North Wales

C3222	BANGOR
C3229	NORTH ANGLESEY
C3231	PWLLHELI
C3232	[SOUTH ANGLESEY PSD]
C3232A	BEAUMARIS
C3232B	MENAI BRIDGE
C3232C	LLANGEFNI
C3234	CAERNARFON & GWYRFAI
C3236	DWYFOR

C3237	[ABERCONWY PSD]
C3237A	CONWY AND LLANDUDNO
C3238	YNYS MON/ANGLESEY
C3238A	LLANGEFNI
C3239	DOLGELLAU
C3244	GWYNEDD PSA
C3051A	LLANGOLLEN
C3051C	CORWEN
C3052A	COLWYN (CLWYD)
C3052B	ABERGELE
C3053	DYFFRYN CLWYD (PSD DELETED)
C3054	FLINT
C3055	HAWARDEN
C3056	MOLD
C3057	RHUDDLAN (PRESTATYN) (PSD DELETED)
C3058	WREXHAM MAELOR
C3059	FLINTSHIRE
C3061	DENBIGHSHIRE
C3061A	LLANDUDNO
C3061B	PRESTATYN
C3061C	DENBIGH
C3062	CONWY
C7055	HAWARDEN YOUTH

North Yorkshire

C2527	HARROGATE (PSD)
C2534	RIPON LIBERTY
C2536	SCARBOROUGH
C2537	SELBY
C2538	[SKIPTON PSD]
C2538A	SKIPTON
C2538B	INGLETON
C2538C	SETTLE
C2540	WHITBY STRAND
C2541	YORK
C2543A	THIRSK
C2543B	BEDALE
C2543C	NORTHALLERTON
C2543D	STOKESLEY
C2544	EASINGWOLD
C2545A	RICHMOND (NORTH YORKS)
C2545B	LEYBURN
C2546A	MALTON
C2546B	PICKERING
C1905B	POCKLINGTON
C1905C	MARKET WEIGHTON

Nottinghamshire

C2553	EAST RETFORD
C2560	WORKSOP

C2566	MANSFIELD
C2567	NEWARK & SOUTHWELL
C2568	NOTTINGHAM
C2569	WORKSOP & RETFORD PSA

South Wales

C3201	[BEDWELLTY PSD]
C3201A	TREDEGAR
C3201B	ABERTILLERY
C3201C	EBBW VALE
C3201D	BLACKWOOD
C3262	CYNON VALLEY
C3263	LWR RHYMNEY VALLEY (CAERPHILLY)
C3264	MERTHYR TYDFIL
C3265	MISKIN
C3266	NEWCASTLE AND OGMORE
C3267	UPPER RHYMNEY VALLEY
C3348	CARDIFF
C3349	VALE OF GLAMORGAN
C3358	[LLIW VALLEY]
C3359	NEATH PORT TALBOT PSA
C3359A	NEATH
C3359B	PORT TALBOT
C3360	[SWANSEA PSD]
C3360A	SWANSEA
C3360B	LLIW VALLEY

South Yorkshire

C2770	BARNSLEY
C2771	[DONCASTER PSD]
C2771A	DONCASTER
C2771B	THORNE
C2772	ROTHERHAM
C2773	SHEFFIELD

Staffordshire

C2780	BURTON-UPON-TRENT
C2781	CANNOCK
C2784	LEEK
C2785	LICHFIELD
C2786	NEWCASTLE-UNDER-LYME
C2788	RUGELEY
C2790	STAFFORD
C2791	NORTH STAFFORDSHIRE (STOKE-ON-TRENT)
C2793	TAMWORTH
C2795	MID-STAFFORDSHIRE DIVISION
C2795A	STAFFORD
C2795D	UTTOXETER
C2796	STAFF. MOORLANDS DIVISION PSD
C2796A	LEEK

C2796B	CHEADLE
C2797	[N'CASTLE/LYME & P'HILL PSD]
C2797A	NEWCASTLE UNDER LYME
C2797B	PIREHILL NORTH
C2797C	KIDSGROVE
C2798	NORTH STAFFORDSHIRE MAGISTRATES' COURT
C2799	CENTRAL & SOUTHWEST STAFFORDSHIRE PSA
C2859	CANNOCK & SEISDON MAGISTRATES' COURT
C2860	SE STAFFORDSHIRE (LICHFIELD & TAMWORTH)

Suffolk

C2821	MILDENHALL
C2823	NEWMARKET (SUFF)
C2825	HAVERHILL (PSD DELETED)
C2828	SUDBURY (PSD DELETED)
C2830	IPSWICH
C2832	ST EDMUNDSBURY (PSD DELETED)
C2833	STOWMARKET (PSD DELETED)
C2861A	FELIXSTOWE (DEBEN)
C2862	[NORTHWEST SUFFOLK PSD]
C2862A	MILDENHALL (NW SUFFOLK)
C2862B	NEWMARKET (NW SUFFOLK)
C2863	NORTHEAST SUFFOLK MAGISTRATES' COURT
C2863A	LOWESTOFT
C2863C	SAXMUNDHAM
C2864	HAVERHILL AND SUDBURY
C2865	ST EDMUNDSBURY & STOWMARKET
C2866	SOUTHEAST SUFFOLK
C2867	WEST SUFFOLK
C6816	BECCLES
C6831	SAXMUNDHAM

Surrey

C2845	NORTH & EAST SURREY DIVISION
C2845A	EPSOM
C2845B	STAINES & SUNBURY
C2846	NORTHWEST SURREY DIVISION
C2846A	CHERTSEY
C2846B	WOKING
C2846C	CAMBERLEY
C2847	SOUTHEAST SURREY DIVISION
C2847A	REIGATE
C2847B	DORKING
C2847C	GODSTONE
C2848	SOUTHWEST SURREY DIVISION
C2848A	FARNHAM

C2848B	GUILDFORD
C2849	NORTH & EAST SURREY DIVISION
C2856	SOUTHEAST SURREY
C2856A	SOUTHEAST SURREY (REDHILL)

Sussex

C1597	BRIGHTON
C1598	[CROWBOROUGH PSD]
C1598A	CROWBOROUGH
C1598B	CROWBOROUGH (MARK CROSS)
C1602	HOVE
C1603	LEWES
C1604A	BRIGHTON (BRIGHTON & HOVE)
C1604B	HOVE (BRIGHTON & HOVE)
C1605A	EASTBOURNE (EASTBOURNE & HAILSHAM)
C1605B	HAILSHAM (EASTBOURNE & HAILSHAM)
C1606A	BATTLE & RYE
C1606B	BEXHILL
C1606C	HASTINGS (HASTINGS & ROTHER)
C1607A	CROWBOROUGH (LEWES & CROWBOROUGH)
C1607B	LEWES (LEWES & CROWBOROUGH)
C2927	ARUNDEL
C2929	CRAWLEY
C2930	HORSHAM
C2932	[MID SUSSEX PSD]
C2932A	HAYWARDS HEATH
C2932B	EAST GRINSTEAD
C2934	STEYNING
C2935	WORTHING
C2936	CHICHESTER AND DISTRICT
C2937	WORTHING AND DISTRICT
C2947	SUSSEX (NORTH) (CRAWLEY/HORSHAM/MID-SUSSEX)
C2948	SUSSEX (EASTERN) PSA (EASTBOURNE)
C2949	SUSSEX (WESTERN) (WORTHING)
C2950	SUSSEX (CENTRAL) PSA (BRIGHTON)

Thames Valley

C1066	BRACKNELL (FOREST)
C1068	MAIDENHEAD
C1072	EAST BERKSHIRE PSA (SLOUGH)
C1074	WINDSOR
C1075	NEWBURY (WEST BERKS)
C1076	READING (READING AND SONNING)
C1124	MILTON KEYNES
C1125	AYLESBURY
C1129	[CENTRAL BUCKINGHAMSHIRE PSD]
C1129A	AYLESBURY (CENTRAL BUCKS)
C1129B	BUCKINGHAM (CENTRAL BUCKS)
C1129C	AMERSHAM (CENTRAL BUCKS)
C1130A	BEACONSFIELD (WYCOMBE & BEACONSFIELD)

C1130B	WYCOMBE (WYCOMBE & BEACONSFIELD)
C2671	BICESTER
C2681	ABINGDON
C2701	WOODSTOCK
C2702	BANBURY/CHIPPING NORTON

West Mercia

C1840	[BROMSGROVE & REDDITCH PSD]
C1840A	BROMSGROVE (COURT CLOSED)
C1840B	REDDITCH
C1841A	HEREFORD (HEREFORDSHIRE)
C1841B	LEOMINSTER (HEREFORDSHIRE)
C1841C	SOUTH HEREFORDSHIRE
C1842A	SEVERNMINSTER (KIDDERMINSTER)
C1843A	DROITWICH (SOUTH WORCESTERSHIRE)
C1843B	EVESHAM (SOUTH WORCESTERSHIRE)
C1843C	WORCESTER (SOUTH WORCESTERSHIRE)
C1843D	WORCESTER (SOUTH WORCESTERSHIRE)
C1846	BROMSGROVE (CLOSED)
C3275	DRAYTON DIVISION
C3275A	MARKET DRAYTON
C3275B	WHITCHURCH
C3276	LUDLOW
C3277	OSWESTRY
C3279	SHREWSBURY
C3282	TELFORD

West Midlands

C2789	SEISDON
C2908	BIRMINGHAM
C2909	SUTTON COLDFIELD
C2910	COVENTRY
C2911	DUDLEY
C2912	STOURBRIDGE & HALESOWEN
C2913	STOURBRIDGE
C2914	WARLEY
C2915	WEST BROMWICH
C2916	SOLIHULL
C2917	WALSALL & ALDRIDGE
C2918	WALSALL
C2919	WOLVERHAMPTON
C3274	BRIDGNORTH

Warwickshire

C2894	ATHERSTONE & COLESHILL
C2896	NUNEATON
C2897	RUGBY DIVISION
C2902	SOUTH WARWICKSHIRE (STRATFORD)

C2903	MID WARWICKSHIRE (WARWICK)
C2904	WARWICKSHIRE PSA (NUNEATON/RUGBY)

West Yorkshire

C2978	BRADFORD
C2979	[KEIGHLEY PSD]
C2979A	KEIGHLEY
C2979B	BINGLEY
C2984	CALDER (HALIFAX)
C2987	HUDDERSFIELD
C2988	LEEDS
C2989	MORLEY
C2990A	PUDSEY
C2990B	OTLEY
C2991	SKYRACK & WETHERBY
C2992	LEEDS
C2994	[PONTEFRACT PSD]
C2994A	PONTEFRACT
C2994B	CASTLEFORD
C2995	WAKEFIELD
C2996	BATLEY & DEWSBURY
C2997	CALDERDALE
C6988	LEEDS

Wiltshire

C3015	SWINDON
C3022	CHIPPENHAM (NORTH WILTSHIRE)
C3023	SALISBURY
C3024	TROWBRIDGE
C3025	DEVIZES
C3026	NORTHWEST WILTSHIRE PSA
C3027	SOUTHEAST WILTSHIRE PSA

NOTE: Courts are not allocated to schemes

APPENDIX 8

Billing codes for CDS7

[*LSC Manual*, Vol.4, Part E, release 06]

The following codes are to be used when completing form CDS7 for non-standard fee and revised non-standard fee claims for work done in the magistrates' court.

Codes to identify person attended upon

Individual	Code	Individual	Code
Client	C	Other defence solicitor	D
Expert witness	E	Probation	PR
Prosecution/police	P	Witness	W
Surety	S	Other	O

Codes to identify hearing type

Hearing type	Code	Hearing type	Code
Defence bail application	DB		
Crown Court bail application	CB	Plea	PL
		Pre-trial review	PTR
		Cracked trial	CT
High Court bail application	HB	Summary trial	ST
Varied bail conditions	VB	Sentence	SE
Prosecution bail application (including judge in chambers)	PB	Transfer to Crown Court	TR
Formal remand (in custody)	FR	S.6(1) Committal (CPIA 1996) (including discontinuance or withdrawal)	SD
Adjournment (client on bail)	AD	S.6(2) Committal (including discontinuance or withdrawal)	SW
Mode of trial	MT	Case remitted from Crown Court to magistrates' (s.51 Crime and Disorder Act 1998)	RE
New offence(s)	NO		

APPENDIX 9

Crown Court offence classes

[Criminal Defence Service (Funding) Order 2007, SI 2007/1174; alphabetical list of offences taken from **www.hmcourts-service.gov.uk**.]

PART 6: TABLE OF OFFENCES

Offence	Contrary to	Year and chapter
Class A: Homicide and related grave offences		
Murder	Common law	
Manslaughter	Common law	
Soliciting to commit murder	Offences against the Person Act 1861 s.4	1861 c.100
Child destruction	Infant Life (Preservation) Act 1929 s.1(1)	1929 c.34
Infanticide	Infanticide Act 1938 s.1(1)	1938 c.36
Causing explosion likely to endanger life or property	Explosive Substances Act 1883 s.2	1883 c.3
Attempt to cause explosion, making or keeping explosive etc.	Explosive Substances Act 1883 s.3	As above
Class B: Offences involving serious violence or damage, and serious drugs offences		
Endangering the safety of an aircraft	Aviation Security Act 1982 s.2(1)(b)	1982 c.36
Racially-aggravated arson (not endangering life)	Crime and Disorder Act 1998 s.30(1)	1998 c.37
Kidnapping	Common law	
False imprisonment	Common law	
Aggravated criminal damage	Criminal Damage Act 1971 s.1(2)	1971 c.48
Aggravated arson	Criminal Damage Act 1971 s.1(2), (3)	As above
Arson (where value exceeds £30,000)	Criminal Damage Act 1971 s.1(3)	As above

Possession of firearm with intent to endanger life	Firearms Act 1968 s.16	1968 c.27
Use of firearm to resist arrest	Firearms Act 1968 s.17	As above
Possession of firearm with criminal intent	Firearms Act 1968 s.18	As above
Possession or acquisition of certain prohibited weapons etc.	Firearms Act 1968 s.5	As above
Aggravated burglary	Theft Act 1968 s.10	1968 c.60
Armed robbery	Theft Act 1968 s.8(1)	As above
Assault with weapon with intent to rob	Theft Act 1968 s.8(2)	As above
Blackmail	Theft Act 1968 s.21	As above
Riot	Public Order Act 1986 s.1	1986 c.64
Violent disorder	Public Order Act 1986 s.2	As above
Contamination of goods with intent	Public Order Act 1986 s.38	As above
Causing death by dangerous driving	Road Traffic Act 1988 s.1	1988 c.52
Causing death by careless driving while under the influence of drink or drugs	Road Traffic Act 1988 s.3A	As above
Aggravated vehicle taking resulting in death	Theft Act 1968 s.12A	1968 c.60
Causing danger to road users	Road Traffic Act 1988 s.22A	1988 c.52
Attempting to choke, suffocate, strangle etc.	Offences against the Person Act 1861 s.21	1861 c.100
Causing miscarriage by poison, instrument	Offences against the Person Act 1861 s.58	As above
Making threats to kill	Offences against the Person Act 1861 s.16	As above
Wounding or grievous bodily harm with intent to cause grievous bodily harm etc.	Offences against the Person Act 1861 s.18	As above
Endangering the safety of railway passengers	Offences against the Person Act 1861 ss.32, 33, 34	As above
Impeding persons endeavouring to escape wrecks	Offences against the Person Act 1861 s.17	As above
Administering chloroform, laudanum etc.	Offences against the Person Act 1861 s.22	As above
Administering poison etc. so as to endanger life	Offences against the Person Act 1861 s.23	As above
Cruelty to persons under 16	Children and Young Persons Act 1933 s.1	1933 c.12
Aiding and abetting suicide	Suicide Act 1961 s.2	1961 c.60
Prison mutiny	Prison Security Act 1992 s.1	1992 c.25

Assaulting prison officer whilst possessing firearm etc.	Criminal Justice Act 1991 s.90	1991 c.53
Producing or supplying a Class A or B drug	Misuse of Drugs Act 1971 s.4	1971 c.38
Possession of a Class A or B drug with intent to supply	Misuse of Drugs Act 1971 s.5(3)	As above
Manufacture and supply of scheduled substances	Criminal Justice (International Co-Operation) Act 1990 s.12	1990 c.5
Fraudulent evasion of controls on Class A and B drugs	Customs and Excise Management Act 1979 s.170(2)(b), (c)	1979 c.2
Illegal importation of Class A and B drugs	Customs and Excise Management Act 1979 s.50	As above
Offences in relation to proceeds of drug trafficking	Drug Trafficking Act 1994 ss.49, 50 and 51	1994 c.37
Offences in relation to money laundering investigations	Drug Trafficking Act 1994 ss.52 and 53	As above
Practitioner contravening drug supply regulations	Misuse of Drugs Act 1971 ss.12 and 13	1971 c.38
Cultivation of cannabis plant	Misuse of Drugs Act 1971 s.6	As above
Occupier knowingly permitting drugs offences etc.	Misuse of Drugs Act 1971 s.8	As above
Activities relating to opium	Misuse of Drugs Act 1971 s.9	As above
Drug trafficking offences at sea	Criminal Justice (International Co-operation) Act 1990 s.18	1990 c.5
Firing on Revenue vessel	Customs and Excise Management Act 1979 s.85	1979 c.2
Making or possession of explosive in suspicious circumstances	Explosive Substances Act 1883 s.4(1)	1883 c.3
Causing bodily injury by explosives	Offences against the Person Act 1861 s.28	1861 c.100
Using explosive or corrosives with intent to cause grievous bodily harm	Offences against the Person Act 1861 s.29	As above
Hostage taking	Taking of Hostages Act 1982 s.1	1982 c.28
Offences against international protection of nuclear material	Nuclear Material (Offences) Act 1983 s.2	1983 c.18
Placing explosives with intent to cause bodily injury	Offences against the Person Act 1861 s.30	1861 c.100
Membership of proscribed organisations	Terrorism Act 2000 s.11	2000 c.11
Support or meeting of proscribed organisations	Terrorism Act 2000 s.12	As above
Uniform of proscribed organisations	Terrorism Act 2000 s.13	As above
Fund-raising for terrorism	Terrorism Act 2000 s.15	As above

Other offences involving money or property to be used for terrorism	Terrorism Act 2000 ss.16–18	As above
Disclosure prejudicing, or interference of material relevant to, investigation of terrorism	Terrorism Act 2000 s.39	As above
Weapons training	Terrorism Act 2000 s.54	As above
Directing terrorist organisation	Terrorism Act 2000 s.56	As above
Possession of articles for terrorist purposes	Terrorism Act 2000 s.57	As above
Unlawful collection of information for terrorist purposes	Terrorism Act 2000 s.58	As above
Incitement of terrorism overseas	Terrorism Act 2000 s.59	As above
Concealing criminal property	Proceeds of Crime Act 2002 s.327	2002 c.29
Involvement in arrangements facilitating the acquisition, retention, use or control of criminal property	Proceeds of Crime Act 2002 s.328	As above
Acquisition, use or possession of criminal property	Proceeds of Crime Act 2002 s.329	As above
Failure to disclose knowledge or suspicion of money laundering: regulated sector	Proceeds of Crime Act 2002 s.330	As above
Failure to disclose knowledge or suspicion of money laundering: nominated officers in the regulated sector	Proceeds of Crime Act 2002 s.331	As above
Failure to disclose knowledge or suspicion of money laundering: other nominated officers	Proceeds of Crime Act 2002 s.332	As above
Tipping off	Proceeds of Crime Act 2002 s.333	As above
Disclosure under sections 330, 331, 332 or 333 of the Proceeds of Crime Act 2002 otherwise than in the form and manner prescribed	Proceeds of Crime Act 2002 s.339(1A)	As above
Causing or allowing the death of a child	Domestic Violence, Crime and Victims Act 2004 s.5	2004 c.28

Class C: Lesser offences involving violence or damage, and less serious drugs offences

Racially-aggravated assault	Crime and Disorder Act 1998 s.29(1)	1998 c.37
Racially-aggravated criminal damage	Crime and Disorder Act 1998 s.30(1)	1998 c.37
Robbery (other than armed robbery)	Theft Act 1968 s.8(1)	1968 c.60

Unlawful wounding	Offences against the Person Act 1861 s.20	1861 c.100
Assault occasioning actual bodily harm	Offences against the Person Act 1861 s.47	As above
Concealment of birth	Offences against the Person Act 1861 s.60	As above
Abandonment of children under two	Offences against the Person Act 1861 s.27	As above
Arson (other than aggravated arson) where value does not exceed £30,000	Criminal Damage Act 1971 s.1(3)	1971 c.48
Criminal damage (other than aggravated criminal damage)	Criminal Damage Act 1971 s.1(1)	As above
Possession of firearm without certificate	Firearms Act 1968 s.1	1968 c.27
Carrying loaded firearm in public place	Firearms Act 1968 s.19	As above
Trespassing with a firearm	Firearms Act 1968 s.20	As above
Shortening of shotgun or possession of shortened shotgun	Firearms Act 1968 s.4	As above
Shortening of smooth bore gun	Firearms Amendment Act 1988 s.6(1)	1988 c.45
Possession or acquisition of shotgun without certificate	Firearms Act 1968 s.2	1968 c.27
Possession of firearms by person convicted of crime	Firearms Act 1968 s.21(4)	As above
Acquisition by or supply of firearms to person denied them	Firearms Act 1968 s.21(5)	As above
Dealing in firearms	Firearms Act 1968 s.3	As above
Failure to comply with certificate when transferring firearm	Firearms Act 1968 s.42	As above
Permitting an escape	Common law	
Rescue	Common law	
Escaping from lawful custody without force	Common law	
Breach of prison	Common law	
Harbouring escaped prisoners	Criminal Justice Act 1961 s.22	1961 c.39
Assisting prisoners to escape	Prison Act 1952 s.39	1952 c.52
Fraudulent evasion of agricultural levy	Customs and Excise Management Act 1979 s.68A(1) and (2)	1979 c.2
Offender armed or disguised	Customs and Excise Management Act 1979 s.86	As above
Making threats to destroy or damage property	Criminal Damage Act 1971 s.2	1971 c.48

Possessing anything with intent to destroy or damage property	Criminal Damage Act 1971 s.3	As above
Child abduction by connected person	Child Abduction Act 1984 s.1	1984 c.37
Child abduction by other person	Child Abduction Act 1984 s.2	As above
Bomb hoax	Criminal Law Act 1977 s.51	1977 c.45
Producing or supplying class C drug	Misuse of Drugs Act 1971 s.4	1971 c.38
Possession of a class C drug with intent to supply	Misuse of Drugs Act 1971 s.5(3)	As above
Fraudulent evasion of controls on class C drugs	Customs and Excise Management Act 1979 s.170(2)(b), (c)	1979 c.2
Illegal importation of class C drugs	Customs and Excise Management Act 1979 s.50	As above
Possession of class A drug	Misuse of Drugs Act 1971 s.5(2)	1971 c.38
Failure to disclose knowledge or suspicion of money laundering	Drug Trafficking Offences Act 1986 s.26B	1986 c.32
Tipping-off in relation to money laundering investigations	Drug Trafficking Offences Act 1986 s.26C	As above
Assaults on officers saving wrecks	Offences against the Person Act 1861 s.37	1861 c.100
Attempting to injure or alarm the sovereign	Treason Act 1842 s.2	1842 c.51
Assisting illegal entry or harbouring persons	Immigration Act 1971 s.25	1971 c.77
Administering poison with intent to injure etc.	Offences against the Person Act 1861 s.24	1861 c.100
Neglecting to provide food for or assaulting servants etc.	Offences against the Person Act 1861 s.26	As above
Setting spring guns with intent to inflict grievous bodily harm	Offences against the Person Act 1861 s.31	As above
Supplying instrument etc. to cause miscarriage	Offences against the Person Act 1861 s.59	As above
Failure to disclose information about terrorism	Terrorism Act 2000 s.19	2000 c.11
Circumcision of females	Prohibition of Female Circumcision Act 1985 s.1	1985 c.38
Breaking or injuring submarine telegraph cables	Submarine Telegraph Act 1885 s.3	1885 c.49
Failing to keep dogs under proper control resulting in injury	Dangerous Dogs Act 1991 s.3	1991 c.65
Making gunpowder etc. to commit offences	Offences against the Person Act 1861 s.64	1861 c.100
Stirring up racial hatred	Public Order Act 1986 ss.18-23	1986 c.64

Class D: Sexual offences and offences against children

Administering drugs to obtain intercourse	Sexual Offences Act 1956 s.4	1956 c.69
Procurement of a defective	Sexual Offences Act 1956 s.9	As above

Incest other than by man with a girl under 13	Sexual Offences Act 1956 ss.10 and 11	As above
Gross indecency between male of 21 or over and male under 16	Sexual Offences Act 1956 s.13	As above
Indecent assault on a woman	Sexual Offences Act 1956 s.14	As above
Indecent assault on a man	Sexual Offences Act 1956 s.15	As above
Abuse of position of trust	Sexual Offences (Amendment) Act 2000 s.3	2000 c.44
Man living on earnings of prostitution	Sexual Offences Act 1956 s.30	1956 c.69
Woman exercising control over prostitute	Sexual Offences Act 1956 s.31	As above
Living on earnings of male prostitution	Sexual Offences Act 1967 s.5	1967 c.60
Incitement to commit incest	Criminal Law Act 1977 s.54	1977 c.45
Ill-treatment of persons of unsound mind	Mental Health Act 1983 s.127	1983 c.20
Abduction of unmarried girl under 18 from parent	Sexual Offences Act 1956 s.19	1956 c.69
Abduction of defective from parent	Sexual Offences Act 1956 s.21	As above
Procuration of girl under 21	Sexual Offences Act 1956 s.23	As above
Permitting defective to use premises for intercourse	Sexual Offences Act 1956 s.27	As above
Causing or encouraging prostitution of defective	Sexual Offences Act 1956 s.29	As above
Sexual assault	Sexual Offences Act 2003 s.3	2003 c.42
Causing sexual activity without penetration	Sexual Offences Act 2003 s.4	As above
Engaging in sexual activity in the presence of a child	Sexual Offences Act 2003 s.11	As above
Causing a child to watch a sexual act	Sexual Offences Act 2003 s.12	As above
Child sex offence committed by person under 18	Sexual Offences Act 2003 s.13	As above
Meeting child following sexual grooming	Sexual Offences Act 2003 s.15	As above
Abuse of trust: sexual activity with a child	Sexual Offences Act 2003 s.16	As above
Abuse of position of trust: causing a child to engage in sexual activity	Sexual Offences Act 2003 s.17	As above
Abuse of trust: sexual activity in the presence of a child	Sexual Offences Act 2003 s.18	As above
Abuse of position of trust: causing a child to watch sexual activity	Sexual Offences Act 2003 s.19	As above

Engaging in sexual activity in the presence of a person with a mental disorder	Sexual Offences Act 2003 s.32	As above
Causing a person with a mental disorder to watch a sexual act	Sexual Offences Act 2003 s.33	As above
Engaging in sexual activity in the presence of a person with a mental disorder	Sexual Offences Act 2003 s.36	As above
Causing a person with a mental disorder to watch a sexual act	Sexual Offences Act 2003 s.37	As above
Care workers: sexual activity in presence of a person with a mental disorder	Sexual Offences Act 2003 s.40	As above
Care workers: causing a person with a mental disorder to watch a sexual act	Sexual Offences Act 2003 s.41	As above
Causing or inciting prostitution for gain	Sexual Offences Act 2003 s.52	As above
Controlling prostitution for gain	Sexual Offences Act 2003 s.53	As above
Administering a substance with intent	Sexual Offences Act 2003 s.61	As above
Committing offence with intent to commit sexual offence	Sexual Offences Act 2003 s.62	As above
Trespass with intent to commit sexual offence	Sexual Offences Act 2003 s.63	As above
Sex with adult relative	Sexual Offences Act 2003 s.64, 65	As above
Exposure	Sexual Offences Act 2003 s.66	As above
Voyeurism	Sexual Offences Act 2003 s.67	As above
Intercourse with an animal	Sexual Offences Act 2003 s.69	As above
Sexual penetration of a corpse	Sexual Offences Act 2003 s.70	As above

Class E: Burglary etc.

Burglary (domestic)	Theft Act 1968 s.9(3)(a)	1968 c.60
Going equipped to steal	Theft Act 1968 s.25	As above
Burglary (non-domestic)	Theft Act 1968 s.9(3)(b)	As above

Classes F, G and K: Other offences of dishonesty

The following offences are always in class F

Destruction of registers of births etc.	Forgery Act 1861 s.36	1861 c.98
Making false entries in copies of registers sent to register	Forgery Act 1861 s.37	As above
Possession (with intention) of false identity documents	Identity Cards Act 2006 s.25(1)	2006 c.15

199

Possession (with intention) of apparatus or material for making false identity documents	Identity Cards Act 2006 s.25(3)	As above
Possession (without reasonable excuse) of false identity documents or apparatus or material for making false identity documents	Identity Cards Act 2006 s.25(5)	As above

The following offences are always in class G

Undischarged bankrupt being concerned in a company	Insolvency Act 1986 s.360	1986 c.45
Counterfeiting notes and coins	Forgery and Counterfeiting Act 1981 s.14	1981 c.45
Passing counterfeit notes and coins	Forgery and Counterfeiting Act 1981 s.15	As above
Offences involving custody or control of counterfeit notes and coins	Forgery and Counterfeiting Act 1981 s.16	As above
Making, custody or control of counterfeiting materials etc.	Forgery and Counterfeiting Act 1981 s.175	As above
Illegal importation: counterfeit notes or coins	Customs and Excise Management Act 1979 s.50	1979 c.2
Fraudulent evasion: counterfeit notes or coins	Customs and Excise Management Act 1979 s.170(2)(b), (c)	As above

The following offences are in class G if the value involved exceeds £30,000, class K if the value exceeds £100,000 and in class F otherwise

VAT offences	Value Added Tax Act 1994 s.72(1-8)	1994 c.23
Fraudulent evasion of duty	Customs and Excise Management Act 1979 s.170(1)(b)	1979 c.2
Theft	Theft Act 1968 s.1	1968 c.60
Removal of articles from places open to the public	Theft Act 1968 s.11	As above
Abstraction of electricity	Theft Act 1968 s.13	As above
Obtaining property by deception	Theft Act 1968 s.15	As above
Obtaining pecuniary advantage by deception	Theft Act 1968 s.16	As above
False accounting	Theft Act 1968 s.17	As above
Handling stolen goods	Theft Act 1968 s.22	As above
Obtaining services by deception	Theft Act 1978 s.1	1978 c.31
Evasion of liability by deception	Theft Act 1978 s.2	As above
Illegal importation: not elsewhere specified	Customs and Excise Management Act 1979 s.50	1979 c.2
Counterfeiting Customs documents	Customs and Excise Management Act 1979 s.168	As above

Fraudulent evasion: not elsewhere specified	Customs and Excise Management Act 1979 s.170(2)(b), (c)	As above
Forgery	Forgery and Counterfeiting Act 1981 s.1	1981 c.45
Copying false instrument with intent	Forgery and Counterfeiting Act 1981 s.2	As above
Using a false instrument	Forgery and Counterfeiting Act 1981 s.3	As above
Using a copy of a false instrument	Forgery and Counterfeiting Act 1981 s.4	As above
Custody or control of false instruments etc.	Forgery and Counterfeiting Act 1981 s.5	As above
Offences in relation to dies or stamps	Stamp Duties Management Act 1891 s.13	1891 c.38
Counterfeiting of dies or marks	Hallmarking Act 1973 s.6	1973 c.43
Fraud by false representation	Fraud Act 2006 s.2	2006 c.35
Fraud by failing to disclose information	Fraud Act 2006 s.3	As above
Fraud by abuse of position	Fraud Act 2006 s.4	As above
Possession etc. of articles for use in frauds	Fraud Act 2006 s.6	As above
Making or supplying articles for use in frauds	Fraud Act 2006 s.7	As above
Participating in fraudulent business carried on by sole trader etc.	Fraud Act 2006 s.9	As above
Obtaining services dishonestly	Fraud Act 2006 s.11	As above

Class H: Miscellaneous other offences

Breach of anti-social behaviour order	Crime and Disorder Act 1998 s.1(10)	1998 c.37
Breach of sex offender order	Crime and Disorder Act 1998 s.2(8)	As above
Racially-aggravated public order offence	Crime and Disorder Act 1998 s.31(1)	As above
Racially aggravated harassment/ putting another in fear of violence	Crime and Disorder Act 1998 s.32(1)	As above
Having an article with a blade or point in a public place	Criminal Justice Act 1988 s.139	1988 c.33
Breach of harassment injunction	Protection from Harassment Act 1997 s.3(6)	1997 c.40
Putting people in fear of violence	Protection from Harassment Act 1997 s.4(1)	As above
Breach of restraining order	Protection from Harassment Act 1997 s.5(5)	As above

Being drunk on an aircraft	Air Navigation Order 2005, article 75	S.I. 2005/1970
Possession of offensive weapon	Prevention of Crime Act 1953 s.1	1953 c.14
Affray	Public Order Act 1986 s.3	1986 c.64
Assault with intent to resist arrest	Offences against the Person Act 1861 s.38	1861 c.100
Unlawful eviction and harassment of occupier	Protection from Eviction Act 1977 s.1	1977 c.43
Obscene articles intended for publication for gain	Obscene Publications Act 1964 s.1	1964 c.74
Gross indecency between males (other than where one is 21 or over and the other is under 16)	Sexual Offences Act 1956 s.13	1956 c.69
Solicitation for immoral purposes	Sexual Offences Act 1956 s.32	As above
Buggery of males of 16 or over otherwise than in private	Sexual Offences Act 1956 s.12	As above
Acts outraging public decency	Common law	
Offences of publication of obscene matter	Obscene Publications Act 1959 s.2	1959 c.66
Keeping a disorderly house	Common law; Disorderly Houses Act 1751 s.8	1751 c.36
Indecent display	Indecent Displays (Control) Act 1981 s.1	1981 c.42
Presentation of obscene performance	Theatres Act 1968 s.2	1968 c.54
Procurement of intercourse by threats etc.	Sexual Offences Act 1956 s.2	1956 c.69
Causing prostitution of women	Sexual Offences Act 1956 s.22	As above
Detention of woman in brothel or other premises	Sexual Offences Act 1956 s.24	As above
Procurement of a woman by false pretences	Sexual Offences Act 1956 s.3	As above
Procuring others to commit homosexual acts	Sexual Offences Act 1967 s.4	1967 c.60
Trade description offences (9 offences)	Trade Descriptions Act 1968 ss.1, 8, 9, 12, 13, 14	1968 c.29
Misconduct endangering ship or persons on board ship	Merchant Shipping Act 1970 s.27	1970 c.36
Obstructing engine or carriage on railway	Malicious Damage Act 1861 s.36	1861 c.97
Offences relating to the safe custody of controlled drugs	Misuse of Drugs Act 1971 s.11	1971 c.38
Possession of Class B or C drug	Misuse of Drugs Act 1971 s.5(2)	As above

Wanton or furious driving	Offences against the Person Act 1861 s.35	1861 c.100
Dangerous driving	Road Traffic Act 1988 s.2	1988 c.52
Forgery and misuse of driving documents	Public Passenger Vehicles Act 1981 s.65	1981 c.14
Forgery of driving documents	Road Traffic Act 1960 s.233	1960 c.16
Forgery etc. of licences and other documents	Road Traffic Act 1988 s.173	1988 c.52
Mishandling or falsifying parking documents etc.	Road Traffic Regulation Act 1984 s.115	1984 c.27
Aggravated vehicle taking	Theft Act 1968 s.12A	1968 c.60
Forgery, alteration, fraud of licences etc.	Vehicle Excise and Registration Act 1994 s.44	1994 c.22
Making off without payment	Theft Act 1978 s.3	1978 c.31
Agreeing to indemnify sureties	Bail Act 1976 s.9(1)	1976 c.63
Sending prohibited articles by post	Post Office Act 1953 s.11	1953 c.36
Impersonating Customs officer	Customs and Excise Management Act 1979 s.13	1979 c.2
Obstructing Customs officer	Customs and Excise Management Act 1979 s.16	As above

Class I: Offences against public justice and similar offences

Conspiring to commit offences outside the United Kingdom	Criminal Justice (Terrorism and Conspiracy) Act 1998 s.5	1998 c.40
Perverting the course of public justice	Common law	
Perjuries (7 offences)	Perjury Act 1911 ss.1–7(2)	1911 c.6
Corrupt transactions with agents	Prevention of Corruption Act 1906 s.1	1906 c.34
Corruption in public office	Public Bodies Corrupt Practices Act 1889 s.1	1889 c.69
Embracery	Common law	
Fabrication of evidence with intent to mislead a tribunal	Common law	
Personation of jurors	Common law	
Concealing an arrestable offence	Criminal Law Act 1967 s.5	1967 c.58
Assisting offenders	Criminal Law Act 1967 s.4(1)	As above
False evidence before European Court	European Communities Act 1972 s.11	1972 c.68
Personating for purposes of bail etc.	Forgery Act 1861 s.34	1861 c.98
Intimidating a witness, juror etc.	Criminal Justice and Public Order Act 1994 s.51(1)	1994 c.33

Harming, threatening to harm a witness, juror etc.	Criminal Justice and Public Order Act 1994 s.51(2)	As above
Prejudicing a drug trafficking investigation	Drug Trafficking Act 1994 s.58(1)	1994 c.37
Giving false statements to procure cremation	Cremation Act 1902 s.8(2)	1902 c.8
False statement tendered under section 9 of the Criminal Justice Act 1967	Criminal Justice Act 1967 s.89	1967 c.80
Making a false statement to obtain interim possession order	Criminal Justice and Public Order Act 1994 s.75(1)	1994 c.33
Making false statement to resist making of interim possession order	Criminal Justice and Public Order Act 1994 s.75(2)	As above
False statement tendered under section 5B of the Magistrates' Courts Act 1980	Magistrates' Courts Act 1980 s.106	1980 c.43
Making false statement to authorised officer	Trade Descriptions Act 1968 s.29(2)	1968 c.29

Class J: Serious sexual offences

Rape	Sexual Offences Act 1956 s.1(1)	1956 c.69
Sexual intercourse with girl under 13	Sexual Offences Act 1956 s.5	As above
Sexual intercourse with girl under 16	Sexual Offences Act 1956 s.6	As above
Sexual intercourse with defective	Sexual Offences Act 1956 s.7	As above
Incest by man with a girl under 13	Sexual Offences Act 1956 s.10	As above
Buggery of person under 16	Sexual Offences Act 1956 s.12	As above
Indecency with children under 14	Indecency with Children Act 1960 s.1(1)	1960 c.33
Taking, having etc. indecent photographs of children	Protection of Children Act 1978 s.1	1978 c.37
Assault with intent to commit buggery	Sexual Offences Act 1956 s.16	1956 c.69
Abduction of woman by force	Sexual Offences Act 1956 s.17	As above
Permitting girl under 13 to use premises for sexual intercourse	Sexual Offences Act 1956 s.25	As above
Allowing or procuring child under 16 to go abroad to perform	Children and Young Persons Act 1933 ss.25, 26	1933 c.12
Sexual intercourse with patients	Mental Health Act 1959 s.128	1959 c.72
Abduction of unmarried girl under 16 from parent	Sexual Offences Act 1956 s.20	1956 c.69
Permitting girl under 16 to use premises for intercourse	Sexual Offences Act 1956 s.26	As above
Causing or encouraging prostitution of girl under 16	Sexual Offences Act 1956 s.28	As above

Rape	Sexual Offences Act 2003 s.1	2003 c.42
Assault by penetration	Sexual Offences Act 2003 s.2	As above
Causing sexual activity with penetration	Sexual Offences Act 2003 s.4	As above
Rape of child under 13	Sexual Offences Act 2003 s.5	As above
Assault of child under 13 by penetration	Sexual Offences Act 2003 s.6	As above
Sexual assault of child under 13	Sexual Offences Act 2003 s.7	As above
Causing a child under 13 to engage in sexual activity	Sexual Offences Act 2003 s.8	As above
Sexual activity with a child	Sexual Offences Act 2003 s.9	As above
Causing a child to engage in sexual activity	Sexual Offences Act 2003 s.10	As above
Arranging child sex offence	Sexual Offences Act 2003 s.14	As above
Sexual activity with a child family member, with penetration	Sexual Offences Act 2003 s.25	As above
Inciting a child family member to engage in sexual activity	Sexual Offences Act 2003 s.26	As above
Sexual activity with a person with a mental disorder	Sexual Offences Act 2003 s.30	As above
Causing or inciting a person with a mental disorder to engage in sexual activity	Sexual Offences Act 2003 s.31	As above
Offering inducement to procure sexual activity with a person with a mental disorder	Sexual Offences Act 2003 s.34	As above
Inducing person with mental disorder to engage in sexual activity	Sexual Offences Act 2003 s.35	As above
Care workers: sexual activity with a person with a mental disorder	Sexual Offences Act 2003 s.38	As above
Care workers: inciting person with mental disorder to engage in sexual act	Sexual Offences Act 2003 s.39	As above
Paying for sexual services of a child	Sexual Offences Act 2003 s.47	As above
Causing or inciting child prostitution or pornography	Sexual Offences Act 2003 s.48	As above
Controlling a child prostitute	Sexual Offences Act 2003 s.49	As above
Facilitating child prostitution	Sexual Offences Act 2003 s.50	As above
Trafficking into UK for sexual exploitation	Sexual Offences Act 2003 s.57	As above
Trafficking within UK for sexual exploitation	Sexual Offences Act 2003 s.58	As above
Trafficking out of UK for sexual exploitation	Sexual Offences Act 2003 s.59	As above

Class K: Other offences of dishonesty (high value)

Class K Offences are listed under Class F and G.

OFFENCES LISTED IN ALPHABETICAL ORDER

Classes

Class A: Homicide and related grave offences
Class B: Offences involving serious violence or damage, and serious drugs offences
Class C: Lesser offences involving violence or damage, and less serious drugs offences
Class D: Sexual offences and offences against children
Class E: Burglary etc.
Classes F, G and K: Other offences of dishonesty
Class H: miscellaneous other offences
Class I: Offences against public justice and similar offences
Class J: Serious sexual offences
Class K: Other offences of dishonesty (high value)

Note:

Within the F class there are specific offences that will always be F (these are shown as F on the list). However, on the list you will see that there are offences whose class is listed as F**. This is because the offence will be in Class G if the value involved exceeds £30,000, class K if the value exceeds £100,000 and in class F otherwise. A note has been inserted beneath each of the F** entries on the list.

Class K offences are listed under Class F and G.

Offence	Contrary to	Class
Abandonment of children under two	Offences against the Person Act 1861 s.27	C
Abduction of defective from parent	Sexual Offences Act 1956 s.21	D
Abduction of unmarried girl under 16 from parent	Sexual Offences Act 1956 s.20	J
Abduction of unmarried girl under 18 from parent	Sexual Offences Act 1956 s.19	D
Abduction of woman by force	Sexual Offences Act 1956 s.17	J
Abstraction of electricity	Theft Act 1968 s.13	F**

** The above offence is in class G if the value involved exceeds £30,000, class K if the value exceeds £100,000 and in class F otherwise

Abuse of position of trust	Sexual Offences (Amendment) Act 2000 s.3	D
Abuse of position of trust: causing a child to engage in sexual activity	Sexual Offences Act 2003 s.17	D

Abuse of position of trust: causing a child to watch sexual activity	Sexual Offences Act 2003 s.19	D
Abuse of trust: sexual activity in the presence of a child	Sexual Offences Act 2003 s.18	D
Abuse of trust: sexual activity with a child	Sexual Offences Act 2003 s.16	D
Acquisition by or supply of firearms to person denied them	Firearms Act 1968 s.21(5)	C
Acquisition, use or possession of criminal property	Proceeds of Crime Act 2002 s.329	B
Activities relating to opium	Misuse of Drugs Act 1971 s.9	B
Acts outraging public decency	Common law	H
Administering a substance with intent	Sexual Offences Act 2003 s.61	D
Administering chloroform, laudanum etc.	Offences against the Person Act 1861 s.22	B
Administering drugs to obtain intercourse	Sexual Offences Act 1956 s.4	D
Administering poison etc. so as to endanger life	Offences against the Person Act 1861 s.23	B
Administering poison with intent to injure etc.	Offences against the Person Act 1861 s.24	C
Affray	Public Order Act 1986 s.3	H
Aggravated arson	Criminal Damage Act 1971 s.1(2), (3)	B
Aggravated burglary	Theft Act 1968 s.10	B
Aggravated criminal damage	Criminal Damage Act 1971 s.1(2)	B
Aggravated vehicle taking	Theft Act 1968 s.12A	H
Aggravated vehicle taking resulting in death	Theft Act 1968 s.12A	B
Agreeing to indemnify sureties	Bail Act 1976 s.9(1)	H
Aiding and abetting suicide	Suicide Act 1961 s.2	B
Allowing or procuring child under 16 to go abroad to perform	Children and Young Persons Act 1933 ss.25, 26	J
Allowing the death of a child	Under Section 5 of the Domestic Violence Act 2004	B
Armed robbery	Theft Act 1968 s.8(1)	B
Arranging child sex offence	Sexual Offences Act 2003 s.14	J
Arson (other than aggravated arson) where value does not exceed £30,000	Criminal Damage Act 1971 s.1(3)	C
Arson (where value exceeds £30,000)	Criminal Damage Act 1971 s.1(3)	B

Assault by penetration	Sexual Offences Act 2003 s.2	J
Assault occasioning actual bodily harm	Offences against the Person Act 1861 s.47	C
Assault of child under 13 by penetration	Sexual Offences Act 2003 s.6	J
Assault with intent to commit buggery	Sexual Offences Act 1956 s.16	J
Assault with intent to resist arrest	Offences against the Person Act 1861 s.38	H
Assault with weapon with intent to rob	Theft Act 1968 s.8(2)	B
Assaulting prison officer whilst possessing firearm etc.	Criminal Justice Act 1991 s.90	B
Assaults on officers saving wrecks	Offences against the Person Act 1861 s.37	C
Assisting illegal entry or harbouring persons	Immigration Act 1971 s.25	C
Assisting offenders	Criminal Law Act 1967 s.4(1)	I
Assisting prisoners to escape	Prison Act 1952 s.39	C
Attempt to cause explosion, making or keeping explosive etc.	Explosive Substances Act 1883 s.3	A
Attempting to choke, suffocate, strangle etc.	Offences against the Person Act 1861 s.21	B
Attempting to injure or alarm the Sovereign	Treason Act 1842 s.2	C
Being drunk on an aircraft	Air Navigation Order 2005, article 75	H
Blackmail	Theft Act 1968 s.21	B
Bomb hoax	Criminal Law Act 1977 s.51	C
Breach of anti-social behaviour order	Crime and Disorder Act 1998 s.1(10)	H
Breach of harassment injunction	Protection from Harassment Act 1997 s.3(6)	H
Breach of prison	Common law	C
Breach of restraining order	Protection from Harassment Act 1997 s.5(5)	H
Breach of sex offender order	Crime and Disorder Act 1998 s.2(8)	H
Breaking or injuring submarine telegraph cables	Submarine Telegraph Act 1885 s.3	C
Buggery of males of 16 or over otherwise than in private	Sexual Offences Act 1956 s.12	H
Buggery of person under 16	Sexual Offences Act 1956 s.12	J

Burglary (domestic)	Theft Act 1968 s.9(3)(a)	E
Burglary (non-domestic)	Theft Act 1968 s.9(3)(b)	E
Care workers: causing a person with a mental disorder to watch a sexual act	Sexual Offences Act 2003 s.41	D
Care workers: inciting person with mental disorder to engage in sexual act	Sexual Offences Act 2003 s.39	J
Care workers: sexual activity in presence of a person with a mental disorder	Sexual Offences Act 2003 s.40	D
Care workers: sexual activity with a person with a mental disorder	Sexual Offences Act 2003 s.38	J
Carrying loaded firearm in public place	Firearms Act 1968 s.19	C
Causing a child to engage in sexual activity	Sexual Offences Act 2003 s.10	J
Causing a child to watch a sexual act	Sexual Offences Act 2003 s.12	D
Causing a child under 13 to engage in sexual activity	Sexual Offences Act 2003 s.8	J
Causing a person with a mental disorder to watch a sexual act	Sexual Offences Act 2003 s.33	D
Causing a person with a mental disorder to watch a sexual act	Sexual Offences Act 2003 s.37	D
Causing bodily injury by explosives	Offences against the Person Act 1861 s.28	B
Causing danger to road users	Road Traffic Act 1988 s.22A	B
Causing death by careless driving while under the influence of drink or drugs	Road Traffic Act 1988 s.3A	B
Causing death by dangerous driving	Road Traffic Act 1988 s.1	B
Causing explosion likely to endanger life or property	Explosive Substances Act 1883 s.2	A
Causing miscarriage by poison, instrument	Offences against the Person Act 1861 s.58	B
Causing or allowing the death of a child	Domestic Violence, Crime and Victims Act 2004 s.5	B
Causing or encouraging prostitution of defective	Sexual Offences Act 1956 s.29	D
Causing or encouraging prostitution of girl under 16	Sexual Offences Act 1956 s.28	J
Causing or inciting a person with a mental disorder to engage in sexual activity	Sexual Offences Act 2003 s.31	J

209

Causing or inciting child prostitution or pornography	Sexual Offences Act 2003 s.48	J
Causing or inciting prostitution for gain	Sexual Offences Act 2003 s.52	D
Causing prostitution of women	Sexual Offences Act 1956 s.22	H
Causing sexual activity with penetration	Sexual Offences Act 2003 s.4	J
Causing sexual activity without penetration	Sexual Offences Act 2003 s.4	D
Child abduction by connected person	Child Abduction Act 1984 s.1	C
Child abduction by other person	Child Abduction Act 1984 s.2	C
Child destruction	Infant Life (Preservation) Act 1929 s.1(1)	A
Child sex offence committed by person under 18	Sexual Offences Act 2003 s.13	D
Circumcision of females	Prohibition of Female Circumcision Act 1985 s.1	C
Committing offence with intent to commit sexual offence	Sexual Offences Act 2003 s.62	D
Concealing an arrestable offence	Criminal Law Act 1967 s.5	I
Concealing criminal property	Proceeds of Crime Act 2002 s.327	B
Concealment of birth	Offences against the Person Act 1861 s.60	C
Conspiring to commit offences outside the United Kingdom	Criminal Justice (Terrorism and Conspiracy) Act 1998 s.5	I
Contamination of goods with intent	Public Order Act 1986 s.38	B
Controlling a child prostitute	Sexual Offences Act 2003 s.49	J
Controlling prostitution for gain	Sexual Offences Act 2003 s.53	D
Copying false instrument with intent	Forgery and Counterfeiting Act 1981 s.2	F **

*** The above offence is in class G if the value involved exceeds £30,000, class K if the value exceeds £100,000 and in class F otherwise*

Corrupt transactions with agents	Prevention of Corruption Act 1906 s.1	I
Corruption in public office	Public Bodies Corrupt Practices Act 1889 s.1	I
Counterfeiting Customs documents	Customs and Excise Management Act 1979 s.168	F **

*** The above offence is in class G if the value involved exceeds £30,000, class K if the value exceeds £100,000 and in class F otherwise*

Counterfeiting notes and coins	Forgery and Counterfeiting Act 1981 s.14	G
Counterfeiting of dies or marks	Hallmarking Act 1973 s.6	F **

*** The above offence is in class G if the value involved exceeds £30,000, class K if the value exceeds £100,000 and in class F otherwise*

Criminal damage (other than aggravated criminal damage)	Criminal Damage Act 1971 s.1(1)	C
Cruelty to persons under 16	Children and Young Persons Act 1933 s.1	B
Cultivation of cannabis plant	Misuse of Drugs Act 1971 s.6	B
Custody or control of false instruments etc.	Forgery and Counterfeiting Act 1981 s.5	F **

*** The above offence is in class G if the value involved exceeds £30,000, class K if the value exceeds £100,000 and in class F otherwise*

Dangerous driving	Road Traffic Act 1988 s.2	H
Dealing in firearms	Firearms Act 1968 s.3	C
Destruction of registers of births etc.	Forgery Act 1861 s.36	F
Detention of woman in brothel or other premises	Sexual Offences Act 1956 s.24	H
Directing terrorist organisation	Terrorism Act 2000 s.56	B
Disclosure prejudicing, or interference of material relevant to, investigation of terrorism	Terrorism Act 2000 s.39	B
Disclosure under sections 330, 331, 332 or 333 of the Proceeds of Crime Act 2002 otherwise than in the form and manner prescribed	Proceeds of Crime Act 2002 s.339(1A)	B
Drug trafficking offences at sea	Criminal Justice (International Co-operation) Act 1990 s.18	B
Embracery	Common law	I
Endangering the safety of an aircraft	Aviation Security Act 1982 s.2(1)(b)	B
Endangering the safety of railway passengers	Offences against the Person Act 1861 ss.32, 33, 34	B
Engaging in sexual activity in the presence of a child	Sexual Offences Act 2003 s.11	D
Engaging in sexual activity in the presence of a person with a mental disorder	Sexual Offences Act 2003 s.32	D
Engaging in sexual activity in the presence of a person with a mental disorder	Sexual Offences Act 2003 s.36	D
Escaping from lawful custody without force	Common law	C
Evasion of liability by deception	Theft Act 1978 s.2	F **

*** The above offence is in class G if the value involved exceeds £30,000, class K if the value exceeds £100,000 and in class F otherwise*

Exposure	Sexual Offences Act 2003 s.66	D
Fabrication of evidence with intent to mislead a tribunal	Common law	I
Facilitating child prostitution	Sexual Offences Act 2003 s.50	J
Failing to keep dogs under proper control resulting in injury	Dangerous Dogs Act 1991 s.3	C
Failure to comply with certificate when transferring firearm	Firearms Act 1968 s.42	C
Failure to disclose information about terrorism	Terrorism Act 2000 s.19	C
Failure to disclose knowledge or suspicion of money laundering	Drug Trafficking Offences Act 1986 s.26B	C
Failure to disclose knowledge or suspicion of money laundering: nominated officers in the regulated sector	Proceeds of Crime Act 2002 s.331	B
Failure to disclose knowledge or suspicion of money laundering: other nominated officers	Proceeds of Crime Act 2002 s.332	B
Failure to disclose knowledge or suspicion of money laundering: regulated sector	Proceeds of Crime Act 2002 s.330	B
False accounting	Theft Act 1968 s.17	F **

*** The above offence is in class G if the value involved exceeds £30,000, class K if the value exceeds £100,000 and in class F otherwise*

False evidence before European Court	European Communities Act 1972 s.11	I
False imprisonment	Common law	B
False statement tendered under section 5B of the Magistrates' Courts Act 1980	Magistrates' Courts Act 1980 s.106	I
False statement tendered under section 9 of the Criminal Justice Act 1967	Criminal Justice Act 1967 s.89	I
Firing on Revenue vessel	Customs and Excise Management Act 1979 s.85	B
Forgery	Forgery and Counterfeiting Act 1981 s.1	F **

*** The above offence is in class G if the value involved exceeds £30,000, class K if the value exceeds £100,000 and in class F otherwise*

Forgery and misuse of driving documents	Public Passenger Vehicles Act 1981 s.65	H
Forgery etc. of licences and other documents	Road Traffic Act 1988 s.173	H

Forgery of driving documents	Road Traffic Act 1960 s.233	H
Forgery, alteration, fraud of licences etc.	Vehicle Excise and Registration Act 1994 s.44	H
Fraud by abuse of position	Fraud Act 2006 s.4	F **

*** The above offence is in class G if the value involved exceeds £30,000, class K if the value exceeds £100,000 and in class F otherwise*

Fraud by failing to disclose information	Fraud Act 2006 s.3	F **

*** The above offence is in class G if the value involved exceeds £30,000, class K if the value exceeds £100,000 and in class F otherwise*

Fraud by false representation	Fraud Act 2006 s.2	F **

*** The above offence is in class G if the value involved exceeds £30,000, class K if the value exceeds £100,000 and in class F otherwise*

Fraudulent evasion of agricultural levy	Customs and Excise Management Act 1979 s.68A(1) and (2)	C
Fraudulent evasion of controls on Class A and B drugs	Customs and Excise Management Act 1979 s.170(2)(b), (c)	B
Fraudulent evasion of controls on Class C drugs	Customs and Excise Management Act 1979 s.170(2)(b), (c)	C
Fraudulent evasion of duty	Customs and Excise Management Act 1979 s.170(1)(b)	F **

*** The above offence is in class G if the value involved exceeds £30,000, class K if the value exceeds £100,000 and in class F otherwise*

Fraudulent evasion: counterfeit notes or coins	Customs and Excise Management Act 1979 s.170(2)(b), (c)	G
Fraudulent evasion: not elsewhere specified	Customs and Excise Management Act 1979 s.170(2)(b), (c)	F **

*** The above offence is in class G if the value involved exceeds £30,000, class K if the value exceeds £100,000 and in class F otherwise*

Fund-raising for terrorism	Terrorism Act 2000 s.15	B
Giving false statements to procure cremation	Cremation Act 1902 s.8(2)	I
Going equipped to steal	Theft Act 1968 s.25	E
Gross indecency between male of 21 or over and male under 16	Sexual Offences Act 1956 s.13	D
Gross indecency between males (other than where one is 21 or over and the other is under 16)	Sexual Offences Act 1956 s.13	H
Handling stolen goods	Theft Act 1968 s.22	F **

*** The above offence is in class G if the value involved exceeds £30,000, class K if the value exceeds £100,000 and in class F otherwise*

Harbouring escaped prisoners	Criminal Justice Act 1961 s.22	C

Harming, threatening to harm a witness, juror etc.	Criminal Justice and Public Order Act 1994 s.51(2)	I
Having an article with a blade or point in a public place	Criminal Justice Act 1988 s.139	H
Hostage taking	Taking of Hostages Act 1982 s.1	B
Illegal importation of Class A and B drugs	Customs and Excise Management Act 1979 s.50	B
Illegal importation of Class C drugs	Customs and Excise Management Act 1979 s.50	C
Illegal importation: counterfeit notes or coins	Customs and Excise Management Act 1979 s.50	G
Illegal importation: not elsewhere specified	Customs and Excise Management Act 1979 s.50	F **

*** The above offence is in class G if the value involved exceeds £30,000, class K if the value exceeds £100,000 and in class F otherwise*

Ill-treatment of persons of unsound mind	Mental Health Act 1983 s.127	D
Impeding persons endeavouring to escape wrecks	Offences against the Person Act 1861 s.17	B
Impersonating Customs officer	Customs and Excise Management Act 1979 s.13	H
Incest by man with a girl under 13	Sexual Offences Act 1956 s.10	J
Incest other than by man with a girl under 13	Sexual Offences Act 1956 ss.10 and 11	D
Incitement of terrorism overseas	Terrorism Act 2000 s.59	B
Incitement to commit incest	Criminal Law Act 1977 s.54	D
Inciting a child family member to engage in sexual activity	Sexual Offences Act 2003 s.26	J
Indecency with children under 14	Indecency with Children Act 1960 s.1(1)	J
Indecent assault on a man	Sexual Offences Act 1956 s.15	D
Indecent assault on a woman	Sexual Offences Act 1956 s.14	D
Indecent display	Indecent Displays (Control) Act 1981 s.1	H
Inducing person with mental disorder to engage in sexual activity	Sexual Offences Act 2003 s.35	J
Infanticide	Infanticide Act 1938 s.1(1)	A
Intercourse with an animal	Sexual Offences Act 2003 s.69	D
Intimidating a witness, juror etc.	Criminal Justice and Public Order Act 1994 s.51(1)	I
Involvement in arrangements facilitating the acquisition, retention, use or control of criminal property	Proceeds of Crime Act 2002 s.328	B

Keeping a disorderly house	Common law; Disorderly Houses Act 1751 s.8	H
Kidnapping	Common law	B
Living on earnings of male prostitution	Sexual Offences Act 1967 s.5	D
Making a false statement to obtain interim possession order	Criminal Justice and Public Order Act 1994 s.75(1)	I
Making false entries in copies of registers sent to register	Forgery Act 1861 s.37	F
Making false statement to authorised officer	Trade Descriptions Act 1968 s.29(2)	I
Making false statement to resist making of interim possession order	Criminal Justice and Public Order Act 1994 s.75(2)	I
Making gunpowder etc. to commit offences	Offences against the Person Act 1861 s.64	C
Making off without payment	Theft Act 1978 s.3	H
Making or possession of explosive in suspicious circumstances	Explosive Substances Act 1883 s.4(1)	B
Making or supplying articles for use in frauds	Fraud Act 2006 s.7	F **

** *The above offence is in class G if the value involved exceeds £30,000, class K if the value exceeds £100,000 and in class F otherwise*

Making threats to destroy or damage property	Criminal Damage Act 1971 s.2	C
Making threats to kill	Offences against the Person Act 1861 s.16	B
Making, custody or control of counterfeiting materials etc.	Forgery and Counterfeiting Act 1981 s.175	G
Man living on earnings of prostitution	Sexual Offences Act 1956 s.30	D
Manslaughter	Common law	A
Manufacture and supply of scheduled substances	Criminal Justice (International Co-operation) Act 1990 s.12	B
Meeting child following sexual grooming	Sexual Offences Act 2003 s.15	D
Membership of proscribed organisations	Terrorism Act 2000 s.11	B
Misconduct endangering ship or persons on board ship	Merchant Shipping Act 1970 s.27	H
Mishandling or falsifying parking documents etc.	Road Traffic Regulation Act 1984 s.115	H
Murder	Common law	A
Neglecting to provide food for or assaulting servants etc.	Offences against the Person Act 1861 s.26	C

215

Obscene articles intended for publication for gain	Obscene Publications Act 1964 s.1	H
Obstructing Customs officer	Customs and Excise Management Act 1979 s.16	H
Obstructing engine or carriage on railway	Malicious Damage Act 1861 s.36	H
Obtaining pecuniary advantage by deception	Theft Act 1968 s.16	F**

** *The above offence is in class G if the value involved exceeds £30,000, class K if the value exceeds £100,000 and in class F otherwise*

Obtaining property by deception	Theft Act 1968 s.15	F **

** *The above offence is in class G if the value involved exceeds £30,000, class K if the value exceeds £100,000 and in class F otherwise*

Obtaining services by deception	Theft Act 1978 s.1	F **

** *The above offence is in class G if the value involved exceeds £30,000, class K if the value exceeds £100,000 and in class F otherwise*

Obtaining services dishonestly	Fraud Act 2006 s.11	F **

** *The above offence is in class G if the value involved exceeds £30,000, class K if the value exceeds £100,000 and in class F otherwise*

Occupier knowingly permitting drugs offences etc.	Misuse of Drugs Act 1971 s.8	B
Offences against international protection of nuclear material	Nuclear Material (Offences) Act 1983 s.2	B
Offences in relation to dies or stamps	Stamp Duties Management Act 1891 s.13	F **

** *The above offence is in class G if the value involved exceeds £30,000, class K if the value exceeds £100,000 and in class F otherwise*

Offences in relation to money laundering investigations	Drug Trafficking Act 1994 ss.52 and 53	B
Offences in relation to proceeds of drug trafficking	Drug Trafficking Act 1994 ss.49, 50 and 51	B
Offences involving custody or control of counterfeit notes and coins	Forgery and Counterfeiting Act 1981 s.16	G
Offences of publication of obscene matter	Obscene Publications Act 1959 s.2	H
Offences relating to the safe custody of controlled drugs	Misuse of Drugs Act 1971 s.11	H
Offender armed or disguised	Customs and Excise Management Act 1979 s.86	C
Offering inducement to procure sexual activity with a person with a mental disorder	Sexual Offences Act 2003 s.34	J

Other offences involving money or property to be used for terrorism	Terrorism Act 2000 ss.16-18	B
Participating in fraudulent business carried on by sole trader etc.	Fraud Act 2006 s.9	F **

*** The above offence is in class G if the value involved exceeds £30,000, class K if the value exceeds £100,000 and in class F otherwise*

Passing counterfeit notes and coins	Forgery and Counterfeiting Act 1981 s.15	G
Paying for sexual services of a child	Sexual Offences Act 2003 s.47	J
Perjuries (7 offences)	Perjury Act 1911 ss.1–7(2)	I
Permitting an escape	Common law	C
Permitting defective to use premises for intercourse	Sexual Offences Act 1956 s.27	D
Permitting girl under 13 to use premises for sexual intercourse	Sexual Offences Act 1956 s.25	J
Permitting girl under 16 to use premises for intercourse	Sexual Offences Act 1956 s.26	J
Personating for purposes of bail etc.	Forgery Act 1861 s.34	I
Personation of jurors	Common law	I
Perverting the course of public justice	Common law	I
Placing explosives with intent to cause bodily injury	Offences against the Person Act 1861 s.30	B
Possessing anything with intent to destroy or damage property	Criminal Damage Act 1971 s.3	C
Possession (with intention) of apparatus or material for making false identity documents	Identity Cards Act 2006 s.25(3)	F
Possession (with intention) of false identity documents	Identity Cards Act 2006 s.25(1)	F
Possession of false identify documents	Section 25(1) and (3) of the Identity Cards Act	F
Possession (without reasonable excuse) of false identity documents or apparatus or material for making false identity documents	Identity Cards Act 2006 s.25(5)	F
Possession etc of articles for use in frauds	Fraud Act 2006 s.6	F **

*** The above offence is in class G if the value involved exceeds £30,000, class K if the value exceeds £100,000 and in class F otherwise*

Possession of a Class A or B drug with intent to supply	Misuse of Drugs Act 1971 s.5(3)	B
Possession of a Class C drug with intent to supply	Misuse of Drugs Act 1971 s.5(3)	C

Possession of articles for terrorist purposes	Terrorism Act 2000 s.57	B
Possession of Class A drug	Misuse of Drugs Act 1971 s.5(2)	C
Possession of Class B or C drug	Misuse of Drugs Act 1971 s.5(2)	H
Possession of firearm with criminal intent	Firearms Act 1968 s.18	B
Possession of firearm with intent to endanger life	Firearms Act 1968 s.16	B
Possession of firearm without certificate	Firearms Act 1968 s.1	C
Possession of firearms by person convicted of crime	Firearms Act 1968 s.21(4)	C
Possession of offensive weapon	Prevention of Crime Act 1953 s.1	H
Possession or acquisition of certain prohibited weapons etc.	Firearms Act 1968 s.5	B
Possession or acquisition of shotgun without certificate	Firearms Act 1968 s.2	C
Practitioner contravening drug supply regulations	Misuse of Drugs Act 1971 ss.12 and 13	B
Prejudicing a drug trafficking investigation	Drug Trafficking Act 1994 s.58(1)	I
Presentation of obscene performance	Theatres Act 1968 s.2	H
Prison mutiny	Prison Security Act 1992 s.1	B
Procuration of girl under 21	Sexual Offences Act 1956 s.23	D
Procurement of a defective	Sexual Offences Act 1956 s.9	D
Procurement of a woman by false pretences	Sexual Offences Act 1956 s.3	H
Procurement of intercourse by threats etc.	Sexual Offences Act 1956 s.2	H
Procuring others to commit homosexual acts	Sexual Offences Act 1967 s.4	H
Producing or supplying a Class A or B drug	Misuse of Drugs Act 1971 s.4	B
Producing or supplying Class C drug	Misuse of Drugs Act 1971 s.4	C
Putting people in fear of violence	Protection from Harassment Act 1997 s.4(1)	H
Racially aggravated harassment/ putting another in fear of violence	Crime and Disorder Act 1998 s.32(1)	H
Racially-aggravated arson (not endangering life)	Crime and Disorder Act 1998 s.30(1)	B
Racially-aggravated assault	Crime and Disorder Act 1998 s.29(1)	C
Racially-aggravated criminal damage	Crime and Disorder Act 1998 s.30(1)	C

Racially-aggravated public order offence	Crime and Disorder Act 1998 s.31(1)	H
Rape	Sexual Offences Act 1956 s.1(1)	J
Rape	Sexual Offences Act 2003 s.1	J
Rape of child under 13	Sexual Offences Act 2003 s.5	J
Removal of articles from places open to the public	Theft Act 1968 s.11	G
Rescue	Common law	C
Riot	Public Order Act 1986 s.1	B
Robbery (other than armed robbery)	Theft Act 1968 s.8(1)	C
Sending prohibited articles by post	Post Office Act 1953 s.11	H
Setting spring guns with intent to inflict grievous bodily harm	Offences against the Person Act 1861 s.31	C
Sex with adult relative	Sexual Offences Act 2003 s.64, 65	D
Sexual activity with a child	Sexual Offences Act 2003 s.9	J
Sexual activity with a child family member, with penetration	Sexual Offences Act 2003 s.25	J
Sexual activity with a person with a mental disorder	Sexual Offences Act 2003 s.30	J
Sexual assault	Sexual Offences Act 2003 s.3	D
Sexual assault of child under 13	Sexual Offences Act 2003 s.7	J
Sexual intercourse with defective	Sexual Offences Act 1956 s.7	J
Sexual intercourse with girl under 13	Sexual Offences Act 1956 s.5	J
Sexual intercourse with girl under 16	Sexual Offences Act 1956 s.6	J
Sexual intercourse with patients	Mental Health Act 1959 s.128	J
Sexual penetration of a corpse	Sexual Offences Act 2003 s.70	D
Shortening of shotgun or possession of shortened shotgun	Firearms Act 1968 s.4	C
Shortening of smooth bore gun	Firearms Amendment Act 1988 s.6(1)	C
Solicitation for immoral purposes	Sexual Offences Act 1956 s.32	H
Soliciting to commit murder	Offences against the Person Act 1861 s.4	A
Stirring up racial hatred	Public Order Act 1986 ss.18–23	C
Supplying instrument etc. to cause miscarriage	Offences against the Person Act 1861 s.59	C
Support or meeting of proscribed organisations	Terrorism Act 2000 s.12	B
Taking, having etc. indecent photographs of children	Protection of Children Act 1978 s.1	J
Theft	Theft Act 1968 s.1	F**

*** The above offence is in class G if the value involved exceeds £30,000, class K if the value exceeds £100,000 and in class F otherwise*

Tipping off	Proceeds of Crime Act 2002 s.333	B
Tipping-off in relation to money laundering investigations	Drug Trafficking Offences Act 1986 s.26C	C
Trade description offences (9 offences)	Trade Descriptions Act 1968 ss.1, 8, 9, 12, 13, 14	H
Trafficking into UK for sexual exploitation	Sexual Offences Act 2003 s.57	J
Trafficking out of UK for sexual exploitation	Sexual Offences Act 2003 s.59	J
Trafficking within UK for sexual exploitation	Sexual Offences Act 2003 s.58	J
Trespass with intent to commit sexual offence	Sexual Offences Act 2003 s.63	D
Trespassing with a firearm	Firearms Act 1968 s.20	C
Undischarged bankrupt being concerned in a company	Insolvency Act 1986 s.360	G
Uniform of proscribed organisations	Terrorism Act 2000 s.13	B
Unlawful collection of information for terrorist purposes	Terrorism Act 2000 s.58	B
Unlawful eviction and harassment of occupier	Protection from Eviction Act 1977 s.1	H
Unlawful wounding	Offences against the Person Act 1861 s.20	C
Use of firearm to resist arrest	Firearms Act 1968 s.17	B
Using a copy of a false instrument	Forgery and Counterfeiting Act 1981 s.4	F **

*** The above offence is in class G if the value involved exceeds £30,000, class K if the value exceeds £100,000 and in class F otherwise*

Using a false instrument	Forgery and Counterfeiting Act 1981 s.3	F**

*** The above offence is in class G if the value involved exceeds £30,000, class K if the value exceeds £100,000 and in class F otherwise*

Using explosive or corrosives with intent to cause grievous bodily harm	Offences against the Person Act 1861 s.29	B
VAT offences	Value Added Tax Act 1994 s.72(1)–(8)	F **

*** The above offence is in class G if the value involved exceeds £30,000, class K if the value exceeds £100,000 and in class F otherwise*

Violent disorder	Public Order Act 1986 s.2	B
Voyeurism	Sexual Offences Act 2003 s.67	D

Wanton or furious driving	Offences against the Person Act 1861 s.35	H
Weapons training	Terrorism Act 2000 s.54	B
Woman exercising control over prostitute	Sexual Offences Act 1956 s.31	D
Wounding or grievous bodily harm with intent to cause grievous bodily harm etc.	Offences against the Person Act 1861 s.18	B

APPENDIX 10

Litigators' graduated fee tables

[Criminal Defence Service (Funding) Order 2007, SI 2007/1174, Sched.2, as amended by Criminal Defence Service (Funding) (Amendment) Orders 2007, SI 2007/3552 and 2009, SI 2009/1843]

(1)   CRACKED TRIALS AND GUILTY PLEAS

(a)   PPE Cut-off figures in cracked trials and guilty pleas [para.4]

Class of offence

Type of case	A	B	C	D	E	F	G	H	I	J	K
Cracked trial or guilty plea	150	70	40	80	40	50	120	40	40	80	120

(b)   Cracked trial or guilty plea where the number of pages of prosecution evidence is less than or equal to the PPE Cut-off [para.5]

Class of offence

Type of case	A	B	C	D	E	F
Cracked trial	2785.18	1036.20	766.89	1255.67	340.50	327.63
Guilty plea	1907.11	609.44	485.38	708.34	202.41	214.59

Class of offence

Type of case	G	H	I	J	K
Cracked trial	1074.22	346.31	370.66	1321.76	1130.76
Guilty plea	667.17	209.28	191.34	745.63	702.29

(c)   Cracked trials and guilty pleas where the number of pages of prosecution evidence exceeds the PPE Cut-off [para.7]

7.   (1)   Where in a cracked trial or guilty plea the number of pages of prosecution evidence exceeds the PPE Cut-off specified in the tables following paragraph

4(1) as appropriate to the offence with which the assisted person is charged, the total fee payable to the litigator will be –

(a) the final fee, calculated in accordance with sub-paragraph (2) of this paragraph;
(b) the defendant uplift, if any, calculated in accordance with the table following paragraph 9; and
(c) the adjustment for transfers and retrials, if any, calculated in accordance with paragraph 10.

(2) For the purposes of sub-paragraph (1), the final fee payable to a litigator in a cracked trial or guilty plea will be calculated in accordance with the following formula –

$$F = I + (D \times i)$$

(3) In the formula in sub-paragraph (2) –

F is the amount of the final fee;
I is the initial fee specified in the tables following this paragraph, as appropriate to the type of case, the offence with which the assisted person is charged and the number of pages of prosecution evidence;
D is the difference between –

(a) the number of pages of prosecution evidence in the case; and
(b) the lower number in the PPE range as specified in the tables following this paragraph, as appropriate to the type of case, the offence with which the assisted person is charged and the number of pages of prosecution evidence in the case;

i is the incremental fee per page of prosecution evidence specified in the tables following this paragraph, as appropriate to the type of case, the offence with which the assisted person is charged and the number of pages of prosecution evidence in the case.

(d)   Table of final fees in cracked trials [para.7]

Class of offence	PPE range	Initial fee (£)	Incremental fee per page of prosecution evidence (£)
A	0–149	2,785.18	0
A	150–249	2,785.18	16.5771
A	250–499	4,442.89	16.2953
A	500–999	8,516.71	8.9555
A	1000–2799	12,994.44	5.7143
A	2800–4599	23,280.20	5.7143
A	4600–6399	33,565.95	5.7143
A	6400–8199	43,851.70	5.7143
A	8200–9999	54,137.46	5.7143
A	10,000	64,417.49	0
B	0–69	1,036.20	0
B	70–249	1,036.20	11.4339
B	250–999	3,094.31	5.3516

B	1000–2799	7,108.03	3.5644
B	2800–4599	13,524.03	3.5644
B	4600–6399	19,940.03	2.9971
B	6400–8199	25,334.77	2.9971
B	8200–9999	30,729.49	2.9971
B	10,000	36,121.23	0
C	0–39	766.89	0
C	40–249	766.89	5.7329
C	250–999	1,970.80	3.2814
C	1000–2799	4,431.86	2.0898
C	2800–4599	8,193.57	2.0898
C	4600–6399	11,955.28	2.0898
C	6400–8199	15,716.99	2.0898
C	8200–9999	19,478.70	2.0898
C	10,000	23,238.32	0
D	0–79	1,255.67	0
D	80–249	1,255.67	14.8109
D	250–999	3,773.52	8.9254
D	1000–2799	10,467.60	5.2700
D	2800–4599	19,953.59	5.2700
D	4600–6399	29,439.57	4.3244
D	6400–8199	37,223.44	4.3244
D	8200–9999	45,007.29	4.3244
D	10,000	52,786.83	0
E	0–39	340.50	0
E	40–249	340.50	6.7242
E	250–999	1,752.59	2.1277
E	1000–2799	3,348.37	0.8919
E	2800–4599	4,953.80	0.8919
E	4600–6399	6,559.23	0.8919
E	6400–8199	8,164.66	0.8919
E	8200–9999	9,770.09	0.8919
E	10,000	11,374.63	0
F	0–49	327.63	0
F	50–249	327.63	6.4534
F	250–999	1,618.30	2.6162
F	1000–2799	3,580.48	1.0182
F	2800–4599	5,413.21	1.0182
F	4600–6399	7,245.94	1.0182
F	6400–8199	9,078.67	1.0182
F	8200–9999	10,911.40	1.0182
F	0	12,743.11	0
G	0–119	1,074.22	0
G	120–249	1,074.22	9.0709
G	250–999	2,253.44	6.8647
G	1000–2799	7,401.94	6.0530
G	2800–4599	18,297.33	6.0530
G	4600–6399	29,192.73	5.2019
G	6400–8199	38,556.20	5.2019
G	8200–9999	47,919.68	5.2019
G	10,000	57,277.96	0
H	0–39	346.31	0
H	40–249	346.31	6.2247
H	250–999	1,653.49	2.2728

H	1000–2799	3,358.10	1.0168
H	2800–4599	5,188.37	1.0168
H	4600–6399	7,018.63	1.0168
H	6400–8199	8,848.89	1.0168
H	8200–9999	10,679.16	1.0168
H	10,000	12,508.40	0
I	0–39	370.66	0
I	40–249	370.66	8.6497
I	250–999	2,187.10	3.3804
I	1000–2799	4,722.43	1.3114
I	2800–4599	7,082.89	1.3114
I	4600–6399	9,443.34	1.3114
I	6400–8199	11,803.80	1.3114
I	8200–9999	14,164.26	1.3114
I	10,000	16,523.40	0
J	0–79	1,321.76	0
J	80–249	1,321.76	15.6288
J	250–999	3,978.65	9.8095
J	1000–2799	11,335.74	5.7334
J	2800–4599	21,655.89	5.7334
J	4600–6399	31,976.05	4.5514
J	6400–8199	40,168.54	4.5514
J	8200–9999	48,361.04	4.5514
J	10,000	56,548.99	0
K	0–119	1,130.76	0
K	120–249	1,130.76	9.5650
K	250–999	2,374.21	7.3335
K	1000–2799	7,874.30	6.4212
K	2800–4599	19,432.39	6.4212
K	4600–6399	30,990.49	5.4755
K	6400–8199	40,846.45	5.4755
K	8200–9999	50,702.41	5.4755
K	10,000	60,552.89	0

(e)   Table of final fees in guilty pleas

Class of offence	PPE range	Initial fee (£)	Incremental fee per page of prosecution evidence (£)
A	0–149	1,907.11	0
A	150–399	1,907.11	9.2742
A	400–999	4,225.66	5.3634
A	1000–2799	7,443.69	3.8000
A	2800–4599	14,283.77	3.8001
A	4600–6399	21,123.86	3.8001
A	6400–8199	27,963.96	3.8001
A	8200–9999	34,804.05	3.8001
A	10,000	41,640.34	0
B	0–69	609.44	0
B	70–399	609.44	4.9497
B	400–999	2,242.84	2.4934
B	1000–2799	3,738.90	1.5916
B	2800–4599	6,603.75	1.5916

B	4600–6399	9,468.61	1.1661
B	6400–8199	11,567.51	1.1661
B	8200–9999	13,666.41	1.1661
B	10,000	15,764.14	0
C	0–39	485.38	0
C	40–399	485.38	2.9193
C	400–999	1,536.31	1.5971
C	1000–2799	2,494.54	0.8668
C	2800–4599	4,054.72	0.8668
C	4600–6399	5,614.91	0.8668
C	6400–8199	7,175.10	0.8668
C	8200–9999	8,735.29	0.8668
C	10,000	10,294.60	0
D	0–79	708.34	0
D	80–399	708.34	5.7339
D	400–999	2,543.19	3.0095
D	1000–2799	4,348.90	1.8739
D	2800–4599	7,721.86	1.8739
D	4600–6399	11,094.83	1.1647
D	6400–8199	13,191.21	1.1646
D	8200–9999	15,287.57	1.1647
D	10,000	17,382.78	0
E	0–39	202.41	0
E	40–399	202.41	3.2041
E	400–999	1,355.88	1.3732
E	1000–2799	2,179.80	0.5057
E	2800–4599	3,090.08	0.5057
E	4600–6399	4,000.36	0.5057
E	6400–8199	4,910.64	0.5057
E	8200–9999	5,820.92	0.5057
E	10,000	6,730.69	0
F	0–49	214.59	0
F	50–399	214.59	3.1058
F	400–999	1,301.62	1.0840
F	1000–2799	1,952.01	0.3488
F	2800–4599	2,579.80	0.3488
F	4600–6399	3,207.59	0.3488
F	6400–8199	3,835.38	0.3488
F	8200–9999	4,463.17	0.3488
F	10,000	5,090.61	0
G	0–119	667.17	0
G	120–399	667.17	4.7216
G	400–999	1,989.23	3.0953
G	1000–2799	3,846.43	2.7317
G	2800–4599	8,763.51	2.7317
G	4600–6399	13,680.59	2.1643
G	6400–8199	17,576.39	2.1643
G	8200–9999	21,472.20	2.1643
G	10,000	25,365.84	0
H	0–39	209.28	0
H	40–399	209.28	3.0613
H	400–999	1,311.33	1.0852
H	1000–2799	1,962.46	0.3465
H	2800–4599	2,586.14	0.3465

H	4600–6399	3,209.84	0.3465
H	6400–8199	3,833.53	0.3465
H	8200–9999	4,457.23	0.3465
H	10,000	5,080.55	0
I	0–39	191.34	0
I	40–399	191.34	3.4214
I	400–999	1,423.04	1.4936
I	1000–2799	2,319.22	0.5581
I	2800–4599	3,323.86	0.5581
I	4600–6399	4,328.49	0.5581
I	6400–8199	5,333.13	0.5581
I	8200–9999	6,337.78	0.5581
I	10,000	7,341.86	0
J	0–79	745.63	0
J	80–399	745.63	6.1572
J	400–999	2,715.93	3.2471
J	1000–2799	4,664.21	2.0766
J	2800–4599	8,402.07	2.0766
J	4600–6399	12,139.92	1.2255
J	6400–8199	14,345.86	1.2255
J	8200–9999	16,551.81	1.2255
J	10,000	18,756.53	0
K	0–119	702.29	0
K	120–399	702.29	5.7624
K	400–999	2,315.76	3.2075
K	1000–2799	4,240.26	2.9871
K	2800–4599	9,617.04	2.9871
K	4600–6399	14,993.82	2.2779
K	6400–8199	19,094.01	2.2779
K	8200–9999	23,194.20	2.2779
K	10,000	27,292.10	0

(2)   TRIALS

(a)   Trials where the number of pages of prosecution evidence exceeds the PPE Cut-off [para.8]

8.   (1)   Where in a trial the number of pages of prosecution evidence exceeds the PPE Cut-off figure specified in the table following paragraph 4(2) as appropriate to the offence for which the assisted person is tried and the length of trial, the total fee payable to the litigator will be –

(a)   the final fee, calculated in accordance with sub-paragraph (2) of this paragraph;

(b)   the defendant uplift, if any, calculated in accordance with the table following paragraph 9; and

(c)   the adjustment for transfers and retrials, if any, calculated in accordance with paragraph 10.

(2)   For the purposes of sub-paragraph (1), the final fee will be calculated in accordance with the following formula –

227

$$F = I + (D \times i)$$

(3)   In the formula in sub-paragraph (2) –

F is the amount of the final fee;

I is the initial fee specified in the table following this paragraph, as appropriate to the offence for which the assisted person is tried and the number of pages of prosecution evidence;

D is the difference between –

(a)   the number of pages of prosecution evidence in the case; and

(b)   the lower number in the PPE range as specified in the table following this paragraph, as appropriate to the offence for which the assisted person is tried and the number of pages of prosecution evidence in the case;

i is the incremental fee per page of prosecution evidence specified in the table following this paragraph, as appropriate to the offence for which the assisted person is tried and the number of pages of prosecution evidence in the case.

(b)   Basic fees for trials (£) [para.6]

Class of offence

Type of case	A	B	C	D	E	F
Trial	2785.18	1202.92	810.51	1527.89	386.54	391.89

Class of offence

Type of case	G	H	I	J	K
Trial	1074.22	392.05	391.72	1608.31	1130.76

(c) PPE cut-off figures in trials [para.4]

Trial length in days	PPE cut off A	PPE cut off B	PPE cut off C	PPE cut off D	PPE cut off E	PPE cut off F	PPE cut off G	PPE cut off H	PPE cut off I	PPE cut off J	PPE cut off K
1	150	70	40	80	40	50	120	40	40	80	120
2	150	70	40	80	40	50	120	40	40	80	120
3	246	105	81	95	120	138	186	122	134	95	186
4	341	139	120	126	158	173	252	157	185	126	252
5	431	170	157	156	195	206	314	191	232	156	314
6	523	203	193	186	229	240	372	225	281	186	372
7	615	238	230	218	265	276	433	260	329	218	433
8	716	274	267	257	301	310	495	301	376	257	495
9	807	306	301	293	333	342	550	338	420	293	550
10	898	338	339	330	365	373	606	374	464	330	606
11	991	370	378	367	399	405	663	412	509	367	663
12	1,084	402	417	404	433	437	721	449	554	404	721
13	1,184	434	455	440	467	470	779	486	598	440	779
14	1,286	465	493	477	500	501	836	523	642	477	836
15	1,389	497	531	514	532	533	894	559	686	514	894
16	1,491	535	569	551	565	564	951	596	730	551	951
17	1,594	573	607	587	598	596	1,007	637	774	587	1,007
18	1,696	611	646	624	646	627	1,063	687	818	624	1,063
19	1,798	649	684	661	696	659	1,119	736	862	661	1,119
20	1,901	687	722	697	746	690	1,174	786	907	697	1,174
21	2,017	722	753	742	787	720	1,230	826	943	742	1,230
22	2,132	757	785	786	828	752	1,286	867	980	786	1,286
23	2,247	792	819	830	868	784	1,341	908	1,017	830	1,341
24	2,362	826	857	874	908	816	1,396	948	1,053	874	1,396
25	2,477	860	894	917	948	848	1,451	988	1,088	917	1,451
26	2,593	895	931	961	988	880	1,505	1,028	1,124	961	1,505
27	2,708	935	967	1,005	1,028	912	1,560	1,068	1,160	1,005	1,560
28	2,823	975	1,004	1,049	1,068	944	1,615	1,107	1,196	1,049	1,615
29	2,938	1,016	1,041	1,099	1,108	976	1,670	1,147	1,231	1,099	1,670

Trial length in days	PPE cut off A	PPE cut off B	PPE cut off C	PPE cut off D	PPE cut off E	PPE cut off F	PPE cut off G	PPE cut off H	PPE cut off I	PPE cut off J	PPE cut off K
30	3,053	1,057	1,077	1,150	1,148	1,007	1,725	1,187	1,267	1,150	1,725
31	3,168	1,098	1,114	1,200	1,188	1,039	1,780	1,226	1,303	1,200	1,780
32	3,284	1,138	1,151	1,251	1,228	1,070	1,835	1,266	1,349	1,251	1,835
33	3,399	1,179	1,187	1,301	1,268	1,102	1,889	1,307	1,394	1,301	1,889
34	3,514	1,220	1,224	1,352	1,308	1,133	1,944	1,357	1,439	1,352	1,944
35	3,629	1,261	1,262	1,402	1,347	1,165	1,999	1,407	1,485	1,402	1,999
36	3,744	1,302	1,303	1,453	1,435	1,196	2,054	1,457	1,530	1,453	2,054
37	3,859	1,348	1,345	1,503	1,526	1,228	2,109	1,507	1,575	1,503	2,109
38	3,975	1,395	1,386	1,554	1,617	1,259	2,164	1,557	1,621	1,554	2,164
39	4,090	1,441	1,428	1,604	1,708	1,291	2,219	1,607	1,666	1,604	2,219
40	4,178	1,484	1,444	1,652	1,745	1,314	2,271	1,629	1,704	1,652	2,271
41	4,266	1,527	1,461	1,700	1,782	1,338	2,324	1,651	1,742	1,700	2,324
42	4,355	1,570	1,477	1,748	1,820	1,361	2,377	1,673	1,780	1,748	2,377
43	4,443	1,613	1,494	1,796	1,857	1,384	2,430	1,695	1,818	1,796	2,430
44	4,532	1,656	1,511	1,844	1,895	1,410	2,483	1,716	1,856	1,844	2,483
45	4,621	1,699	1,527	1,892	1,932	1,440	2,536	1,738	1,894	1,892	2,536
46	4,709	1,742	1,544	1,939	1,970	1,470	2,589	1,760	1,932	1,939	2,589
47	4,798	1,785	1,560	1,987	2,007	1,501	2,642	1,782	1,970	1,987	2,642
48	4,887	1,828	1,577	2,039	2,045	1,531	2,695	1,804	2,008	2,039	2,695
49	4,975	1,871	1,594	2,091	2,082	1,561	2,749	1,826	2,046	2,091	2,749
50	5,064	1,914	1,610	2,144	2,120	1,591	2,802	1,848	2,084	2,144	2,802
51	5,153	1,957	1,627	2,196	2,158	1,622	2,855	1,870	2,122	2,196	2,855
52	5,242	2,000	1,644	2,249	2,195	1,652	2,908	1,892	2,160	2,249	2,908
53	5,330	2,043	1,660	2,301	2,233	1,682	2,962	1,914	2,198	2,301	2,962
54	5,419	2,086	1,677	2,354	2,271	1,712	3,015	1,936	2,236	2,354	3,015
55	5,508	2,129	1,694	2,406	2,308	1,743	3,068	1,958	2,275	2,406	3,068
56	5,597	2,172	1,710	2,459	2,346	1,773	3,121	1,980	2,313	2,459	3,121
57	5,686	2,215	1,727	2,512	2,384	1,803	3,175	2,002	2,351	2,512	3,175
58	5,775	2,258	1,744	2,564	2,422	1,833	3,228	2,024	2,389	2,564	3,228
59	5,863	2,301	1,760	2,617	2,459	1,864	3,281	2,046	2,427	2,617	3,281
60	5,952	2,345	1,777	2,669	2,497	1,894	3,335	2,068	2,465	2,669	3,335

61	6,041	2,388	1,794	2,722	2,535	1,924	3,388	2,090	2,503	2,722	3,388
62	6,130	2,431	1,811	2,775	2,572	1,959	3,442	2,112	2,542	2,775	3,442
63	6,219	2,474	1,827	2,827	2,610	2,020	3,495	2,134	2,580	2,827	3,495
64	6,308	2,517	1,844	2,880	2,648	2,081	3,549	2,156	2,618	2,880	3,549
65	6,397	2,561	1,861	2,933	2,686	2,141	3,602	2,178	2,656	2,933	3,602
66	6,486	2,604	1,877	2,985	2,723	2,202	3,656	2,200	2,694	2,985	3,656
67	6,575	2,647	1,894	3,038	2,761	2,263	3,709	2,222	2,776	3,038	3,709
68	6,664	2,690	1,911	3,091	2,799	2,323	3,763	2,244	2,865	3,091	3,763
69	6,754	2,734	1,927	3,144	2,836	2,384	3,816	2,266	2,954	3,144	3,816
70	6,843	2,777	1,944	3,196	2,874	2,445	3,870	2,288	3,043	3,196	3,870
71	6,932	2,820	1,961	3,249	2,912	2,506	3,923	2,310	3,132	3,249	3,923
72	7,021	2,864	1,978	3,302	2,950	2,566	3,977	2,332	3,221	3,302	3,977
73	7,110	2,907	1,994	3,355	2,987	2,627	4,031	2,354	3,310	3,355	4,031
74	7,199	2,950	2,016	3,407	3,025	2,688	4,084	2,376	3,399	3,407	4,084
75	7,289	2,994	2,040	3,460	3,063	2,749	4,138	2,398	3,488	3,460	4,138
76	7,378	3,037	2,064	3,513	3,101	2,809	4,192	2,420	3,577	3,513	4,192
77	7,467	3,080	2,089	3,566	3,138	2,870	4,245	2,442	3,666	3,566	4,245
78	7,556	3,124	2,113	3,619	3,176	2,931	4,299	2,464	3,755	3,619	4,299
79	7,646	3,167	2,137	3,672	3,214	2,992	4,353	2,486	3,844	3,672	4,353
80	7,735	3,211	2,161	3,724	3,251	3,052	4,406	2,508	3,933	3,724	4,406
81	7,824	3,254	2,185	3,777	3,289	3,113	4,460	2,530	4,023	3,777	4,460
82	7,914	3,297	2,210	3,830	3,327	3,174	4,514	2,552	4,112	3,830	4,514
83	8,003	3,341	2,234	3,883	3,365	3,235	4,568	2,575	4,201	3,883	4,568
84	8,093	3,384	2,258	3,936	3,402	3,295	4,622	2,597	4,290	3,936	4,622
85	8,182	3,428	2,282	3,989	3,440	3,356	4,675	2,619	4,379	3,989	4,675
86	8,271	3,471	2,307	4,042	3,478	3,417	4,729	2,641	4,469	4,042	4,729
87	8,361	3,515	2,331	4,095	3,516	3,478	4,783	2,663	4,558	4,095	4,783
88	8,450	3,558	2,355	4,148	3,553	3,539	4,837	2,685	4,647	4,148	4,837
89	8,540	3,602	2,379	4,201	3,591	3,599	4,891	2,707	4,737	4,201	4,891
90	8,629	3,645	2,404	4,254	3,629	3,660	4,945	2,729	4,826	4,254	4,945
91	8,719	3,689	2,428	4,307	3,666	3,721	4,999	2,751	4,915	4,307	4,999
92	8,809	3,733	2,452	4,360	3,704	3,782	5,053	2,774	5,005	4,360	5,053
93	8,898	3,776	2,477	4,413	3,742	3,843	5,107	2,796	5,094	4,413	5,107

Trial length in days	PPE cut off A	PPE cut off B	PPE cut off C	PPE cut off D	PPE cut off E	PPE cut off F	PPE cut off G	PPE cut off H	PPE cut off I	PPE cut off J	PPE cut off K
94	8,988	3,820	2,501	4,466	3,780	3,903	5,161	2,818	5,183	4,466	5,161
95	9,077	3,863	2,525	4,519	3,817	3,964	5,215	2,840	5,273	4,519	5,215
96	9,167	3,907	2,549	4,572	3,855	4,025	5,269	2,862	5,362	4,572	5,269
97	9,257	3,951	2,574	4,625	3,893	4,086	5,323	2,884	5,452	4,625	5,323
98	9,346	3,994	2,598	4,679	3,930	4,147	5,377	2,906	5,541	4,679	5,377
99	9,436	4,038	2,622	4,732	3,968	4,207	5,431	2,929	5,631	4,732	5,431
100	9,526	4,082	2,647	4,785	4,006	4,268	5,485	2,951	5,720	4,785	5,485
101	9,616	4,125	2,671	4,838	4,044	4,329	5,539	2,973	5,810	4,838	5,539
102	9,705	4,169	2,695	4,891	4,081	4,390	5,593	2,995	5,899	4,891	5,593
103	9,795	4,213	2,720	4,944	4,119	4,451	5,647	3,032	5,989	4,944	5,647
104	9,885	4,257	2,744	4,997	4,157	4,512	5,702	3,073	6,079	4,997	5,702
105	9,975	4,300	2,768	5,051	4,195	4,573	5,756	3,114	6,168	5,051	5,756
106	10,065	4,344	2,793	5,104	4,232	4,633	5,810	3,155	6,258	5,104	5,810
107	10,155	4,388	2,817	5,157	4,270	4,694	5,864	3,196	6,348	5,157	5,864
108	10,245	4,432	2,841	5,210	4,308	4,755	5,918	3,237	6,437	5,210	5,918
109	10,334	4,475	2,866	5,264	4,345	4,816	5,973	3,278	6,527	5,264	5,973
110	10,424	4,519	2,890	5,317	4,383	4,877	6,027	3,319	6,617	5,317	6,027
111	10,514	4,563	2,914	5,370	4,421	4,938	6,081	3,361	6,706	5,370	6,081
112	10,604	4,607	2,939	5,423	4,459	4,999	6,135	3,402	6,796	5,423	6,135
113	10,694	4,650	2,963	5,477	4,496	5,059	6,189	3,443	6,886	5,477	6,189
114	10,784	4,694	2,987	5,530	4,534	5,120	6,244	3,484	6,976	5,530	6,244
115	10,874	4,738	3,012	5,583	4,572	5,181	6,298	3,525	7,066	5,583	6,298
116	10,964	4,782	3,036	5,637	4,610	5,242	6,352	3,566	7,155	5,637	6,352
117	11,054	4,826	3,060	5,690	4,647	5,303	6,406	3,607	7,245	5,690	6,406
118	11,145	4,869	3,085	5,743	4,685	5,364	6,460	3,648	7,335	5,743	6,460
119	11,235	4,913	3,109	5,797	4,723	5,425	6,514	3,689	7,425	5,797	6,514
120	11,325	4,957	3,133	5,850	4,760	5,486	6,569	3,730	7,515	5,850	6,569
121	11,415	5,001	3,158	5,904	4,798	5,547	6,623	3,771	7,605	5,904	6,623
122	11,504	5,044	3,182	5,956	4,836	5,607	6,677	3,812	7,693	5,956	6,677
123	11,593	5,088	3,206	6,009	4,874	5,668	6,731	3,853	7,782	6,009	6,731
124	11,681	5,131	3,230	6,061	4,911	5,729	6,785	3,895	7,871	6,061	6,785

125	11,770	5,175	3,254	6,114	4,949	5,789	6,839	3,936	7,959	6,114	6,839
126	11,859	5,218	3,278	6,167	4,987	5,850	6,892	3,977	8,048	6,167	6,892
127	11,948	5,261	3,302	6,219	5,025	5,911	6,945	4,017	8,137	6,219	6,945
128	12,037	5,304	3,326	6,272	5,062	5,971	6,999	4,058	8,225	6,272	6,999
129	12,125	5,347	3,350	6,324	5,100	6,032	7,052	4,098	8,314	6,324	7,052
130	12,214	5,390	3,374	6,377	5,138	6,093	7,106	4,139	8,403	6,377	7,106
131	12,303	5,433	3,398	6,430	5,175	6,153	7,159	4,179	8,491	6,430	7,159
132	12,392	5,476	3,422	6,482	5,213	6,214	7,212	4,219	8,580	6,482	7,212
133	12,481	5,520	3,446	6,535	5,251	6,274	7,266	4,260	8,669	6,535	7,266
134	12,570	5,563	3,470	6,588	5,289	6,335	7,319	4,300	8,757	6,588	7,319
135	12,658	5,606	3,494	6,640	5,326	6,396	7,373	4,341	8,846	6,640	7,373
136	12,747	5,649	3,518	6,693	5,364	6,456	7,426	4,381	8,935	6,693	7,426
137	12,836	5,692	3,542	6,745	5,402	6,517	7,479	4,422	9,023	6,745	7,479
138	12,925	5,735	3,566	6,798	5,439	6,578	7,533	4,462	9,112	6,798	7,533
139	13,014	5,778	3,590	6,851	5,477	6,638	7,586	4,503	9,201	6,851	7,586
140	13,102	5,821	3,614	6,903	5,515	6,699	7,639	4,543	9,289	6,903	7,639
141	13,191	5,864	3,638	6,956	5,553	6,760	7,693	4,584	9,378	6,956	7,693
142	13,280	5,908	3,662	7,008	5,590	6,820	7,746	4,624	9,467	7,008	7,746
143	13,369	5,951	3,686	7,061	5,628	6,881	7,800	4,664	9,555	7,061	7,800
144	13,458	5,994	3,709	7,114	5,666	6,942	7,853	4,705	9,644	7,114	7,853
145	13,546	6,037	3,733	7,166	5,704	7,002	7,906	4,745	9,733	7,166	7,906
146	13,635	6,080	3,757	7,219	5,741	7,063	7,960	4,786	9,821	7,219	7,960
147	13,724	6,123	3,781	7,272	5,779	7,124	8,013	4,826	9,910	7,272	8,013
148	13,813	6,166	3,805	7,324	5,817	7,184	8,067	4,867	9,999	7,324	8,067
149	13,902	6,209	3,829	7,377	5,854	7,245	8,120	4,907	10,087	7,377	8,120
150	13,990	6,252	3,853	7,429	5,892	7,305	8,173	4,948	10,176	7,429	8,173
151	14,079	6,296	3,877	7,482	5,930	7,366	8,227	4,988	10,265	7,482	8,227
152	14,168	6,339	3,901	7,535	5,968	7,427	8,280	5,029	10,353	7,535	8,280
153	14,257	6,382	3,925	7,587	6,005	7,487	8,333	5,069	10,442	7,587	8,333
154	14,346	6,425	3,949	7,640	6,043	7,548	8,387	5,110	10,531	7,640	8,387
155	14,435	6,468	3,973	7,692	6,081	7,609	8,440	5,150	10,619	7,692	8,440
156	14,523	6,511	3,997	7,745	6,119	7,669	8,494	5,190	10,708	7,745	8,494
157	14,612	6,554	4,021	7,798	6,156	7,730	8,547	5,231	10,797	7,798	8,547

Trial length in days	PPE cut off A	PPE cut off B	PPE cut off C	PPE cut off D	PPE cut off E	PPE cut off F	PPE cut off G	PPE cut off H	PPE cut off I	PPE cut off J	PPE cut off K
158	14,701	6,597	4,045	7,850	6,194	7,791	8,600	5,271	10,885	7,850	8,600
159	14,790	6,641	4,069	7,903	6,232	7,851	8,654	5,312	10,974	7,903	8,654
160	14,879	6,684	4,093	7,956	6,269	7,912	8,707	5,352	11,063	7,956	8,707
161	14,967	6,727	4,117	8,008	6,307	7,973	8,760	5,393	11,151	8,008	8,760
162	15,056	6,770	4,141	8,061	6,345	8,033	8,814	5,433	11,240	8,061	8,814
163	15,145	6,813	4,165	8,113	6,383	8,094	8,867	5,474	11,329	8,113	8,867
164	15,234	6,856	4,189	8,166	6,420	8,155	8,921	5,514	11,417	8,166	8,921
165	15,323	6,899	4,213	8,219	6,458	8,215	8,974	5,555	11,506	8,219	8,974
166	15,411	6,942	4,237	8,271	6,496	8,276	9,027	5,595	11,595	8,271	9,027
167	15,500	6,985	4,261	8,324	6,534	8,337	9,081	5,636	11,683	8,324	9,081
168	15,589	7,029	4,285	8,376	6,571	8,397	9,134	5,676	11,772	8,376	9,134
169	15,678	7,072	4,309	8,429	6,609	8,458	9,188	5,716	11,861	8,429	9,188
170	15,767	7,115	4,333	8,482	6,647	8,518	9,241	5,757	11,949	8,482	9,241
171	15,855	7,158	4,357	8,534	6,684	8,579	9,294	5,797	12,038	8,534	9,294
172	15,944	7,201	4,380	8,587	6,722	8,640	9,348	5,838	12,127	8,587	9,348
173	16,033	7,244	4,404	8,639	6,760	8,700	9,401	5,878	12,215	8,639	9,401
174	16,122	7,287	4,428	8,692	6,798	8,761	9,454	5,919	12,304	8,692	9,454
175	16,211	7,330	4,452	8,745	6,835	8,822	9,508	5,959	12,393	8,745	9,508
176	16,300	7,373	4,476	8,797	6,873	8,882	9,561	6,000	12,481	8,797	9,561
177	16,388	7,417	4,500	8,850	6,911	8,943	9,615	6,040	12,570	8,850	9,615
178	16,477	7,460	4,524	8,903	6,948	9,004	9,668	6,081	12,659	8,903	9,668
179	16,566	7,503	4,548	8,955	6,986	9,064	9,721	6,121	12,747	8,955	9,721
180	16,655	7,546	4,572	9,008	7,024	9,125	9,775	6,162	12,836	9,008	9,775
181	16,744	7,589	4,596	9,060	7,062	9,186	9,828	6,202	12,925	9,060	9,828
182	16,832	7,632	4,620	9,113	7,099	9,246	9,881	6,242	13,013	9,113	9,881
183	16,921	7,675	4,644	9,166	7,137	9,307	9,935	6,283	13,102	9,166	9,935
184	17,010	7,718	4,668	9,218	7,174	9,368	9,988	6,323	13,191	9,218	9,988
185	17,099	7,762	4,692	9,271	7,211	9,428	10,042	6,364	13,279	9,271	10,042
186	17,188	7,805	4,716	9,323	7,248	9,489	10,095	6,404	13,368	9,323	10,095
187	17,276	7,848	4,740	9,376	7,285	9,549	10,148	6,445	13,457	9,376	10,148
188	17,365	7,891	4,764	9,429	7,322	9,610	10,202	6,485	13,545	9,429	10,202

189	17,454	7,934	4,788	9,481	7,360	9,671	10,255	6,526	13,634	9,481	10,255
190	17,543	7,977	4,812	9,534	7,397	9,731	10,309	6,566	13,723	9,534	10,309
191	17,632	8,020	4,836	9,587	7,434	9,792	10,362	6,607	13,811	9,587	10,362
192	17,720	8,063	4,860	9,639	7,471	9,853	10,415	6,647	13,900	9,639	10,415
193	17,809	8,106	4,884	9,692	7,508	9,913	10,469	6,687	13,988	9,692	10,469
194	17,898	8,150	4,908	9,744	7,545	9,974	10,522	6,728	14,077	9,744	10,522
195	17,987	8,193	4,932	9,797	7,582	10,035	10,575	6,768	14,166	9,797	10,575
196	18,076	8,236	4,956	9,850	7,620	10,095	10,629	6,809	14,254	9,850	10,629
197	18,165	8,279	4,980	9,902	7,657	10,156	10,682	6,849	14,343	9,902	10,682
198	18,253	8,322	5,004	9,955	7,694	10,217	10,736	6,890	14,432	9,955	10,736
199	18,342	8,365	5,028	10,007	7,731	10,277	10,789	6,930	14,520	10,007	10,789
200	18,431	8,408	5,051	10,060	7,768	10,338	10,842	6,971	14,609	10,060	10,842

(d) Length of trial proxy [para.6]

Trial length in days	Trial length proxy A	Trial length proxy B	Trial length proxy C	Trial length proxy D	Trial length proxy E	Trial length proxy F	Trial length proxy G	Trial length proxy H	Trial length proxy I	Trial length proxy J	Trial length proxy K
1	0.00	0.00	0.00	0.00	0.00	0.00	0.00	0.00	0.00	0.00	0.00
2	0.00	0.00	0.00	0.00	0.00	0.00	0.00	0.00	0.00	0.00	0.00
3	1,567.39	496.31	473.98	262.93	785.29	706.78	597.73	771.17	945.08	276.76	629.18
4	3,125.99	964.00	924.20	801.42	1,132.77	984.95	1,187.50	1,106.66	1,447.59	843.60	1,250.00
5	4,606.67	1,408.31	1,351.90	1,312.99	1,462.86	1,249.21	1,747.80	1,425.36	1,924.97	1,382.09	1,839.79
6	6,102.89	1,858.61	1,776.66	1,833.56	1,772.17	1,519.38	2,270.67	1,741.43	2,411.61	1,930.05	2,390.18
7	7,586.15	2,303.80	2,203.87	2,346.50	2,099.12	1,789.40	2,824.77	2,059.74	2,890.57	2,469.99	2,973.44
8	9,069.42	2,748.97	2,631.09	2,859.44	2,426.07	2,055.07	3,378.86	2,378.05	3,369.53	3,009.93	3,556.69
9	10,404.37	3,149.63	3,015.57	3,342.88	2,720.32	2,294.19	3,877.54	2,664.53	3,806.50	3,518.82	4,081.63
10	11,739.31	3,550.30	3,400.07	3,826.32	3,014.59	2,533.30	4,376.22	2,951.00	4,243.47	4,027.71	4,606.55
11	13,101.98	3,951.50	3,794.99	4,313.36	3,322.37	2,779.24	4,897.29	3,245.35	4,689.34	4,540.38	5,155.06
12	14,465.79	4,352.20	4,190.10	4,797.10	3,630.24	3,025.17	5,418.70	3,539.33	5,135.58	5,049.58	5,703.89
13	15,805.12	4,752.90	4,576.22	5,280.84	3,937.70	3,270.12	5,940.11	3,826.93	5,574.00	5,558.78	6,252.75
14	17,144.46	5,153.61	4,962.33	5,764.59	4,235.69	3,510.51	6,461.49	4,114.53	6,012.41	6,067.98	6,801.57
15	18,483.80	5,554.31	5,348.45	6,248.32	4,532.77	3,750.89	6,982.85	4,402.14	6,450.82	6,577.18	7,350.37
16	19,823.13	5,955.02	5,734.56	6,732.06	4,829.87	3,991.29	7,503.38	4,689.74	6,889.23	7,086.38	7,898.30
17	21,162.47	6,355.73	6,120.68	7,215.80	5,126.96	4,231.68	8,010.04	4,977.34	7,327.64	7,595.57	8,431.63
18	22,501.80	6,756.43	6,506.79	7,699.54	5,424.05	4,472.07	8,516.70	5,264.94	7,766.05	8,104.77	8,964.95
19	23,841.14	7,157.13	6,892.90	8,183.28	5,721.14	4,712.46	9,023.36	5,552.54	8,204.46	8,613.97	9,498.27
20	25,180.48	7,557.84	7,279.02	8,667.02	6,018.23	4,952.85	9,530.02	5,840.14	8,642.88	9,123.17	10,031.60
21	26,528.83	7,927.97	7,596.29	9,159.97	6,263.74	5,149.52	10,036.68	6,076.67	9,003.14	9,642.08	10,564.93
22	27,868.58	8,298.07	7,913.63	9,652.84	6,509.26	5,346.28	10,543.34	6,313.31	9,363.42	10,160.89	11,098.26
23	29,208.32	8,668.15	8,231.00	10,137.38	6,747.46	5,543.04	11,050.01	6,549.95	9,723.73	10,670.92	11,631.58
24	30,548.08	9,029.83	8,548.37	10,621.91	6,985.68	5,739.80	11,556.66	6,786.59	10,080.08	11,180.95	12,164.91
25	31,887.82	9,391.50	8,864.09	11,106.44	7,223.89	5,936.55	12,063.32	7,019.41	10,431.95	11,691.00	12,698.24

26	33,227.57	9,753.17	9,174.28	11,590.99	7,462.10	6,133.31	12,569.98	7,250.40	10,783.83	12,201.03	13,231.57
27	34,567.32	10,114.85	9,484.49	12,075.51	7,700.31	6,330.07	13,076.64	7,481.38	11,135.70	12,711.06	13,764.89
28	35,907.06	10,476.53	9,794.68	12,560.05	7,938.53	6,526.83	13,583.31	7,712.37	11,487.57	13,221.10	14,298.22
29	37,246.82	10,838.20	10,104.88	13,044.58	8,176.73	6,721.29	14,089.97	7,943.34	11,839.46	13,731.14	14,831.54
30	38,586.56	11,199.87	10,415.07	13,529.11	8,414.94	6,914.62	14,596.63	8,174.32	12,191.33	14,241.17	15,364.87
31	39,926.31	11,561.55	10,725.27	14,013.65	8,653.16	7,107.96	15,103.29	8,405.31	12,543.20	14,751.21	15,898.20
32	41,266.06	11,923.23	11,035.47	14,498.18	8,891.37	7,301.29	15,609.95	8,636.29	12,895.08	15,261.24	16,431.52
33	42,605.81	12,284.90	11,345.67	14,982.72	9,129.58	7,494.62	16,116.60	8,867.28	13,246.95	15,771.29	16,964.85
34	43,945.56	12,646.57	11,655.86	15,467.26	9,367.79	7,687.96	16,623.27	9,098.26	13,598.83	16,281.32	17,498.18
35	45,285.31	13,008.25	11,966.06	15,951.79	9,606.00	7,881.29	17,129.93	9,329.24	13,950.71	16,791.35	18,031.51
36	46,625.06	13,369.92	12,276.26	16,436.32	9,844.21	8,074.63	17,636.59	9,560.22	14,302.58	17,301.39	18,564.83
37	47,964.81	13,731.60	12,586.46	16,920.86	10,082.43	8,267.96	18,143.25	9,791.21	14,654.45	17,811.43	19,098.16
38	49,304.55	14,093.27	12,896.66	17,405.39	10,320.64	8,461.29	18,649.91	10,022.19	15,006.33	18,321.46	19,631.49
39	50,644.31	14,454.94	13,206.85	17,889.92	10,558.84	8,654.63	19,156.57	10,253.17	15,358.20	18,831.50	20,164.82
40	51,667.89	14,785.90	13,329.94	18,346.59	10,654.34	8,797.55	19,641.20	10,353.05	15,651.51	19,312.20	20,674.95
41	52,697.86	15,119.38	13,454.39	18,805.74	10,752.37	8,940.76	20,129.41	10,454.14	15,946.54	19,795.51	21,188.86
42	53,728.06	15,452.95	13,578.88	19,265.01	10,850.45	9,083.97	20,617.80	10,555.27	16,241.65	20,278.95	21,702.94
43	54,758.50	15,786.64	13,703.38	19,724.39	10,948.58	9,227.20	21,106.33	10,656.41	16,536.81	20,762.51	22,217.20
44	55,789.17	16,120.43	13,827.90	20,183.88	11,046.75	9,370.43	21,595.04	10,757.57	16,832.03	21,246.19	22,731.63
45	56,820.09	16,454.31	13,952.45	20,643.48	11,144.95	9,513.67	22,083.91	10,858.77	17,127.33	21,729.98	23,246.22
46	57,851.23	16,788.30	14,077.02	21,103.21	11,243.21	9,656.92	22,572.94	10,959.97	17,422.67	22,213.90	23,761.00
47	58,882.61	17,122.39	14,201.62	21,563.03	11,341.51	9,800.18	23,062.14	11,061.21	17,718.09	22,697.92	24,275.94
48	59,914.23	17,456.59	14,326.24	22,022.98	11,439.86	9,943.44	23,551.50	11,162.47	18,013.57	23,182.08	24,791.06
49	60,946.09	17,790.89	14,450.89	22,483.03	11,538.24	10,086.71	24,041.02	11,263.74	18,309.10	23,666.34	25,306.34
50	61,978.18	18,125.29	14,575.55	22,943.19	11,636.66	10,230.00	24,530.71	11,365.05	18,604.70	24,150.72	25,821.80
51	63,010.50	18,459.79	14,700.25	23,403.47	11,735.14	10,373.29	25,020.57	11,466.37	18,900.37	24,635.23	26,337.44
52	64,043.06	18,794.39	14,824.96	23,863.86	11,833.66	10,516.60	25,510.58	11,567.72	19,196.09	25,119.85	26,853.24
53	65,075.86	19,129.10	14,949.70	24,324.37	11,932.22	10,659.90	26,000.76	11,669.09	19,491.87	25,604.59	27,369.22
54	66,108.89	19,463.91	15,074.46	24,784.97	12,030.83	10,803.22	26,491.11	11,770.48	19,787.72	26,089.45	27,885.37
55	67,142.16	19,798.82	15,199.24	25,245.69	12,129.47	10,946.54	26,981.61	11,871.89	20,083.63	26,574.42	28,401.69

Trial length in days	Trial length proxy A	Trial length proxy B	Trial length proxy C	Trial length proxy D	Trial length proxy E	Trial length proxy F	Trial length proxy G	Trial length proxy H	Trial length proxy I	Trial length proxy J	Trial length proxy K
56	68,175.66	20,133.84	15,324.06	25,706.54	12,228.16	11,089.88	27,472.28	11,973.33	20,379.61	27,059.51	28,918.19
57	69,209.40	20,468.95	15,448.89	26,167.49	12,326.89	11,233.23	27,963.11	12,074.78	20,675.64	27,544.72	29,434.86
58	70,243.38	20,804.17	15,573.74	26,628.55	12,425.63	11,376.58	28,454.11	12,176.26	20,971.74	28,030.05	29,951.69
59	71,277.59	21,139.50	15,698.63	27,089.73	12,524.37	11,519.94	28,945.28	12,277.77	21,267.90	28,515.50	30,468.71
60	72,312.03	21,474.92	15,823.53	27,551.00	12,623.11	11,663.31	29,436.60	12,379.29	21,564.12	29,001.06	30,985.90
61	73,346.71	21,810.44	15,948.46	28,012.41	12,721.86	11,806.69	29,928.09	12,480.84	21,860.41	29,486.75	31,503.25
62	74,381.63	22,146.08	16,073.41	28,473.92	12,820.60	11,950.07	30,419.74	12,582.42	22,156.76	29,972.54	32,020.78
63	75,416.78	22,481.80	16,198.38	28,935.55	12,919.34	12,093.46	30,911.56	12,684.01	22,453.17	30,458.47	32,538.49
64	76,452.18	22,817.64	16,323.39	29,397.28	13,018.08	12,236.87	31,403.54	12,785.63	22,749.63	30,944.50	33,056.36
65	77,487.80	23,153.57	16,448.41	29,859.12	13,116.82	12,380.28	31,895.69	12,887.26	23,046.17	31,430.66	33,574.41
66	78,523.66	23,489.62	16,573.46	30,321.09	13,215.56	12,523.70	32,387.99	12,988.92	23,342.77	31,916.93	34,092.62
67	79,559.75	23,825.76	16,698.52	30,783.16	13,314.30	12,667.13	32,880.47	13,090.60	23,639.42	32,403.32	34,611.01
68	80,596.09	24,162.01	16,823.62	31,245.34	13,413.04	12,810.57	33,373.11	13,192.31	23,936.14	32,889.83	35,129.58
69	81,632.66	24,498.35	16,948.73	31,707.63	13,511.78	12,954.02	33,865.90	13,294.04	24,232.93	33,376.46	35,648.31
70	82,669.46	24,834.80	17,073.87	32,170.04	13,610.52	13,097.48	34,358.87	13,395.79	24,529.77	33,863.20	36,167.23
71	83,706.49	25,171.35	17,199.04	32,632.57	13,709.26	13,240.94	34,851.99	13,497.57	24,826.68	34,350.07	36,686.31
72	84,743.77	25,508.01	17,324.22	33,095.20	13,808.00	13,384.42	35,345.28	13,599.36	25,123.65	34,837.05	37,205.57
73	85,781.29	25,844.77	17,449.44	33,557.95	13,906.74	13,527.90	35,838.74	13,701.17	25,420.68	35,324.14	37,724.99
74	86,819.03	26,181.63	17,574.67	34,020.80	14,005.48	13,671.39	36,332.36	13,803.02	25,717.78	35,811.36	38,244.59
75	87,857.00	26,518.59	17,699.93	34,483.76	14,104.22	13,814.89	36,826.14	13,904.89	26,014.94	36,298.70	38,764.36
76	88,895.23	26,855.65	17,825.21	34,946.85	14,202.96	13,958.39	37,320.09	14,006.77	26,312.15	36,786.15	39,284.30
77	89,933.68	27,192.82	17,950.52	35,410.04	14,301.70	14,101.91	37,814.19	14,108.67	26,609.43	37,273.73	39,804.42
78	90,972.37	27,530.09	18,075.85	35,873.35	14,400.44	14,245.43	38,308.47	14,210.60	26,906.77	37,761.41	40,324.71
79	92,011.29	27,867.46	18,201.20	36,336.77	14,499.18	14,388.97	38,802.91	14,312.56	27,204.19	38,249.23	40,845.17
80	93,050.45	28,204.93	18,326.58	36,800.29	14,597.92	14,532.51	39,297.51	14,414.54	27,501.65	38,737.15	41,365.80
81	94,089.85	28,542.51	18,451.97	37,263.94	14,696.66	14,676.06	39,792.27	14,516.54	27,799.18	39,225.19	41,886.60
82	95,129.47	28,880.19	18,577.40	37,727.69	14,795.40	14,819.62	40,287.21	14,618.55	28,096.77	39,713.35	42,407.58

83	96,169.34	29,217.97	18,702.85	38,191.56	14,894.14	14,963.18	40,782.29	14,720.60	28,394.43	40,201.63	42,928.73
84	97,209.45	29,555.86	18,828.31	38,655.53	14,992.89	15,106.77	41,277.55	14,822.66	28,692.14	40,690.03	43,450.06
85	98,249.78	29,893.84	18,953.81	39,119.62	15,091.63	15,250.35	41,772.98	14,924.75	28,989.92	41,178.54	43,971.55
86	99,290.36	30,231.93	19,079.34	39,583.83	15,190.37	15,393.94	42,268.55	15,026.86	29,287.77	41,667.18	44,493.22
87	100,331.17	30,570.12	19,204.88	40,048.14	15,289.11	15,537.54	42,764.31	15,129.00	29,585.68	42,155.93	45,015.06
88	101,372.21	30,908.42	19,330.44	40,512.57	15,387.85	15,681.16	43,260.22	15,231.15	29,883.64	42,644.81	45,537.07
89	102,413.49	31,246.81	19,456.03	40,977.11	15,486.59	15,824.77	43,756.29	15,333.33	30,181.67	43,133.80	46,059.26
90	103,455.00	31,585.31	19,581.64	41,441.75	15,585.33	15,968.40	44,252.53	15,435.52	30,479.76	43,622.90	46,581.62
91	104,496.76	31,923.91	19,707.28	41,906.52	15,684.07	16,112.04	44,748.94	15,537.75	30,777.91	44,112.13	47,104.14
92	105,538.75	32,262.61	19,832.94	42,371.40	15,782.81	16,255.69	45,245.50	15,639.99	31,076.13	44,601.46	47,626.84
93	106,580.97	32,601.42	19,958.62	42,836.38	15,881.55	16,399.34	45,742.23	15,742.26	31,374.41	45,090.93	48,149.72
94	107,623.43	32,940.33	20,084.33	43,301.48	15,980.29	16,543.00	46,239.13	15,844.55	31,672.75	45,580.50	48,672.77
95	108,666.13	33,279.34	20,210.06	43,766.69	16,079.03	16,686.67	46,736.19	15,946.87	31,971.15	46,070.20	49,195.98
96	109,709.06	33,618.46	20,335.82	44,232.02	16,177.77	16,830.35	47,233.40	16,049.19	32,269.62	46,560.02	49,719.38
97	110,752.22	33,957.68	20,461.60	44,697.46	16,276.51	16,974.04	47,730.79	16,151.51	32,568.14	47,049.95	50,242.94
98	111,795.63	34,297.00	20,587.40	45,163.00	16,375.25	17,117.74	48,228.34	16,253.84	32,866.73	47,540.00	50,766.68
99	112,839.26	34,636.42	20,713.23	45,628.66	16,473.99	17,261.45	48,726.06	16,356.16	33,165.39	48,030.17	51,290.59
100	113,883.13	34,975.94	20,839.07	46,094.43	16,572.73	17,405.16	49,223.93	16,458.49	33,464.09	48,520.45	51,814.66
101	114,927.24	35,315.57	20,964.94	46,560.32	16,671.47	17,548.89	49,721.97	16,560.81	33,762.88	49,010.86	52,338.92
102	115,971.58	35,655.29	21,090.84	47,026.31	16,770.21	17,692.61	50,220.18	16,663.13	34,061.71	49,501.38	52,863.34
103	117,016.17	35,995.12	21,216.77	47,492.43	16,868.95	17,836.35	50,718.54	16,765.46	34,360.61	49,992.03	53,387.95
104	118,060.98	36,335.06	21,342.70	47,958.65	16,967.69	17,980.10	51,217.08	16,867.78	34,659.57	50,482.78	53,912.71
105	119,106.03	36,675.10	21,468.63	48,424.97	17,066.43	18,123.86	51,715.78	16,970.10	34,958.60	50,973.66	54,437.66
106	120,151.32	37,015.23	21,594.56	48,891.42	17,165.17	18,267.63	52,214.52	17,072.43	35,257.69	51,464.66	54,962.66
107	121,196.84	37,355.44	21,720.49	49,357.97	17,263.91	18,411.40	52,713.27	17,174.75	35,556.84	51,955.77	55,487.65
108	122,242.60	37,695.64	21,846.43	49,824.66	17,362.66	18,555.18	53,212.02	17,277.07	35,856.05	52,447.00	56,012.65
109	123,288.60	38,035.85	21,972.36	50,291.43	17,461.40	18,698.98	53,710.76	17,379.40	36,155.33	52,938.35	56,537.64

Trial length in days	Trial length proxy A	Trial length proxy B	Trial length proxy C	Trial length proxy D	Trial length proxy E	Trial length proxy F	Trial length proxy G	Trial length proxy H	Trial length proxy I	Trial length proxy J	Trial length proxy K
110	124,334.83	38,376.05	22,098.29	50,758.32	17,560.14	18,842.77	54,209.51	17,481.72	36,454.66	53,429.81	57,062.64
111	125,381.29	38,716.26	22,224.22	51,225.34	17,658.88	18,986.59	54,708.26	17,584.04	36,754.06	53,921.40	57,587.63
112	126,427.99	39,056.46	22,350.15	51,692.45	17,757.62	19,130.40	55,207.00	17,686.37	37,053.52	54,413.10	58,112.63
113	127,474.93	39,396.66	22,476.09	52,159.69	17,856.36	19,274.23	55,705.74	17,788.69	37,353.05	54,904.92	58,637.63
114	128,522.10	39,736.87	22,602.02	52,627.02	17,955.10	19,418.07	56,204.49	17,891.01	37,652.64	55,396.86	59,162.62
115	129,569.51	40,077.07	22,727.95	53,094.47	18,053.84	19,561.91	56,703.23	17,993.34	37,952.28	55,888.92	59,687.62
116	130,617.15	40,417.28	22,853.88	53,562.04	18,152.58	19,705.76	57,201.98	18,095.66	38,251.99	56,381.10	60,212.61
117	131,665.03	40,757.48	22,979.81	54,029.72	18,251.32	19,849.62	57,700.72	18,197.98	38,551.77	56,873.39	60,737.61
118	132,713.15	41,097.69	23,105.74	54,497.51	18,350.06	19,993.49	58,199.47	18,300.31	38,851.60	57,365.80	61,262.60
119	133,761.50	41,437.89	23,231.68	54,965.41	18,448.80	20,137.37	58,698.22	18,402.63	39,151.50	57,858.33	61,787.60
120	134,810.09	41,778.09	23,357.61	55,433.43	18,547.54	20,281.26	59,196.96	18,504.95	39,451.46	58,350.98	62,312.60
121	135,858.91	42,118.30	23,483.54	55,901.56	18,646.28	20,425.15	59,695.71	18,607.28	39,751.48	58,843.74	62,837.59
122	136,892.03	42,458.50	23,609.47	56,362.76	18,745.02	20,568.43	60,194.46	18,709.60	40,047.31	59,329.22	63,362.59
123	137,925.16	42,798.71	23,735.40	56,823.97	18,843.76	20,711.70	60,693.20	18,811.92	40,343.13	59,814.69	63,887.58
124	138,958.29	43,134.92	23,859.50	57,285.16	18,942.50	20,854.97	61,190.98	18,914.25	40,638.96	60,300.17	64,411.56
125	139,991.41	43,470.02	23,983.54	57,746.36	19,041.24	20,998.25	61,682.25	19,016.57	40,934.79	60,785.64	64,928.68
126	141,024.54	43,805.11	24,107.58	58,207.57	19,139.98	21,141.51	62,173.51	19,118.83	41,230.61	61,271.11	65,445.80
127	142,057.67	44,140.22	24,231.63	58,668.77	19,238.72	21,284.79	62,664.77	19,219.63	41,526.44	61,756.60	65,962.93
128	143,090.79	44,475.32	24,355.67	59,129.97	19,337.46	21,428.07	63,156.04	19,320.42	41,822.27	62,242.07	66,480.04
129	144,123.92	44,810.42	24,479.71	59,591.17	19,436.20	21,571.34	63,647.30	19,421.20	42,118.09	62,727.54	66,997.17
130	145,157.05	45,145.52	24,603.75	60,052.37	19,534.94	21,714.61	64,138.57	19,521.99	42,413.92	63,213.02	67,514.29
131	146,190.17	45,480.62	24,727.80	60,513.57	19,633.69	21,857.89	64,629.84	19,622.78	42,709.75	63,698.49	68,031.40
132	147,223.30	45,815.73	24,851.84	60,974.77	19,732.43	22,001.16	65,121.10	19,723.57	43,005.57	64,183.97	68,548.53
133	148,256.43	46,150.83	24,975.88	61,435.97	19,831.17	22,144.43	65,612.37	19,824.36	43,301.40	64,669.45	69,065.65
134	149,289.56	46,485.92	25,099.92	61,897.17	19,929.91	22,287.70	66,103.63	19,925.15	43,597.23	65,154.92	69,582.77
135	150,322.68	46,821.03	25,223.97	62,358.37	20,028.65	22,430.98	66,594.89	20,025.93	43,893.06	65,640.39	70,099.89

136	151,355.80	47,156.13	25,348.02	62,819.57	20,127.39	22,574.26	67,086.16	20,126.72	44,188.89	66,125.87	70,617.01
137	152,388.94	47,491.23	25,472.06	63,280.77	20,226.13	22,717.52	67,577.42	20,227.51	44,484.71	66,611.34	71,134.14
138	153,422.06	47,826.33	25,596.10	63,741.98	20,324.87	22,860.80	68,068.69	20,328.30	44,780.54	67,096.82	71,651.25
139	154,455.18	48,161.43	25,720.14	64,203.18	20,423.61	23,004.08	68,559.96	20,429.09	45,076.37	67,582.29	72,168.37
140	155,488.31	48,496.54	25,844.19	64,664.38	20,522.35	23,147.34	69,051.22	20,529.88	45,372.20	68,067.77	72,685.50
141	156,521.44	48,831.63	25,968.23	65,125.58	20,621.09	23,290.62	69,542.49	20,630.66	45,668.02	68,553.24	73,202.61
142	157,554.57	49,166.74	26,092.27	65,586.78	20,719.83	23,433.90	70,033.75	20,731.46	45,963.85	69,038.71	73,719.74
143	158,587.69	49,501.84	26,216.31	66,047.99	20,818.57	23,577.17	70,525.01	20,832.25	46,259.68	69,524.20	74,236.86
144	159,620.82	49,836.94	26,340.36	66,509.19	20,917.31	23,720.44	71,016.28	20,933.03	46,555.50	70,009.67	74,753.97
145	160,653.95	50,172.04	26,464.40	66,970.38	21,016.05	23,863.71	71,507.55	21,033.82	46,851.33	70,495.14	75,271.10
146	161,687.07	50,507.14	26,588.44	67,431.59	21,114.79	24,006.99	71,998.81	21,134.60	47,147.16	70,980.62	75,788.22
147	162,720.20	50,842.25	26,712.49	67,892.79	21,213.53	24,150.26	72,490.07	21,235.40	47,442.98	71,466.09	76,305.34
148	163,753.33	51,177.34	26,836.53	68,354.00	21,312.27	24,293.53	72,981.34	21,336.19	47,738.81	71,951.57	76,822.46
149	164,786.45	51,512.44	26,960.57	68,815.19	21,411.01	24,436.81	73,472.60	21,436.97	48,034.64	72,437.05	77,339.58
150	165,819.58	51,847.55	27,084.61	69,276.39	21,509.75	24,580.09	73,963.86	21,537.76	48,330.46	72,922.52	77,856.71
151	166,852.71	52,182.65	27,208.66	69,737.60	21,608.49	24,723.35	74,455.13	21,638.55	48,626.29	73,407.99	78,373.82
152	167,885.84	52,517.74	27,332.70	70,198.80	21,707.23	24,866.63	74,946.39	21,739.34	48,922.12	73,893.47	78,890.94
153	168,918.96	52,852.85	27,456.74	70,660.00	21,805.97	25,009.91	75,437.66	21,840.13	49,217.94	74,378.94	79,408.07
154	169,952.09	53,187.95	27,580.78	71,121.20	21,904.71	25,153.17	75,928.92	21,940.92	49,513.77	74,864.42	79,925.18
155	170,985.22	53,523.06	27,704.83	71,582.40	22,003.46	25,296.45	76,420.19	22,041.70	49,809.60	75,349.90	80,442.31
156	172,018.34	53,858.15	27,828.87	72,043.61	22,102.20	25,439.72	76,911.46	22,142.49	50,105.42	75,835.37	80,959.43
157	173,051.46	54,193.25	27,952.91	72,504.80	22,200.94	25,583.00	77,402.71	22,243.29	50,401.25	76,320.84	81,476.54
158	174,084.60	54,528.36	28,076.95	72,966.01	22,299.68	25,726.27	77,893.98	22,344.07	50,697.08	76,806.32	81,993.67
159	175,117.72	54,863.46	28,201.00	73,427.21	22,398.42	25,869.54	78,385.25	22,444.86	50,992.90	77,291.80	82,510.79
160	176,150.85	55,198.56	28,325.05	73,888.41	22,497.16	26,012.82	78,876.51	22,545.65	51,288.73	77,777.27	83,027.91
161	177,183.97	55,533.66	28,449.09	74,349.61	22,595.90	26,156.09	79,367.78	22,646.43	51,584.56	78,262.75	83,545.03
162	178,217.10	55,868.76	28,573.13	74,810.81	22,694.64	26,299.36	79,859.05	22,747.23	51,880.38	78,748.22	84,062.15
163	179,250.23	56,203.86	28,697.17	75,272.02	22,793.38	26,442.64	80,350.31	22,848.02	52,176.21	79,233.69	84,579.28
164	180,283.35	56,538.96	28,821.22	75,733.22	22,892.12	26,585.91	80,841.57	22,948.80	52,472.04	79,719.17	85,096.39

Trial length in days	Trial length proxy A	Trial length proxy B	Trial length proxy C	Trial length proxy D	Trial length proxy E	Trial length proxy F	Trial length proxy G	Trial length proxy H	Trial length proxy I	Trial length proxy J	Trial length proxy K
165	181,316.49	56,874.07	28,945.26	76,194.41	22,990.86	26,729.18	81,332.84	23,049.59	52,767.86	80,204.65	85,613.51
166	182,349.61	57,209.17	29,069.30	76,655.62	23,089.60	26,872.46	81,824.10	23,150.38	53,063.69	80,690.12	86,130.64
167	183,382.73	57,544.26	29,193.34	77,116.82	23,188.34	27,015.73	82,315.37	23,251.17	53,359.52	81,175.59	86,647.75
168	184,415.86	57,879.37	29,317.39	77,578.03	23,287.08	27,159.00	82,806.64	23,351.96	53,655.34	81,661.07	87,164.88
169	185,448.99	58,214.47	29,441.43	78,039.22	23,385.82	27,302.28	83,297.90	23,452.75	53,951.17	82,146.54	87,682.00
170	186,482.11	58,549.57	29,565.47	78,500.42	23,484.56	27,445.55	83,789.17	23,553.53	54,247.00	82,632.02	88,199.11
171	187,515.24	58,884.67	29,689.51	78,961.63	23,583.30	27,588.83	84,280.43	23,654.32	54,542.83	83,117.50	88,716.24
172	188,548.37	59,219.77	29,813.56	79,422.83	23,682.04	27,732.10	84,771.69	23,755.11	54,838.66	83,602.97	89,233.36
173	189,581.50	59,554.88	29,937.60	79,884.03	23,780.78	27,875.37	85,262.95	23,855.90	55,134.49	84,088.44	89,750.49
174	190,614.62	59,889.97	30,061.64	80,345.23	23,879.52	28,018.65	85,754.22	23,956.69	55,430.31	84,573.92	90,267.60
175	191,647.74	60,225.07	30,185.69	80,806.43	23,978.26	28,161.92	86,245.48	24,057.47	55,726.14	85,059.40	90,784.72
176	192,680.88	60,560.18	30,309.73	81,267.63	24,077.00	28,305.19	86,736.75	24,158.26	56,021.97	85,544.87	91,301.85
177	193,714.00	60,895.28	30,433.77	81,728.83	24,175.74	28,448.47	87,228.01	24,259.06	56,317.79	86,030.35	91,818.96
178	194,747.13	61,230.38	30,557.81	82,190.03	24,274.49	28,591.74	87,719.28	24,359.84	56,613.62	86,515.82	92,336.09
179	195,780.26	61,565.48	30,681.86	82,651.23	24,373.23	28,735.01	88,210.54	24,460.63	56,909.45	87,001.29	92,853.21
180	196,813.38	61,900.58	30,805.90	83,112.43	24,471.97	28,878.29	88,701.80	24,561.42	57,205.27	87,486.77	93,370.32
181	197,846.51	62,235.69	30,929.95	83,573.63	24,570.71	29,021.56	89,193.07	24,662.20	57,501.10	87,972.25	93,887.45
182	198,879.63	62,570.78	31,053.99	84,034.83	24,669.45	29,164.83	89,684.34	24,763.00	57,796.93	88,457.72	94,404.57
183	199,912.76	62,905.89	31,178.03	84,496.04	24,766.77	29,308.11	90,175.60	24,863.79	58,092.75	88,943.20	94,921.69
184	200,945.89	63,240.99	31,302.08	84,957.24	24,864.03	29,451.38	90,666.87	24,964.57	58,388.58	89,428.67	95,438.81
185	201,979.01	63,576.09	31,426.12	85,418.43	24,961.29	29,594.66	91,158.14	25,065.36	58,684.41	89,914.14	95,955.93
186	203,012.14	63,911.19	31,550.16	85,879.64	25,058.55	29,737.93	91,649.40	25,166.15	58,980.23	90,399.63	96,473.06
187	204,045.27	64,246.29	31,674.20	86,340.84	25,155.81	29,881.20	92,140.66	25,266.94	59,276.06	90,885.10	96,990.17
188	205,078.39	64,581.39	31,798.25	86,802.05	25,253.07	30,024.48	92,631.93	25,367.73	59,571.89	91,370.57	97,507.29
189	206,111.52	64,916.49	31,922.29	87,263.24	25,350.33	30,167.74	93,123.19	25,468.52	59,867.71	91,856.04	98,024.42
190	207,144.65	65,251.59	32,046.33	87,724.44	25,447.59	30,311.02	93,614.46	25,569.30	60,163.54	92,341.52	98,541.53
191	208,177.78	65,586.70	32,170.37	88,185.65	25,544.85	30,454.30	94,105.73	25,670.09	60,459.37	92,827.00	99,058.66

192	209,210.90	65,921.80	32,294.42	88,646.85	25,642.11	30,597.57	94,596.99	25,770.89	60,755.19	93,312.47	99,575.78
193	210,244.03	66,256.89	32,418.46	89,108.05	25,739.37	30,740.84	95,088.26	25,871.67	61,051.02	93,797.95	100,092.89
194	211,277.16	66,592.00	32,542.50	89,569.25	25,836.63	30,884.12	95,579.52	25,972.46	61,346.85	94,283.42	100,610.02
195	212,310.28	66,927.10	32,666.54	90,030.45	25,933.89	31,027.39	96,070.78	26,073.25	61,642.67	94,768.89	101,127.14
196	213,343.40	67,262.20	32,790.59	90,491.66	26,031.15	31,170.66	96,562.05	26,174.03	61,938.50	95,254.37	101,644.26
197	214,376.54	67,597.30	32,914.63	90,952.85	26,128.41	31,313.93	97,053.30	26,274.83	62,234.33	95,739.85	102,161.38
198	215,409.66	67,932.40	33,038.67	91,414.06	26,225.67	31,457.21	97,544.57	26,375.62	62,530.15	96,225.32	102,678.50
199	216,442.79	68,267.51	33,162.71	91,875.26	26,322.93	31,600.49	98,035.84	26,476.40	62,825.98	96,710.80	103,195.63
200	217,475.91	68,602.60	33,286.76	92,336.46	26,420.19	31,743.75	98,527.10	26,577.19	63,121.81	97,196.27	103,712.74

(e) Table of final fees in trials [para.8]

Offence class	PPE range	Initial fee	Incremental fee per page
A	0–149	2,785.18	0
A	150–599	2,785.18	16.3759
A	600–1099	10,154.34	14.6753
A	1100–1899	17,491.98	13.0799
A	1900–3299	27,955.92	11.6330
A	3300–4999	44,242.16	11.6330
A	5000–5999	64,018.33	11.6331
A	6000–6999	75,651.38	11.6330
A	7000–7999	87,284.42	11.6330
A	8000–8999	98,917.44	11.6330
A	9000–9999	110,550.46	11.6330
A	10,000	122,171.85	0
B	0–69	1,202.92	0
B	70–199	1,202.92	14.0353
B	200–499	3,027.51	12.5398
B	500–899	6,789.46	10.5557
B	900–1299	11,011.74	8.8680
B	1300–1999	14,558.94	7.7722
B	2000–3299	19,999.46	7.7722
B	3300–4999	30,103.28	7.7722
B	5000–5999	43,315.97	7.7722
B	6000–7999	51,088.14	7.7722
B	8000–8999	66,632.48	7.7722
B	9000–9999	74,404.65	7.7722
B	10,000	82,169.05	0
C	0–39	810.51	0
C	40–299	810.51	11.5783
C	300–799	3,820.87	10.1155
C	800–1249	8,878.62	8.4660
C	1250–1999	12,688.32	7.4854
C	2000–3199	18,302.39	5.1761
C	3200–4559	24,513.74	5.1761
C	4560–5919	31,553.29	5.1761
C	5920–7279	38,592.83	5.1761
C	7280–8639	45,632.37	5.1761
C	8640–9999	52,671.91	5.1762
C	10,000	59,706.30	0
D	0–79	1,527.89	0
D	80–209	1,527.89	17.2578
D	210–699	3,771.41	13.1781
D	700–1049	10,228.68	11.0609
D	1050–1999	14,100.00	9.5912
D	2000–3599	23,211.67	8.7658
D	3600–5199	37,236.90	8.7658
D	5200–6799	51,262.14	8.7658
D	6800–8399	65,287.39	8.7658
D	8400–9999	79,312.63	8.7658
D	10,000	93,329.10	0
E	0–39	386.54	0
E	40–69	386.54	10.4287

Offence class	PPE range	Initial fee	Incremental fee per page
E	70–129	699.40	9.3950
E	130–599	1,263.10	9.0869
E	600–1349	5,533.96	5.9649
E	1350–2999	10,007.63	2.6174
E	3000–4749	14,326.32	2.6174
E	4750–6499	18,906.75	2.6174
E	6500–8249	23,487.17	2.6174
E	8250–9999	28,067.60	2.6174
E	10,000	32,645.40	0
F	0–49	391.89	0
F	50–229	391.89	8.0098
F	230–699	1,833.66	7.6326
F	700–1399	5,420.98	6.1357
F	1400–1949	9,715.95	4.7354
F	1950–3549	12,320.41	2.3624
F	3550–5149	16,100.18	2.3624
F	5150–6749	19,879.95	2.3624
F	6750–8349	23,659.72	2.3624
F	8350–9999	27,439.49	2.3624
F	10,000	31,335.02	0
G	0–119	1,074.22	0
G	120–734	1,074.22	9.0131
G	735–1289	6,617.28	9.0746
G	1290–2399	11,653.69	9.2375
G	2400–4499	21,907.31	9.2029
G	4500–7999	41,233.37	9.2029
G	8000–8399	73,443.48	9.2029
G	8400–8799	77,124.64	9.2029
G	8800–9199	80,805.79	9.2029
G	9200–9599	84,486.95	9.2029
G	9600–9999	88,168.10	9.2029
G	10,000	91,840.06	0
H	0–39	392.05	0
H	40–249	392.05	9.4203
H	250–619	2,370.32	7.8338
H	620–1299	5,268.81	5.8194
H	1300–2999	9,226.02	4.6188
H	3000–4999	17,077.91	2.4911
H	5000–5999	22,060.10	2.4910
H	6000–6999	24,551.12	2.4911
H	7000–7999	27,042.22	2.4911
H	8000–8999	29,533.32	2.4911
H	9000–9999	32,024.42	2.4911
H	10,000	34,513.02	0
I	0–39	391.72	0
I	40–369	391.72	10.0165
I	370–799	3,697.16	9.9618
I	800–1299	7,980.75	9.8555
I	1300–2699	12,908.52	7.7641
I	2700–4199	23,778.23	3.3365
I	4200–5359	28,783.04	3.3365

Offence class	PPE range	Initial fee	Incremental fee per page
I	5360–6519	32,653.42	3.3365
I	6520–7679	36,523.80	3.3366
I	7680–8839	40,394.20	3.3365
I	8840–9999	44,264.58	3.3365
I	10,000	48,131.63	0
J	0–79	1,608.31	0
J	80–209	1,608.31	18.1662
J	210–699	3,969.91	13.8717
J	700–1049	10,767.03	11.6431
J	1050–1999	14,842.10	10.0960
J	2000–3599	24,433.34	9.2271
J	3600–5199	39,196.75	9.2271
J	5200–6799	53,960.15	9.2271
J	6800–8399	68,723.57	9.2271
J	8400–9999	83,486.98	9.2271
J	10,000	98,241.16	0
K	0–119	1,130.76	0
K	120–734	1,130.76	9.4875
K	735–1289	6,965.55	9.5522
K	1290–2399	12,267.04	9.7237
K	2400–4499	23,060.31	9.6873
K	4500–7999	43,403.55	9.6873
K	8000–8399	77,308.93	9.6872
K	8400–8799	81,183.82	9.6872
K	8800–9199	85,058.72	9.6873
K	9200–9599	88,933.63	9.6872
K	9600–9999	92,808.53	9.6872
K	10,000	96,673.74	0

(3) DEFENDANT UPLIFTS

Total number of defendants represented by litigator	Percentage uplift to total fee
2–4	20%
5+	30%

(4) RETRIALS AND TRANSFERS

Scenario	Percentage of the total fee	Case type used to determine total fee	Claim period
Cracked trial before retrial, where there is no change of litigator	25%	Cracked trial	–
Retrial, where there is no change of litigator	25%	Trial	–

Up to and including plea and case management hearing transfer (original litigator)	25%	Cracked trial	–
Up to and including plea and case management hearing transfer – guilty plea (new litigator)	100%	Guilty plea	–
Up to and including plea and case management hearing transfer – cracked trial (new litigator)	100%	Cracked trial	–
Up to and including plea and case management hearing transfer – trial (new litigator)	100%	Trial	–
Before trial transfer (original litigator)	75%	Cracked trial	–
Before trial transfer - cracked trial (new litigator)	100%	Cracked trial	–
Before trial transfer – trial (new litigator)	100%	Trial	–
During trial transfer (original litigator)	100%	Trial	Claim up to and including the day before the transfer
During trial transfer (new litigator)	50%	Trial	Claim for the full trial length
During trial transfer – retrial (new litigator)	25%	Trial	Claim for the full retrial length
Transfer after trial and before sentencing hearing (original litigator)	100%	Trial	–
Transfer after trial and before sentencing hearing (new litigator)	10%	Trial	–
Transfer after retrial and before sentencing hearing (original litigator)	25%	Trial	–

Transfer after retrial and before sentencing hearing (new litigator)	10%	Trial	–
Transfer before retrial (original litigator)	25%	Cracked trial	–
Transfer before cracked retrial (new litigator)	50%	Cracked trial	
Transfer before retrial (new litigator)	50%	Trial	Claim for the full retrial length
Transfer during retrial (original litigator)	25%	Trial	Claim up to and including the day before the transfer
Transfer during retrial (new litigator)	50%	Trial	Claim for the full retrial length

APPENDIX 11

Advocates' graduated fee tables

[Criminal Defence Service (Funding) Order 2007, SI 2007/1174, Sched.2, as amended by Criminal Defence Service (Funding) (Amendment) Orders 2007, SI 2007/3552 and 2009, SI 2009/1843]

(a) Table of fees and uplifts [para.5]

Class of offence	Basic fee (B)	Daily attendance fee (D)	Evidence uplift (E)	Witness uplift (W)
QC				
A	£4,434	£1,321	£1.89	£7.55
B	£2,924	£991	£1.89	£7.55
C	£2,275	£943	£1.89	£7.55
D	£2,641	£943	£1.89	£7.55
E	£1,750	£708	£1.89	£7.55
F	£1,750	£708	£1.89	£7.55
G	£2,200	£943	£1.89	£7.55
H	£2,200	£943	£1.89	£7.55
I	£2,453	£943	£1.89	£7.55
J	£3,302	£1,132	£1.89	£7.55
K	£3,302	£1,132	£1.89	£7.55
Leading junior				
A	£3,325	£991	£1.42	£5.66
B	£2,193	£743	£1.42	£5.66
C	£1,706	£708	£1.42	£5.66
D	£1,981	£708	£1.42	£5.66
E	£1,313	£531	£1.42	£5.66
F	£1,313	£531	£1.42	£5.66
G	£1,650	£708	£1.42	£5.66
H	£1,650	£708	£1.42	£5.66
I	£1,840	£708	£1.42	£5.66
J	£2,476	£849	£1.42	£5.66
K	£2,476	£849	£1.42	£5.66
Led junior				
A	£2,217	£660	£0.94	£3.77
B	£1,462	£495	£0.94	£3.77

C	£1,038	£472	£0.94	£3.77
D	£1,300	£472	£0.94	£3.77
E	£802	£354	£0.94	£3.77
F	£802	£354	£0.94	£3.77
G	£1,100	£472	£0.94	£3.77
H	£943	£472	£0.94	£3.77
I	£1,132	£472	£0.94	£3.77
J	£1,887	£566	£0.94	£3.77
K	£1,651	£566	£0.94	£3.77
Junior alone				
A	£2,547	£778	£1.13	£5.66
B	£1,509	£542	£1.13	£5.66
C	£1,038	£472	£1.13	£5.66
D	£1,300	£472	£1.13	£5.66
E	£755	£377	£1.13	£5.66
F	£802	£377	£1.13	£5.66
G	£1,415	£472	£1.13	£5.66
H	£943	£472	£1.13	£5.66
I	£1,132	£472	£1.13	£5.66
J	£1,887	£613	£1.13	£5.66
K	£1,887	£613	£1.13	£5.66

(b)   Fees and uplifts in guilty pleas and trials which crack in the first third [para.7, Table A]

Class of offence	Basic fee	Evidence uplift per page of prosecution evidence (pages 1 to 1,000)	Evidence uplift per page of prosecution evidence (1,001 to 10,000)
QC			
A	£2,358.00	£2.53	£1.17
B	£1,509.00	£2.08	£1.04
C	£1,415.00	£1.48	£0.74
D	£1,509.00	£3.30	£1.65
E	£1,250.00	£1.06	£0.53
F	£1,250.00	£1.39	£0.70
G	£1,415.00	£1.84	£0.92
H	£1,415.00	£1.91	£0.95
I	£1,415.00	£1.86	£0.92
J	£1,981.00	£3.30	£1.65
K	£1,981.00	£1.84	£0.92
Leading junior			
A	£1,768.50	£1.90	£0.88
B	£1,131.75	£1.56	£0.78
C	£1,061.25	£1.11	£0.56
D	£1,131.75	£2.48	£1.24
E	£937.50	£0.80	£0.40
F	£937.50	£1.04	£0.53
G	£1,061.25	£1.38	£0.69

H	£1,061.25	£1.43	£0.71
I	£1,061.25	£1.40	£0.69
J	£1,485.75	£2.48	£1.24
K	£1,485.75	£1.38	£0.69
Led junior			
A	£1,179.00	£1.27	£0.59
B	£754.50	£1.04	£0.52
C	£707.50	£0.74	£0.37
D	£754.50	£1.65	£0.83
E	£625.00	£0.53	£0.27
F	£625.00	£0.70	£0.35
G	£707.50	£0.92	£0.46
H	£707.50	£0.96	£0.48
I	£707.50	£0.93	£0.46
J	£990.50	£1.65	£0.83
K	£990.50	£0.92	£0.46
Junior alone			
A	£1,312.00	£1.08	£0.54
B	£802.00	£0.94	£0.47
C	£519.00	£0.69	£0.35
D	£802.00	£1.37	£0.68
E	£472.00	£0.41	£0.20
F	£472.00	£0.63	£0.31
G	£755.00	£1.18	£0.59
H	£566.00	£0.63	£0.32
I	£660.00	£0.49	£0.25
J	£1,132.00	£1.37	£0.68
K	£1,132.00	£1.18	£0.59

(c)   **Fees and uplifts in trials which crack in the second or final third [para.7, Table B]**

				A case that cracks in the second third	A case that cracks in the final third
Class of offence	Basic fee	Evidence uplift per page of prosecution evidence (pages 1 to 250)	Evidence uplift per page of prosecution evidence (pages 251 to 1,000)	Evidence uplift per page of prosecution evidence (pages 1,001 to 10,000)	Evidence uplift per page of prosecution evidence (pages 1,001 to 10,000)
QC					
A	£3,585.00	£4.70	£1.17	£1.55	£4.70
B	£2,264.00	£4.16	£1.04	£1.38	£4.16
C	£1,975.00	£2.95	£0.74	£0.97	£2.95
D	£2,264.00	£6.59	£1.65	£2.18	£6.59
E	£1,600.00	£2.11	£0.53	£0.70	£2.11

F	£1,600.00	£2.77	£0.70	£0.92	£2.77
G	£2,000.00	£3.68	£0.92	£1.22	£3.68
H	£2,000.00	£3.80	£0.95	£1.25	£3.80
I	£2,075.00	£3.72	£0.92	£1.23	£3.72
J	£3,019.00	£6.59	£1.65	£2.18	£6.59
K	£3,019.00	£3.68	£0.92	£1.22	£3.68
Leading junior					
A	£2,688.75	£3.53	£0.88	£1.16	£3.53
B	£1,698.00	£3.12	£0.78	£1.04	£3.12
C	£1,481.25	£2.21	£0.56	£0.73	£2.21
D	£1,698.00	£4.94	£1.24	£1.64	£4.94
E	£1,200.00	£1.58	£0.40	£0.53	£1.58
F	£1,200.00	£2.08	£0.53	£0.69	£2.08
G	£1,500.00	£2.76	£0.69	£0.92	£2.76
H	£1,500.00	£2.85	£0.71	£0.94	£2.85
I	£1,556.25	£2.79	£0.69	£0.92	£2.79
J	£2,264.25	£4.94	£1.24	£1.64	£4.94
K	£2,264.25	£2.76	£0.69	£0.92	£2.76
Led junior					
A	£1,792.50	£2.35	£0.59	£0.78	£2.35
B	£1,132.00	£2.08	£0.52	£0.69	£2.08
C	£987.50	£1.48	£0.37	£0.49	£1.48
D	£1,132.00	£3.30	£0.83	£1.09	£3.30
E	£800.00	£1.06	£0.27	£0.35	£1.06
F	£800.00	£1.39	£0.35	£0.46	£1.39
G	£1,000.00	£1.84	£0.46	£0.61	£1.84
H	£1,000.00	£1.90	£0.48	£0.63	£1.90
I	£1,037.50	£1.86	£0.46	£0.62	£1.86
J	£1,509.50	£3.30	£0.83	£1.09	£3.30
K	£1,509.50	£1.84	£0.46	£0.61	£1.84
Junior alone					
A	£1,981.00	£4.63	£2.15	£0.71	£2.15
B	£1,179.00	£4.03	£1.88	£0.62	£1.88
C	£755.00	£2.99	£1.39	£0.46	£1.39
D	£1,050.00	£5.87	£2.73	£0.90	£2.73
E	£660.00	£1.75	£0.82	£0.27	£0.82
F	£660.00	£2.70	£1.25	£0.42	£1.25
G	£1,132.00	£5.08	£2.37	£0.78	£2.37
H	£802.00	£2.71	£1.26	£0.42	£1.26
I	£943.00	£2.11	£0.98	£0.32	£0.98
J	£1,698.00	£5.87	£2.73	£0.90	£2.73
K	£1,604.00	£5.08	£2.37	£0.78	£2.37

(d) Noting brief fees – fixed fees [para.19]

Category of work	Paragraph providing for fee	Fee for qc	Fee for leading junior	Fee for led junior or junior alone
Standard appearance	9(2)	£200 per day	£150 per day	£100 per day
Paper plea and case management hearing	9(3)	£30 per case	£30 per case	£30 per case
Abuse of process hearing	10(1)(a)	Half day £300	Half day £225	Half day £150
		Full day £575	Full day £400	Full day £275
Hearings relating to disclosure	10(1)(b) and (c)	Half day £300	Half day £225	Half day £150
		Full day £575	Full day £400	Full day £275
Hearings relating to the admissibility of evidence	10(1)(d)	Half day £300	Half day £225	Half day £150
		Full day £575	Full day £400	Full day £275
Hearings on withdrawal of a plea of guilty	10(1)(e)	Half day £300	Half day £225	Half day £150
		Full day £575	Full day £400	Full day £275
Confiscation hearings	11	Half day £300	Half day £225	Half day £150
		Full day £575	Full day £400	Full day £275
Deferred sentencing hearing	12(1)(a)	£375 per day	£275 per day	£200 per day
Sentencing hearing	12(1)(b)	£300 per day	£200 per day	£125 per day
Ineffective trial payment	13	£325 per day	£225 per day	£150 per day
Special preparation	14	£85 per hour	£65 per hour	£45 per hour
Wasted preparation	15	£85 per hour	£65 per hour	£45 per hour
Conferences and views	16	£85 per hour	£65 per hour	£45 per hour
Appeals to the Crown Court against conviction	17(1)	£300 per day	£225 per day	£150 per day
Appeals to the Crown Court against sentence	17(1)	£250 per day	£175 per day	£125 per day

Proceedings relating to breach of an order of the Crown Court	17(1)	£250 per day	£175 per day	£125 per day
Committal for sentence	17(1)	£300 per day	£225 per day	£150 per day
Adjourned appeals, committals for sentence and breach hearings	17(2)	£200 per day	£150 per day	£100 per day
Bail applications, mentions and other applications in appeals, committals for sentence and breach hearings	17(3)	£200 per day	£150 per day	£100 per day
Second and subsequent days of an application to dismiss	18(6)	Half day £300		
Full day £575	Half day £225			
Full day £400	Half day £150			
Full day £275				
Noting brief	19	–	–	£125 per day

(e) Daily rates payable where a trial lasts over 40 days [para.25]

Class of offence	Daily rate payable for days 41 to 50	Daily rate payable for days 51 and over
QC		
A	£635	£680
B	£447	£479
C	£447	£479
D	£447	£479
E	£447	£479
F	£447	£479
G	£447	£479
H	£447	£479
I	£447	£479
J	£447	£479
K	£447	£479
Leading junior		
A	£544	£583
B	£383	£411

C	£383	£411
D	£383	£411
E	£383	£411
F	£383	£411
G	£383	£411
H	£383	£411
I	£383	£411
J	£383	£411
K	£383	£411
Led junior		
A	£363	£389
B	£256	£274
C	£256	£274
D	£256	£274
E	£256	£274
F	£256	£274
G	£256	£274
H	£256	£274
I	£256	£274
J	£256	£274
K	£256	£274
Junior acting alone		
A	£435	£467
B	£286	£306
C	£286	£306
D	£307	£329
E	£260	£279
F	£260	£279
G	£307	£329
H	£286	£306
I	£286	£306
J	£307	£329
K	£307	£329

Provisional grant of representation/very high cost cases

PROVISIONAL GRANT OF REPRESENTATION

The following rates will be payable for work agreed with the Contract Manager (see **1.3** and **3.2**):

(a) travel and waiting at £25 per hour;
(b) mileage at 45 pence per mile;
(c) disbursements at costs.

Other work shall be paid at the following rates:

	Preparation £ hour	Standard rate work £ hour
Solicitor		
Level A	119.00	55.75
Level B	104.50	47.25
Level C	69.00	34.00
Counsel		
QC	119.00	
Led junior	85.50	
Junior alone	76.00	
Solicitor advocate		
Level A alone	115.00	
Level B alone	99.50	
Led level A	104.50	
Led level B	90.50	

VERY HIGH COST CRIMINAL CASES: REMUNERATION RATES AND NOTIFICATION FORM

[LSC, Contract Annexes for Panel Advocates, Annex 7, 13 November 2008. For work between January 2008 and 13 November 2008 reference should be made to the first edition of this book.]

VHCC RATES OF PAY

Preparation (hourly rates)

	Category 1 (£)	Category 2 (£)	Category 3 (£)	Category 4 (£)	Standard rates (£)
Solicitor					
Level A sol	152.50	119.00	95.50	95.50	55.75
Level B sol	133.00	104.50	83.50	83.50	47.25
Level C sol	88.50	69.00	54.00	54.00	34.00
Pupil/junior[1]	48.00	38.50	31.50	31.50	
Counsel					
QC	152.50	119.00	95.50	95.50	
Leading junior	133.00	104.50	83.50	83.50	
Led junior	95.50	76.00	65.00	65.00	
Junior alone	104.50	85.50	74.00	74.00	
2nd led junior	67.00	53.00	46.00	46.00	
Solicitor advocate					
Leading level a	152.50	119.00	95.50	95.50	
Led level A	133.00	104.50	83.50	83.50	
Leading level B	133.00	104.50	83.50	83.50	
Led level B	110.00	90.50	69.00	69.00	
Level A alone	138.00	115.00	93.50	93.50	
Level B alone	116.00	99.50	78.50	78.50	
Second advocate	67.00	53.00	46.00	46.00	

Advocacy[2]

Advocacy rates for counsel are paid per hearing or per day depending upon the duration of the court sitting time. Advocacy rates are non-category specific.

	Preliminary hearing (£)	Half day (£)	Full day (£)
QC	119.00	250.00	500.00
Leading junior	90.50	205.25	410.50
Led junior	61.00	132.75	265.50
Junior alone	70.00	150.00	300.00
Second led junior	35.50	67.50	135.00
Noter	30.580	57.50	115.00

Attendance at court with counsel (hourly rates for solicitors)

Level A	£42.25
Level B	£34.00
Level C	£20.50

Travelling and waiting

£25 per hour regardless of Litigator Level or Advocacy role

Mileage

£0.45 per mile

1. This is to cover situations where the representation order cannot be amended to provide for a second junior counsel but the Case Manager determines that to achieve value for money certain items of work should be done by a third counsel.
2. Solicitor-advocates will be paid the appropriate rate for a leading junior, a led junior, or a junior alone.

legal services
COMMISSION

Complex Crime Unit

VHCC Notification Request Form

Please complete this form answering all questions. Where a question does not apply, please state that this is so. Do not leave the box blank.

This information should also be typed.

Please use additional sheets if necessary.

Information	Details where available

1) Firm Information

Firm Name	
Firm Address	
Primary contact details Fee Earner Telephone Fax Email	
Is your firm a member of the VHCC (Crime) Panel	
If your client has been charged with a fraud related offence, state how your firm will satisfy the requirements of s.15(4) of the VHCC Panel Member's Contract	

2) Defendant(s) Information

Total number of defendants with your firm	
Name(s)	
Charge(s) faced	

CCU Notification request form   1

Date of Arrest	
Date of Charge	
Date the defendant instructed your firm	
Is the defendant in custody?	
If so what date does the custody time limit expire?	
Date of Representation Order(s) for your defendant(s) (You should include any amended orders here also)	
Level of counsel authorised by Representation Order	

3) Court Information

Court	
T Number	
Judge (if known)	
Date of committal or transfer to the Crown Court	
Stage of proceedings now reached (state if pre or post arraignment)	
Date and nature of next hearing	
Trial date (if known)	
Court's estimated trial length (where possible please obtain this information from the court)	
Your Estimated Trial Length (if this differs to court's estimate above please detail reasons) * see footnote	

4) Case Information

Prosecuting Authority (Inc. prosecution case manager & case	

---

* In the absence of a court estimated trial length please make every effort, based on the current information, to provide your own estimate.

CCU Notification request form   2

ref. no.)	
Name of all co-defendants & representing solicitors firms (include addresses of firms)	
Brief description of case (please state if the matter is placed in the terrorism list)	
Breakdown of served documentation (please specify number of pages)	Statements: Exhibits: Interviews: Unused: Other (please specify):
Further documentation to be served (if known)	

CCU Notification request form   3

Value of the alleged fraud/drugs (where applicable)	
Please detail your initial views on the likely category of the case (please refer to Annex [5] of the VHCC Panel Contract)	

5) Defence Team Information

Name and role of advocate instructed, if applicable	
Date of instruction of advocate(s)	
Are any of your instructed advocates non-panel Advocates?	
Work done to date (in terms of hours)	

6) Exceptional Circumstances

Please detail any further information in relation to any exceptional circumstances as to why the case should/should not be contracted	
Please detail any further information regarding this case that may be of use when considering this notification (e.g. indication of early guilty pleas, indication of severance, etc)	

Crown Court: pages of prosecution evidence

[LSC, Process Map for Pages of Prosecution Evidence (PPE), last updated 17 September 2009.]

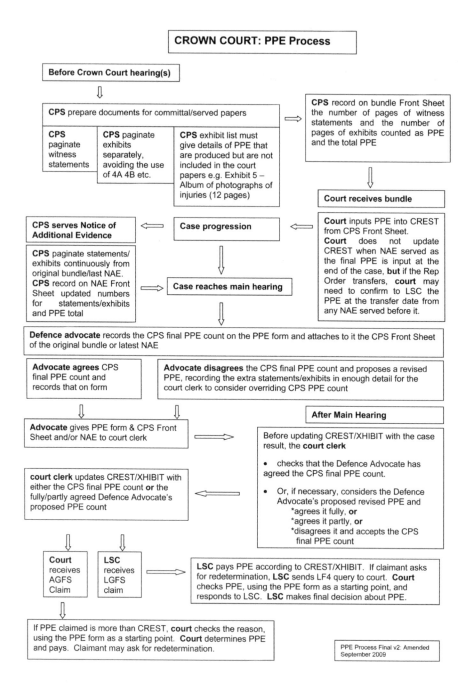

CROWN COURT: PPE Process

Before Crown Court hearing(s)

⇩

CPS prepare documents for committal/served papers

| **CPS** paginate witness statements | **CPS** paginate exhibits separately, avoiding the use of 4A 4B etc. | **CPS** exhibit list must give details of PPE that are produced but are not included in the court papers e.g. Exhibit 5 – Album of photographs of injuries (12 pages) |

⇒ **CPS** record on bundle Front Sheet the number of pages of witness statements and the number of pages of exhibits counted as PPE and the total PPE

⇩

Court receives bundle

⇩

Court inputs PPE into CREST from CPS Front Sheet. **Court** does not update CREST when NAE served as the final PPE is input at the end of the case, **but** if the Rep Order transfers, **court** may need to confirm to LSC the PPE at the transfer date from any NAE served before it.

⇐ **Case progression** ⇐

CPS serves Notice of Additional Evidence

CPS paginate statements/ exhibits continuously from original bundle/last NAE. **CPS** record on NAE Front Sheet updated numbers for statements/exhibits and PPE total

⇒ **Case reaches main hearing**

⇩

Defence advocate records the CPS final PPE count on the PPE form and attaches to it the CPS Front Sheet of the original bundle or latest NAE

Advocate agrees CPS final PPE count and records that on form

Advocate disagrees the CPS final PPE count and proposes a revised PPE, recording the extra statements/exhibits in enough detail for the court clerk to consider overriding CPS PPE count

⇩ ⇩

Advocate gives PPE form & CPS Front Sheet and/or NAE to court clerk

⇒ **After Main Hearing**

Before updating CREST/XHIBIT with the case result, the **court clerk**

- checks that the Defence Advocate has agreed the CPS final PPE count.

court clerk updates CREST/XHIBIT with either the CPS final PPE count **or** the fully/partly agreed Defence Advocate's proposed PPE count

⇐

- Or, if necessary, considers the Defence Advocate's proposed revised PPE and
  *agrees it fully, **or**
  *agrees it partly, **or**
  *disagrees it and accepts the CPS final PPE count

⇩ ⇩

| **Court** receives AGFS Claim | **LSC** receives LGFS claim |

⇒ **LSC** pays PPE according to CREST/XHIBIT. If claimant asks for redetermination, **LSC** sends LF4 query to court. **Court** checks PPE, using the PPE form as a starting point, and responds to LSC. **LSC** makes final decision about PPE.

⇩

If PPE claimed is more than CREST, **court** checks the reason, using the PPE form as a starting point. **Court** determines PPE and pays. Claimant may ask for redetermination.

PPE Process Final v2: Amended September 2009

CROWN COURT: PAGES OF PROSECUTION EVIDENCE (FOR AGFS & LGFS)

Defence Advocate: Fill in this form in all trials, cracked trials and guilty pleas. Attach the CPS Front Sheet and/or latest NAE to show the CPS final PPE count. At the end of the main hearing, give it to the court clerk.

Defendant(s)			Case No.	
CPS final PPE count of statements and exhibits served on the court <u>EITHER</u> from original bundle ☐ OR NAE ☐ **(tick a box & attach a copy of the CPS Front Sheet and/or the NAE)**			**CPS PPE Total**	
Defence Advocate Name (Leader <u>or</u> Junior)		Date	Agreed	Disagreed

                                  ▼ **give form & CPS Front**   ▼ **fill in next box**
                                     Sheet/NAE to court clerk

Name/description, date and number of pages of each witness statement or exhibit to be ADDED to the CPS final PPE count	
	Advocate Proposed Revised Total PPE

                                   ▼ **give form & the CPS Front Sheet/**
                                   NAE to court clerk

Court Clerk: Accept this form only if the Defence Advocate sections are filled in AND a CPS Front Sheet/NAE is attached. You do not have to check PPE in court. This form is to help you later to input the final PPE figure when updating CREST/XHIBIT at the end of the case. When you have done that fill in the boxes below

Your Name	Tick one box			CREST/XHIBIT Updated Tick or date
	CPS count accepted	Advocate count agreed		
		fully	partly	

Guidance

1. Criminal Defence Service (Funding) Order 2007, as amended by the Criminal Defence Service (Funding) (Amendment) Order 2007, Paragraph 1 of Schedule 1 defines "pages of prosecution evidence" as:

1 (2) The number of pages of prosecution evidence served on the court includes – all witness statements, documentary and pictorial exhibits, records of interviews with the assisted person, and records of interviews with other defendants, which form part of the committal or served prosecution documents or which are included in any notice of additional evidence, but does not include any document provided on CD-ROM or by other means of electronic communication.

1 (3) In proceedings on indictment in the Crown Court initiated otherwise than by committal for trial, the appropriate officer must determine the number of pages of prosecution evidence in accordance with sub-paragraph (2) or as nearly in accordance with it as possible as the nature of the case permits.

2. Precis of The Graduated Fee Guidance Manual http://www.hmcourts-service.gov.uk/cms/781.htm:
Count. • Transcripts of video evidence asked for by the judge. • When a transcript has been expanded by the prosecution or the defence, because the one provided by the prosecution was deemed insufficient to go before the jury, count the fullest transcript produced <u>and</u> the version in the committal bundle. • Any page that is allowable is counted as one page regardless of the number of lines, making no allowance for small or large print.

Do Not Count • Documents provided outside the committal bundle or without written notice of additional evidence. • Title pages or separator pages. • Versions of a transcript edited for the purpose of being put before the jury.

PPE Form agreed HMCS/MoJ/LSC/CPS : Final v2 Amended September 2009